D0883493

POLITICS AND EXEGESIS:
ORIGEN AND THE TWO SWORDS

Raphael, *Le Due Spade*, Stanza della Segnatura, Vatican Museums.
Musei Vaticani Archivio Fotografico no. xxx.17.5

POLITICS AND EXEGESIS: ORIGEN AND THE TWO SWORDS

Gerard E. Caspary

UNIVERSITY OF CALIFORNIA PRESS
Berkeley · Los Angeles · London

University of California Press
Berkeley and Los Angeles, California

University of California Press, Ltd.
London, England

ISBN 0-520-03445-7
Library of Congress Catalog Card Number: 77-71058
Printed in the United States of America

1 2 3 4 5 6 7 8 9

CARISSIMIS AVUNCULO UXORIQUE EJUS
PARENTIBUS MEIS
TAM SPIRITUALITER SECUNDUM CARNEM
QUAM LITTERALITER SECUNDUM SPIRITUM
D D D

CONTENTS

PREFACE

This book is part of a much larger study on the history of the political interpretation of the two swords of Luke from the patristic era to the third quarter of the twelfth century. Since this interpretation is emphatically a Western one the emphasis in the study as a whole, to which this volume is only an introduction, will also be on the West. Origen is thus something of an exception. His exegesis forms the basis of later Latin expositions of the fourth and fifth centuries and through these, or directly, of the medieval theory of the two swords of Luke. In the East, on the other hand, his exegesis of the sword pericope seems to have had relatively little influence. This is why I have allowed myself to rely rather heavily though by no means exclusively on the Latin Origen—that is, on those works that have survived in Latin; and why even in the case of those that have come down to us in both Greek and Latin versions I have tended to quote from the Latin rather than the Greek. After all, it was the Latin versions that were destined to be influential in the Latin West.

This book contains a good many quotations in Latin, and I am grateful to the University of California Press for allowing me to keep these in the text instead of relegating all of them to the foot of the page. In every case, these quotations in the text are followed either by a translation or a very close paraphrase.

(The paraphrases usually involve only the necessary changes in person, tense, and incorporate a modern method of biblical citation, to allow for a smoother English text.) This translation or paraphrase is then usually followed by a fairly close and literal exegesis, then by an analysis of possible associations and of deeper structures of interpretation. This method, which to an extent imitates that of patristic or medieval commentators, is meant to engage the reader into a slow, reflective and empathetic *meditatio* upon the text. Exegetical material remains strange, at first perhaps repellent, even to specialists working in the period. It contains, moreover, so many echoes and resonances, so many hidden structures and infrastructures, that it cannot be quickly assimilated. To digest well, to be moved to partake in the slow meditative process of sniffing and tasting and chewing, which patristic and medieval exegetes were themselves practicing, is often necessary. Such is the method attempted in this book.

In writing this book I have incurred many debts of many kinds. Thanks should go to the ACLS and to the Humanities Research Committee of the University of California at Berkeley for generous grants that helped at various stages. I am grateful to the staffs of the *Biblioteca Vaticana* in Rome, of the libraries of Union Theological Seminary in New York and of the Graduate Theological Union in Berkeley, and particularly of the Doe Memorial Library of the University of California at Berkeley. Mrs. Grace O'Connell, a marvellous and most learned typist, deserves special praise. I am also very much indebted to the University of California Press, to its anonymous readers for their most helpful comments, and to my copyeditor, Mr. Stephen Hart, for an excellent job and most particularly for his immense sense of tact. Finally, I wish to thank the Vatican's *Archivio Fotografico* for letting me use Rafael's *Due Spade* for the frontispiece of this book.

My main obligation is however to friends and colleagues, who have read all or parts of the manuscript at various stages of its composition, and have given me the support to persevere in my endeavor. Under this heading, special thanks are due to my late colleague and beloved friend, Professor Paul Alexander, as well as to my former colleague and friend, Mr. Stephen Schneiderman for many things but in particular for their help with Greek texts. I also want to thank my friend and former colleague, Professor Wendell Johnson of the Department of

English at CUNY and Hunter College, for his aid with stylistic problems at a relatively early stage in the genesis of this work. I am very grateful to Professor Robert Benson of the Department of History of the University of California at Los Angeles, who read the manuscript of an earlier and more ambitious version (from the patristic era to the third quarter of the twelfth century) and with whom over the years I seem to have had a never ending dialogue on medieval ecclesiology and political thought. For all sorts of reasons, all my gratitude is extended to my former colleague and friend, Professor Nina G. Garsoïan, Dean of the Graduate School of Princeton University, as well as to my friend Professor Samuel J. Todes of the Philosophy Department of Northwestern University: with them I have discussed various problems arising from this study and without their constant friendship and support this work could never have been written. My greatest thanks, however, must go to two colleagues and their wives in the Department of History here at the University of California at Berkeley: Robert and Carroll Brentano and Irwin and Betsey Scheiner are in fact the midwives of this book. They were the ones who pulled, they were the ones who pushed. Their help, their friendship, their concern and their care were to me winged figures attending the birth of this child.

Berkeley, California
February 1978

ABBREVIATIONS

WORKS OF ORIGEN USED IN THIS BOOK

TITLE USED IN TEXT	ABBREVIATION USED IN NOTES	FULL TITLE
Catena-Fragments	*Frag. Mat.*	*Origenes Matthäuserklärung. III. Fragmente und Indices*, ed. Erich Klostermann, *GCS* 41, *Origenes* 12, Berlin, 1941–55.
Commentary on John*	*Com. Joh.*	*Origenes' Johanneskommentar*, ed. Erwin Preuschen, *GCS* 10, *Origenes* 4, Leipzig, 1903.
Commentary on Matthew	*Com. Mat.*	*Origenes Matthäuserklärung*. I. *Die Griechisch erhaltenen Tomoi*, ed. Erich Klostermann, *GCS* 40, *Origenes* 10, Leipzig, 1935.
Commentariorum Series	*Commentariorum Series*	*Origenes Matthäuserklärung*. II. *Die Lateinische Übersetzung der Commentariorum Series*, ed. Erich Klostermann, *GCS* 38, *Origenes* 11, Leipzig, 1933.
Commentary on Romans	*Com. Rom.*	*Commentariorum in Epistolam Sancti Pauli ad Romanos Libri*, *PG* 14, 837-1292, Paris, 1857.

*With the exception of *Commentariorum Series*, *Contra Celsum* and *De Principiis*, where the Latin title may be said to have entered common usage, I have in the text given an English translation of the title, which, since it is my own, I have not italicized.

*Contra Celsum***	*Contra Celsum*	*Contre Celse*, 5 vols., ed. Marcel Borret, vol. 1: *SC* 132; vol. 2: *SC* 136; vol. 3: *SC* 147; vol. 4: *SC* 150; vol. 5: *SC* 227; Paris 1967–76.
*Contra Celsum***	*GCS* 2 or 3	*Gegen Celsus, GCS* 2 and 3, *Origenes* 1 and 2, ed. Paul Koetschau, Leipzig, 1897–99.
*Contra Celsum***	Chadwick	Henry Chadwick, *Origen: Contra Celsum Translated with an Introduction and Notes*, Cambridge, 1952.
De Principiis	*De Principiis*	*De Principiis (Peri Archōn)*, ed. Paul Koetschau, *GCS* 22, *Origenes* 5, Leipzig, 1913.
Homilies on Genesis	*Hom. Gen.*	"In Genesim Homiliae" in *Homilien zum Hexateuch in Rufins Übersetzung*, ed. W. A. Baehrens, *GCS* 29, *Origenes* 6, 1–144, Leipzig, 1920.
Homilies on Exodus	*Hom. Ex.*	"Origenis in Exodum Homiliae", ibid., 145–280.
Homilies on Ezechiel	*Hom. Ez.*	"Origenis Homiliae in Ezechielen" in *Homilien zu Samuel I, zum Hohenlied und zu den Propheten. Kommentar zum Hohenlied in Rufins und Hieronymus' Übersetzungen*, ed. W. A. Baehrens, *GCS* 33, *Origenes* 8, 318–45, Leipzig, 1925.
Homilies on Isaiah	*Hom. Is.*	"Origenis Homiliae in Isaiam", ibid., 242–89.

**References to *Contra Celsum* are always threefold: first to the book and chapter of the work, followed by the volume and page in Borret's edition; then a citation of the parallel passage in Koetschau's edition in the *GCS*; and finally a reference to Chadwick's translation. Thus *Contra Celsum* 5.61, 3,166; *GCS* 3, 65; Chadwick 311f, should be read as: *Contra Celsum* Bk V, ch. 61 in *Contre Celse*, ed. Borret, vol. 3 (*SC* 147) p. 166; see also *Gegen Celsus*, ed. Koetschau, *GCS* 3, *Origenes* 2, p. 65; see finally, Chadwick, *Origen: Contra Celsum*, p. 311f.

Homilies on Jeremiah	*Hom. Jer.*	*Jeremiahomilien, Klagenliederkommentar, Erklärung der Samuel- und Königsbücher*, ed. Erich Klostermann, *GCS* 6, *Origenes* 3, 1–198, Leipzig, 1901.
Homilies on Leviticus	*Hom. Lev.*	"Origenis in Leviticum Homiliae" in *Die Homilien zum Hexateuch in Rufins Übersetzung*, ed. W. A. Baehrens, *GCS* 29, *Origenes* 6, 280–507, Leipzig, 1920.
Homilies on Luke	*Hom. Luc.*	"In Lucam Homiliae" in *Die Homilien zu Lukas in der Übersetzung des Hieronymus und die Griechische Reste der Homilien und des Lukas-Kommentars*, 2nd ed., Max Rauer, *GCS* 49, *Origenes* 9, 1–222, Berlin, 1959.
Homilies on Numbers	*Hom. Num.*	"In Numeros Homiliae" in *Die Homilien zum Hexateuch in Rufins Übersetzung*, ed. W. A. Baehrens, *GCS* 30, *Origenes* 7, 1–285, Leipzig, 1921.
Homilies on Joshua	*Hom. Jos.*	"In Libro Jesu Nave Homiliae", ibid., 286–463.
Homilies on Judges	*Hom. Jud.*	"In Libro Judicum Homiliae", ibid., 464–522.

INTRODUCTION

Origen and the Two Swords? Politics and Exegesis? The title is (or is at least meant to be) something of a challenge. Politics and the Two Swords is an association, familiar to every medievalist; Origen and exegesis another, familiar to every patristic scholar. But what has Origen to do with the two swords? And what have politics in common with biblical exegesis?

As every medievalist knows, participants in the never-ending confrontation between kingship and priesthood found a curious pleasure, from at least the Investiture Controversy on, in citing Luke 22:38: *Ecce duo gladii hic.* The passage could be used simply as a pious platitude in order to back up the admitted truism that there were indeed two powers, the material and the spiritual. But it could also be used polemically, equally by both sides: by royalists in order to show that the "spiritual" sword of the papacy should not interfere with the "material" sword of the king; and by curialists in order to demonstrate that both swords belonged rightfully to the successor of Peter. There is probably no handbook on medieval history that does not allude to the two swords of Luke; yet there is no major work on the subject.[1] This dearth of secondary material, in contrast to the

1. There are three fundamental articles of which only the first really deals with the material before the Investiture Controversy: Joseph Leclerc, "L'argument des deux

relative abundance of the sources, is curious; particularly, if one compares it with the plethora of books that have been written on the related subject of the Donation of Constantine, a *topos* probably less often mentioned by medieval authors. Most modern writers, one has the feeling, have felt just a little ill at ease with the allegory of the two swords. The Donation of Constantine was no doubt a forgery, but the arguments based on it were at least solid and rational. The two swords of Luke, on the other hand, are usually assumed to be nothing but a quaint and, if truth be told, rather unfortunate, medieval way of attacking the relationship between the two powers. While a good deal has therefore been written on that broader subject, the two swords themselves have normally been dealt with in only cursory fashion.

Yet the allegory itself is an interesting one, and deserves to be treated on its own ground, that is to say from a largely exegetical point of view. Allegorical exegesis may no longer be much in fashion, but it formed the marrow and the bones of a large part of patristic and medieval thought, and a concentration on its methods is essential for an understanding of many of the aspects of Early Christian and medieval theology of politics. (Another work, it is hoped, will show that the medieval allegory of the two swords, far from being a quaint and rather arbitrary exegesis, was solidly built on the tradition of the Fathers and was, in fact, a natural development of some of the basic principles of biblical theology. The present book will limit itself to Origen.)

It is by no means certain that in any of his works Origen even refers to the two swords of Luke.[2] Yet this study will attempt to demonstrate that the later patristic and ultimately medieval interpretation of the sword pericope is based on Origen's exegesis and on his theology of politics. A general outline of the relationship of Origen's theology of politics and what may well be called his theology of exegesis, as well as the interconnection between both and his specific interpretation of the sword pericope, will be provided later in this work. That pericope as it actually appears in the Gospels, the episode as a

---

glaives," *Rech. Sc. Rel.* 21 (1931) 299 ff. and 22 (1932) 151 ff., 280 ff.; Wilhelm Levison, "Die Mittelalterliche Lehre von den beiden Schwertern," *DA* 9 (1951) 14 f.; and Hartmut Hoffmann, "Die beiden Schwerter im hohen Mittelalter," *DA* 20 (1965) 78 ff.

2. But see below, chapter 2 at nn. 109–111.

whole, is in fact composed of two pericopes, probably separate in origin: one, found in Luke alone, that actually mentions "the two swords"; and the second, found in all four Gospels, in which a sword is used to defend the Lord at the time of his arrest. The tradition, however, tends to amalgamate the two episodes, at least to the extent that the Lucan material, when dealt with at all, is usually treated as an introduction to the second episode. From that point of view one can speak of a single sword pericope, composed of six moments or points. The first three are found only in Luke. In the first moment (Luke 22:35 ff.), the Lord at the very end of the Last Supper, intending to warn of His coming Passion and probably of the persecution to which His disciples will now be subject, reminds His disciples that He had heretofore sent them out "without purse and scrip and shoes"; now, however, "he that hath a purse, let him take it . . . and he that hath no sword, let him sell his tunic and buy one."[3] The second moment (Luke 22:38a) describes how the disciples in typical misunderstanding of the Lord's injunction said, "Lord, behold here are two swords"; while the third records Christ's answer, a rather mysterious "That is enough."[4] The fourth moment, found in one form or another in all four of the Gospels (Matthew 26:51; Mark 14:47; Luke 22:49 f.; John 18:10), relates how after the kiss of Judas

3. The full text reads: 35.—"And he said unto them: 'When I sent you without purse and scrip and shoes lacked ye any thing?' And they said: 'Nothing.' 36.—Then he said unto them, 'But now, he that hath a purse, let him take it and likewise his scrip; and he that hath no sword, let him sell his garment and buy one. 37.—For I say unto you that this that is written must yet be accomplished in me, *And he was reckoned among the transgressors.* For the things concerning me have an end." Verse 36 is a reversal of the apostolic marching orders given to the apostles in Luke 9:3 ff. (*et par.*) and to the 72 disciples in Luke 10:4 ff. and of which the apostles are reminded in verse 35a. Verse 37 is one of the few citations from the Servant Songs of Second Isaiah (Isaiah 53:12) that actually occur in the Gospels. It is crucial to the modern interpretation of the sword pericope (see below, n. 11), but plays a relatively small role in patristic and medieval tradition.

When citing the Bible, I rely on the King James Version whenever the translation does not interfere with the use made by Origen of the text, or my own intent. In such cases I have freely made use of other translations or provided my own.

4. The full text in KJ reads: 38.—"And they said 'Lord, behold, here are two swords.' And he said unto them 'It is enough.' " The Greek for "It is enough"—*hikanon estin*—is not idiomatic (it is one of the reasons for assuming a pre-Lucan source behind the sword pericope; see below, n. 10) and probably should be taken as an attempt to end the conversation, possibly even as an expression of impatience as in "That's enough." See Heinz Schürmann, *Jesu Abschiedsrede. Lk 22, 21–38. III. Teil: Einer Quellenkritischen Untersuchung des Lukanischen Abendmahlsberichtes Lk 22, 7–38* (*Neutestamentliche Abhandlungen* 20:5; Münster, 1956) 132 f.; see also the translation in the Jerusalem Bible.

at the time of the Lord's arrest, one of the disciples "that stood by drew a sword and smote a servant of the high priest and cut off his ear." Luke reports that the disciples first asked for permission by saying, "Lord, shall we smite with the sword?" and that it was the slave's right ear that was amputated, while John repeats the detail about the right ear, and adds that the name of the servant was Malchus and that the disciple with the sword was none other than the Apostle Peter.[5] The fifth moment which records the Lord's response is entirely absent in Mark and takes rather different forms in the three other Gospels. In John 18:11 it is simply: "Then said Jesus unto Peter: 'Put up thy sword into the sheath; the cup which my Father hath given me, shall I not drink it?'" In Matthew 26:52 ff., it is much lengthier and seems to combine two distinct *logia:* "Then said Jesus unto him 'Put up again thy sword into his place: for all they that take the sword shall perish with the sword; or thinkest thou that I cannot now pray to my Father and he shall presently give me more than twelve legions of angels? But how then shall the scriptures be fulfilled that thus it must be?'" Finally, in Luke 22:51, the Lord's response involves not only a *logion* but a physical act: "And Jesus answered and said: 'Suffer ye thus far.' And he touched his ear and healed him."[6] The sixth and final moment is ignored in John, and in Matthew is part of a transitional section rather than of the pericope itself. In Mark 14:48 f., it reads: "And Jesus answered and said unto them 'Are

5. Mark 14:47: "And one of them that stood by drew a sword and smote a servant of the high priest and cut off his ear." Matthew 26:51 (almost certainly dependent on Mark): "And, behold, one of them which were with Jesus stretched out his hand and drew his sword and struck a servant of the high priest's and smote off his ear." Luke 22:49 f. (Markan basis probably modified by adding an introductory question to dovetail this episode with the two swords pericope, see below, n. 10): 49.—"When they which were about him saw what would follow, they said unto him, 'Lord, shall we smite with the sword?' 50.—And one of them smote the servant of the high priest and cut off his right ear." John 18:10: "Then Simon Peter having a sword drew it and smote the high priest's servant and cut off his right ear. The servant's name was Malchus." KJ slightly exaggerates the verbal resemblances between John and the synoptics: thus, for "cut off" the synoptics use *aphairein* (a very general verb meaning "to take away") while John uses the much more precise *apokoptein:* similarly, "to draw" (the sword) in Mark or Matthew is *spaein* or *apospaein* while John uses the more poetic *helkuein* (on the importance of these differences, see below, n. 8).

6. The three Gospels that record the Lord's response have been cited in full. One should note again that a good many of the verbal resemblances between Matthew and John are due to the translation. Thus "put up" (thy sword) in Matthew is *apostrephein* ("to turn aside," "turn back," or "bring back," but also "to reject" or "repudiate") while in John it is simply *ballein* ("to thrust" or, quite generally, "to put"). Only Matthew, moreover, speaks of putting up *thy* sword; John simply says *the* sword.

ye come out, as against a bandit with swords and with staves to take me? I was daily with you in the temple teaching and ye took me not; but the scriptures must be fulfilled' "; and in Luke 22:52 f.: "Then Jesus said unto the chief priests . . . and the elders . . . 'Be ye come out as against a bandit, with swords and staves? When I was daily with you in the temple, ye stretched forth no hands against me: but this is your hour, and the power of darkness.' "[7]

This is not the place to speculate about the "real" meaning of the two pericopes in their "original" setting. As for the pericope of the ear of the slave, it is perhaps sufficient to point out two complementary aspects. First, it is striking that Mark, which is generally though not universally recognized as earlier than the other Gospels, records no response on the Lord's part to the disciples' act of resistance. But it is equally striking that the other three Gospels are unanimous in reporting some form of disapproval on the part of Christ; the differences in their accounts seem to guarantee their mutual independence and thus to strengthen the likelihood that the tradition of rebuke is as old as the tradition of resistance.[8] If one reads the four Gospels

7. The text cites Mark in full, as well as most of Luke. Here is Matthew 26:55 f.: "In that same hour said Jesus to the multitudes: 'Are ye come out as against a bandit with swords and with staves for to take me? I sat daily with you teaching in the temple and ye laid no hold on me.' 56.—But all this was done that the scriptures of the prophets might be fulfilled. Then all the disciples forsook him and fled." I have changed the "thief" of all three synoptics in KJ into "bandit," as a better translation of the Greek *lēstēs* "robber," "highwayman," "bandit," which by New Testament times had often taken on the meaning of "revolutionary," "insurrectionist," or "Zealot partisan"; see W. Bauer, W. Arndt, and F. W. Gingrich, *A Greek-English Lexicon of the New Testament* (Chicago, 1957), *ad v. lēstēs.* In Mark the passage is obviously part of the pericope and the fulfillment of scripture refers to the Crucifixion itself. In Luke the reference to this fulfillment of scripture is no longer necessary, since Isaiah 53:12 has just been cited in verse 37 in the first sword pericope (see n. 3 above and n. 10 below); but the verse is still very much part of the pericope and the "power of darkness" is in fact a simple parallel to the Time of the Sword (see the following paragraph, and n. 11 below). In Matthew the passage seems transitional and the fulfillment of scripture may well refer to the fleeing of the disciples (and thus to Zachariah 13:7 ff., which, to be sure, would link the scattering of the sheep to the Time of the Sword and the killing of the Shepherd).

8. Agreement in meaning but diversity of expression is particularly striking between Matthew 26:52a: *apostrepson tēn machairan sou eis ton topon autēs* ("put up again thy sword into its place") and John 18:11a: *bale tēn machairan eis tēn thēkēn* ("put up the sword into the sheath"). For some of the other examples of diversity of expression see n. 5 above. In terms of parallel independent traditions, such resemblances between John and Matthew are particularly valuable, since these are the two Gospels for which any interdependence is especially difficult to postulate (see Raymond E. Brown, *The Gospel According to John* [Anchor Bible 29A], 787 ff.). Agreements between John and Luke, such as the detail of the right ear, are much less striking

together—and that is the way they were read from at least the end of the second century—it seems clear that the episode must be understood as an espousal of Zealot terrorism on the part of at least some of the disciples at the moment of the Lord's arrest and a rejection by Christ of this particular form of Jewish Resistance.[9]

As for the episode of the two swords, it is difficult to separate the original pericope from its reworking by the Lucan redactor, who also reshaped the story about the servant's ear in order to fit the two pericopes together.[10] In its Lucan setting the episode seems to mean that the time of peace and the protection which the disciples enjoyed during the Lord's lifetime is coming to an end: the Time of the Sword is now at hand.[11] Taken together,

---

because of the relative frequency of such parallelisms (Brown, 790 f.; yet *contra,* 816). On the chances that "all they that take the sword shall perish with the sword" has a Semitic-Aramean origin, see Hans Kosmala, "Matthew 26.52—A quotation from the Targum," *Novum Testamentum* 4 (1960) 3 ff., and William F. Albright and C. S. Mann, *Matthew* (Anchor Bible 26), 329.

9. That Jesus was in fact a Zealot or at least akin to the Zealot movement has been argued at length by S. G. F. Brandon, *Jesus and the Zealots* (Manchester, 1967); see also the far more complex approach by O. Betz, "Jesu Heiliger Krieg," *Novum Testamentum* 2 (1958) 116 ff. For the overwhelming rejection of this view by modern scholarship see, for instance, *The Jerome Biblical Commentary,* ed. Raymond Brown *et al.* (Englewood Cliffs, N.J., 1968), vol. 2, pp. 110.187, 159.160; also Albright and Mann, *Matthew,* 328 ff., and Joachim Jeremias, *New Testament Theology* (New York, 1971), 241 f., 294. On the other hand, it seems highly probable that both parts of the sword pericope contain allusions to the Zealot movement. Almost certainly significant is the use of the word *lēstēs,* which, as has been seen (n. 7 above), should probably be translated as "highwayman," "terrorist," "revolutionary," or "bandit" rather than as "thief" and which was commonly used (e.g., by Josephus) in reference to Zealot partisans. Moreover, it is by no means impossible that the *machairai* of Luke 22:38 and the *machaira* used in Mark 14:47 and all its parallels were not real swords but knives, easily concealable under a cloak, such as those used by Zealots or *sicarii* (see, e.g., Brandon, *Jesus and the Zealots,* 203 and 306 f.). In that case it is quite likely that the disciples' misunderstanding in Luke 22:38 is based on a Zealot misconstruction of the Lord's Messianic claims. (See, for instance, Hans Conzelmann, *The Theology of Saint Luke* [London, 1961], 82 f., as well as the references given below, n. 11.)

10. Schürmann, *Jesu Abschiedsrede* III, 130 f., on the parallels between Luke 22:49 and 22:38a, as well as between 22:51 and 22:38b. (See nn. 5 and 7 above.)

11. Conzelmann, *Theology of Luke,* 16, 80 ff., 186 n. 1, and 232 f.; Jeremias, *New Testament Theology,* 241, 243, 284, 294; Paul Minear, "A Note on Luke 22:36," *Novum Testamentum* 7 (1964/65) 128 ff. A. Schlatter, "Die Beiden Schwerter. Lukas 22:35–38. Ein Stück aus der besonderen Quelle des Lukas," *Beiträge zur Förderung Christlichen Theologie* 20.6 (1916) 490–557, remains the longest treatment, but is rather out of date. Of interest for the suggestions that the Lucan pericope has Aramean roots with various possible alliterations and puns involving the Aramean words for "sword," "it is accomplished," "the end," and "it is enough" are the apparently quite independent conclusions of I. Zolli, "L'Episodio delle due Spade (Luca 22, 35 ss.)," *Studi e Materali di Storia delle Religioni* 13 (1938) 228 ff., and of Matthew Black, *An Aramaic Approach to the Gospels and Acts* (Oxford, 1946), 136 f. (: p. 179 in the third edition, 1967).

the two episodes therefore indicate that there will indeed be a Time of the Sword, but that this Time of the Sword does not involve material resistance, and is thus a complete transformation of the Zealot dream.

A later work will attempt to show that this fundamentally biblical reading will remain the basis for patristic and medieval interpretations of the sword pericope. The present work will try to establish that it was Origen who laid the foundations for that later exegesis and that his interpretation of the pericope is closely related to some very fundamental aspects of his theology. Origen of Alexandria (ca. 185–252/3), is seen through the eyes of modern authors as something of a split personality. For some (perhaps now in a minority) he is essentially a philosopher, mostly a Platonist, who introduced new and foreign elements into Christianity. For others he remains primarily a biblical scholar and exegete whose thought has been so impregnated by the Bible that his admitted Platonism is little more than a means for occasionally presenting Christianity in more or less philosophical dress. Some of this double vision can no doubt be explained by the biographical data. Born in a Christian family (his father was martyred in the year 202) Origen earned a living at an early age as head of a catechetical school, but soon began directing a school of philosophy to which non-Christians were apparently admitted. It is from this period of essentially philosophical activity that the most platonizing of his works (*On First Principles* and the first books of his Commentary on John) probably date. In 230, however, he was made a priest by the bishop of Caesarea in Palestine, an ordination that provoked a conflict with the Christian authorities in Alexandria, and forced Origen into permanent exile at Caesarea. From this period of his life came the majority (and more "biblicizing") of his works: the latter books of the Commentary on John, the fragmentary commentaries on Genesis, Psalms, and the Song of Songs, the Commentary on Romans and the great Commentary on Matthew; his voluminous homilies usually dated towards the end of his life, such as the Homilies on the Heptateuch, the Homilies on Jeremiah, the Homilies on Ezechiel, the Homilies on the Song of Songs, and the Homilies on Luke; and finally his major apologetic work, the *Contra Celsum*, which is thought to be of roughly the same years as the homilies.[12]

12. On Origen in general, the fundamental study remains Jean Daniélou, *Origen* (London, 1955). This translation of *Origène* (Paris, 1948) was revised by the author

This double vision is probably also the result of the various "Origenist" controversies that flared up at various times after Origen's death, from the early fourth to the middle of the sixth century. As a consequence of these often extremely acrimonious quarrels—some of which concentrated on the more platonizing ideas he is reputed to have held—much of the original version of his works has been lost. The missing material has had to be reconstituted partly from Greek fragments, often collected for a polemical purpose either by friends or enemies of the dead Origen; or from Latin translations of the fourth or sixth century, which, apart from the defects from which most ancient translations suffer, may also be subject to the polemical slants found in some of the Greek fragments. Finally, modern sectarian biases may also have contributed to this double vision.[13]

For the purposes of this work, such platonizing themes as Origen's theology of the fall and return of the soul, of the double creation, of the curious position of matter and the flesh, of the possible ultimate reconciliation of the Devil, and the peculiarities of his Trinitarianism and Christology, will only be heard in the background.[14] The present book will focus on other

---

and constitutes in fact a second edition. On Origen the "Platonist," see Eugène de Faye, *Origène, sa vie, son oeuvre, sa pensée* (Paris, 1923–28); the still excellent study by Hal Koch, *Pronoia und Paideusis. Studien über Origenes und sein Verhältniss zum Platonismus* (Leipzig, 1932); and from a rather different perspective, Walther Völker, *Das Volkommenheitsideal des Origenes* (Tübingen, 1931). On Origen's biblical exegesis, see Daniélou, *Origen*, 133–99; also by the same author, "L'Unité des Deux Testaments dans l'oeuvre d'Origène," *Rev. Sci. Rel.* 22 (1948) 27 ff., and "Origène comme Exégète de la Bible," in *Studia Patristica* 1 (: *TU* 38) (1958) 280 ff.; Henri de Lubac, *Histoire et Esprit. L'Intelligence de l'Ecriture d'après Origène* (Paris, 1950); R. P. C. Hanson, *Allegory and Event. A Study of the Sources and Significance of Origen's Interpretation of Scripture* (London, 1959); and, most recently, M. F. Wiles, "Origen as Biblical Scholar," in P. R. Ackroyd and C. F. Evans, *The Cambridge History of the Bible*, vol. 1: *From the Beginnings to Jerome* (Cambridge, 1970), 454 ff. For the best discussion of the various editions of Origen's own works, see Johannes Quasten, *Patrology*, vol. 2 (Utrecht, 1962), 44–75; also the simpler and extremely useful listing by Marguerite Harl, *Origène et la Fonction Révélatrice du Verbe Incarné* (*Patristica Sorbonensia* 2; Paris, 1958), 36 ff. More specialized bibliographies will be given when needed. On Origen's political thought see the scanty bibliography given below, chapter 4, n. 1.

13. On the Origenist controversies, see, for instance, Henry Chadwick, *The Early Church* (*Pelican History of the Church*, vol. 1, Baltimore, 1967), 112, 180 f., 184 ff., 209 f.; on their consequences for the transmission and interpretation of Origen's works, see de Lubac, *Histoire et Esprit*, 20 ff., and Daniélou, *Origen*, x ff. On the possibility of modern sectarian bias, see Henri Crouzel, *Théologie de l'Image de Dieu chez Origène* (*Théologie* 34. *Etudes publiées sous la direction de la Faculté de Théologie S.J. de Lyon-Fourvière*; Paris, 1956), 137, n. 53. Yet while Protestants and *laïcs* may rejoice in an overly heterodox Origen, de Lubac and his school (which includes Crouzel) may err by de-platonizing and "churchifying" him just a little too much.

14. But see below, chapter 4 at nn. 75–82, nn. 101, 102, and nn. 107–11.

matters: politics and exegesis. As has just been seen, Origen is frequently associated with biblical exegesis, as frequently, in fact, as he is associated with Platonism or philosophy. "Politics," on the other hand, is not a word that normally springs to mind when his name is mentioned. Yet this study will attempt to demonstrate not only that he has a theology of politics, but that that theology is grounded in his theology of exegesis. In his politics the "state" is related to the Church, very much as in his exegesis the letter is related to the spirit. In a sense, this "exegetical" theology of politics goes back to Saint Paul and the *Epistle to the Romans*, but it is Origen who, as the first formulator of an explicit theology of exegesis, may be said to have "found" (and thus "invented") the theology of politics that is implicit in Saint Paul and other Early Christian writers. The close relationship between politics and exegesis in his thought explains why in the present book the "biblical" Origen will make his presence felt much more than the Platonic or "philosophical" Origen. And his theology of politics, itself grounded in a theology of biblical exegesis, will provide the foundation for the medieval doctrine of the two swords of Luke, which for centuries was to dominate Western thinking about the interrelation between Church and state. Because of this seminal importance of Origen for Western political thought I have on the whole preferred the "Latin" Origen—the Origen available to the West—to the Greek original, even in those relatively few cases where both versions happen to have been preserved.[15] Since Origen was thus particularly accessible and

15. As it happens, of the five works of Origen most frequently used in this study, only one, his *Contra Celsum*, has been preserved in Greek alone. The *De Principiis* exists in its entirety (?) only in the late fourth-century Latin translation of Rufinus, which may mislead by trying to correct Origen's errors; but large Greek fragments have been preserved, mostly through the *Philocalia* (a collection of extracts compiled by Basil and Gregory of Nazianzus) but also through fragments collected by his enemies, who may tend to exaggerate his errors. The Greek fragments have been put together, when possible, face to face with Rufinus's translation in Koetschau's edition of *De Principiis* in *GCS*; whether these Greek extracts are in every case more reliable than even Rufinus's Latin is open to some doubt. The Commentary on Matthew (from Matthew 13:36 only) exists in two parts: the *Tomoi* or Commentary on Matthew proper (until Matthew 22:33 only) exists in very large Greek fragments with equally large Latin fragments (from Matthew 16:13 only) from an anonymous Latin translation of the sixth century that is not always very accurate but is at least without any particular *parti-pris* and often parallels (and sometimes complements) the Greek text. The end of the Commentary—which interests us most since it includes a lengthy discussion of the sword pericope and goes on to the end of Matthew 27—has been preserved only in the so-called *Commentariorum Series*, that is, the anonymous Latin translation of the sixth century. The same is true for the all-important Homilies on the Heptateuch and the Commentary on Romans: both are preserved only in the

influential in the West, the actual mechanics of the medieval interpretation of the two swords of Luke are themselves very much dependent on Origen's exegesis of the sword pericope. For this reason, the second and largest chapter of this work is devoted to a detailed examination of Origen's exegesis of that particular pericope. The third chapter will broaden the canvas and attempt to use his exegesis of the sword pericope as a case study for the theoretical foundations of his hermeneutics as a whole. The fourth chapter will conclude with a discussion of his theology of politics in relation to his theology of exegesis. The first chapter attempts to set the stage: it serves as a general introduction to Origen's exegetical methods but will concentrate on his interpretation of warfare (and particularly of uses of the sword) in his exegesis of the Old Testament.

---

translation by Rufinus. (Small sections of the Commentary on Romans in the Greek original have been discovered since the beginning of this century, but they do not include the verses of Romans—mostly Romans 13:1 ff.—that are especially relevant to this study.) The Homilies on Luke (preserved largely in the Latin translation by Saint Jerome) and the Commentary on John (preserved only in Greek fragments) would have been very useful, but in their present state both stop before the story of the Passion and therefore before the sword pericope. Together with a few other works of Origen, e.g., the Fragments on Matthew, the Homilies on Jeremiah (both preserved only in Greek) and the Homilies on Ezechiel (preserved only in Latin), they have proved of some use but only on relatively rare occasions. On the popularity of Origen in the West, on the reason for his survival often in Latin only, and on the whole phenomenon of the "Origenes Latinus," see de Lubac, *Exégèse Médiévale. Les Quatre sens de l'Ecriture* (*Théologie* 41. *Etudes publiées sous la direction de la Faculté de Théologie S.J. de Lyon-Fourvière;* Paris, 1955), vol. 1, 221 ff.

CHAPTER I

THE SWORD AND THE LETTER

Origen's exegetical activity—New Testament as well as Old Testament exegesis—falls into four distinct categories.[1] First, there is the occasional *ex parte* remark in fundamentally nonexegetical works such as *De Principiis* or *Contra Celsum.* Second, there are the usually short and sometimes incomplete glosses scattered throughout the collections of Byzantine *catenae,* the attribution of which is not always too secure.[2] Third, there are the great homilies which date from the end of Origen's life and were delivered at Caesarea. Fourth, and finally, there are the fully sequential commentaries—the first of the genre—such as the Commentary on John or the great Commentary on Matthew.[3]

1. I have simply added the *ex parte* category to the three listed by Daniélou in *Origen,* xii f.

2. The fragments on Matthew edited by Klostermann as the third part of Origen's *Matthäuserklärung* (*Origenes* 12.3, *GCS* 41) mostly come from such *catenae.* (For an example of a gloss from this volume that is incomplete and not necessarily on Matthew see below, chapter 2 at nn. 109–11.) So do the fragments on the Apocalypse edited by A. Harnack and C. Diobouniotis, *Der Scholier-Kommentar des Origenes zur Apokalypse Johannis, TU* 38.3 (1911). Some other of these glosses have been preserved (together with quite different material often not by Origen at all) in the so-called *Selecta in Psalmos* reprinted in Migne, *PG* 12. (See the warnings and some useful hints on the use of this material by Harl, *Fonction Révélatrice,* 38.) Much of this material probably still remains unprinted; see Daniélou, *Origen,* xiii.

3. I have normally cited Origen from the editions in the Berlin Corpus *(:GCS).* Most of his Commentary on Romans (i.e. all of Rufinus' translation; see above,

Origen's exegesis, however, is notable by its quality even more than by its considerable quantity; and especially by the strongly allegorical bent which he imprinted upon the whole subsequent tradition, particularly upon that of the West, where the rival and less allegorically minded school of Antioch was to have relatively little effect.[4] To be sure, patristic scholars are widely and sometimes even wildly at variance in their appreciation of his allegorism. Yet when the smoke of battle has cleared, a fair number of inescapable conclusions will probably appear: for much of the disagreement seems to be merely of degree.[5]

It is hard to deny that, on occasion at least, Origen's allegorism is based on a kind of mythographic esotericism or on the somewhat curious rules of Hellenistic rhetoric more than on traditional Christianity. This is particularly true of his exegesis of certain passages of the Old Testament, especially the opening chapters of Genesis and some of the precepts of the Mosaic Legislation. He may well, for instance, have believed that before the Fall, man had been a sexless creature and that the story of man's creation as "male and female" must be taken to refer to the composition of the human essence, the spirit being called "man" and the soul "woman."[6] Nor can one dispute the fact

---

Introduction, n. 15) still exists only in Migne (:*PG* 14, 837 ff.), while Koetschau's edition of *Contra Celsum* in the Berlin Corpus (*Origenes* 1 and 2, *GCS* 2 and 3) presents some serious problems. While referring to it for the reader's convenience (under the siglum *GCS* 2 and 3) I have preferred to use and cite in the first place the five-volume French edition and translation by Marcel Borret in *Sources Chrétiennes*, vols. 132, 136, 147, 150 and 227 (Paris 1967–76); on Koetschau's edition and its problems, see Borret, *Contre Celse*, vol. 1 (*SC* 132) 22–56 and vol. 5 (*SC* 227) 9–23. For the "fourfold" method I have used in citing *Contra Celsum*, see the second note to the Abbreviations, above p. xiv.

4. See the general remarks by Beryl Smalley, *The Study of the Bible in the Middle Ages*, 2nd ed. (New York, 1958), 13–22; but cf. M. L. W. Laistner, "Antiochene Exegesis in Western Europe," *Harvard Theological Review* 40 (1947), 19–31.

5. Of the authors cited (above, Intro., n. 12), de Lubac is the most favorable to Origen, Hanson the most unfavorable, Daniélou somewhere in between but perhaps a little closer to de Lubac. (Daniélou's sometimes sharp criticism in his book—e.g., *Origen*, 174 ff.—must be read in the context of his glowing appraisal in "L'Unité des Deux Testaments" and of his balanced account in "Origène comme Exégète.") The dispute between de Lubac and Hanson tends to become acrimonious; the disagreements between de Lubac and Daniélou seem partly verbal, partly a matter of degree and of judgment in particular instances: see below, nn. 12, 14, 16. M. F. Wiles is judicious and does not take part in the controversy: his position on the whole is close to that of Daniélou, but see below, n. 12.

6. See the brief resumé on the state of the question in G. B. Ladner, *The Idea of Reform* (New York, 1967), 157, n. 14. For Origen, at least in *De Principiis* 1.8.1, 96 (see the English translation by G. W. Butterworth, *Origen: On First Principles* [New York, 1966], 277 f.), man was first created as a pure spirit, the body being itself a punish-

that Origen can be badly led astray by his principle that every passage must have at least one "spiritual," while it need not necessarily have a literal, meaning.[7] The danger is compounded when this principle is combined with a distinct tendency (indeed sometimes one might well say an almost eager readiness) to borrow a page from Hellenistic literary criticism and to see in often quite superficial difficulties of a text the definite proof that it cannot possibly make sense at a purely literal level.[8] Thus in the Mosaic Law, the prohibition against leaving the house or carrying a burden on the sabbath has no literal meaning for Origen; for he blandly assumes that it cannot be carried out to the letter. Similarly, the Mosaic ban on eating kites or gier-eagles makes no literal sense, for no one, he joyfully remarks, would wish to eat the first, while no one has ever caught the second. Even apart from the story of the Creation and the Mosaic Legislation, there are, finally, a few other passages of the Old Testament which have no historical meaning: it would be absurd to believe that the Temple of Solomon could actually have been built "without the sound of hammer and of axe."[9] In general, such "stumbling blocks and obstacles" to any strictly literal exegesis of the Old Testament were for Origen deliberately "woven into" Scripture by the Holy Spirit to remind the

---

ment—though admittedly a relatively "light" punishment—for an original "cosmic" fall (see also Daniélou, *Origen*, 214 f.). He may well have believed even late in life that the references to the creation of man in Genesis 1 refer to this purely spiritual being and that the "garments of skin" of Genesis 3:21 refer to the creation of bodies after the Fall. At any rate, Gregory of Nyssa seems to have interpreted Origen in this fashion; see Ladner, *Idea of Reform*, loc. cit. Origen, *Hom. Gen.* 13–15, 15–19, moreover, can be interpreted as suggesting that the literal meaning of the creation of woman in Genesis 2 is purely proleptic, the original—pre-Fall—meaning being an allegory of the separation of soul from spirit. See also Jean Daniélou, *From Shadows to Reality. Studies in the Biblical Typology of the Fathers* (London, 1960), 62, who points out the Philonic origin of this particular allegory.

7. Origen, *De Principiis* 4.3.5, 331, Butterworth, 297. "Everything in Scripture has a spiritual meaning but not all of it has a literal meaning" (translation from the Greek in Daniélou, *Origen*, 181). For a discussion of the principle and its dangers, see Daniélou, *Origen*, 178–91, also in "Origène comme Exégète de la Bible," 288 ff.

8. R. M. Grant, *The Earliest Lives of Jesus* (London, 1961), most of which is in fact dedicated to Origen's exegesis of the New Testament, has emphasized the debt this kind of exegesis owes to Hellenistic rhetoric and the rules it had developed for judging the verisimilitude of a particular argument and literary text. For an example of this sort of eagerness on the part of Origen, see in particular Hanson, *Allegory and Event*, 235–310, and Daniélou, *Origen*, 174–99.

9. *Com. Rom.* 1.10, 856; *De Principiis* 4.3.1–2, 323–27, Butterworth, 288–92; *Hom. Gen.* 2.6, 36 f. (The reference to the Temple being constructed "without the sound of hammer and of axe" is to 3 Reg. 6.7.) See the discussion in Hanson, *Allegory and Event*, 239 ff.

Christian that he should everywhere labor to seek out the spiritual meaning.[10]

On the other hand, while it is true that Origen follows a certain strain of Hellenistic rhetoric and believes that the Old Testament, like the *Iliad*, has woven into its narrative certain myths and allegories, for him such cases remain the exception: "the incidents, which are historically true," he insists, are much more numerous than the "spiritual interpretations" which have been woven in by the Holy Ghost for pedagogical reasons.[11] It is clear, moreover, that in a goodly number of instances Origen's allegorization does provide an extension or a deepening of the traditional typology, which is admittedly a central part of the Christian kerygma.[12] Thus, it is Origen who, by extension of the ancient typology of the Crossing of the Red Sea, first develops the theme of the Crossing of the Jordan (under the leadership of Joshua-Jesus) as a type of Baptism.[13] Again, it is he who points up the traditional theme of the Fall of Jericho as a type of the fall of the "world," by restructuring the spiritual meaning of the episode into a series of hierarchical

10. *De Principiis* 4.2.9, 321 f., Butterworth, 285 f. For this theory of "weaving in" and its relationship to Hellenistic rhetoric and literary criticism, see Grant, *Earliest Lives*, esp. 65 ff.

11. *De Principiis* 4.3.4, 329 f. (cf. Butterworth, 294 f.), cited by Hanson, *Allegory and Event*, 263.

12. The quarrel about the value of Origen's method is complicated by a dispute between Daniélou and de Lubac on whether or not to distinguish between "typology" and "allegory." Daniélou, in "Traversée de la Mer Rouge et Baptême aux Premiers Siècles," *Rech. Sc. Rel.* 33 (1946), 402–30, esp. 416 f., has suggested that "typology" should be used exclusively in *bona parte*, "allegory" in *mala parte*. De Lubac, in a whole article devoted to the subject, " 'Typologie' et 'Allégorisme'," *Rech. Sc. Rel.* 34 (1947), 180–226, rejects the distinction partly because it was not made by the Fathers, partly because in his judgment "bad" allegories are relatively rare (but see below, n. 16). The problem is then taken up again by Daniélou in *Origen* 139–99, with a brief answer to de Lubac, 227, n. 2, and more extensively in *Shadows to Reality*, which is basically a discussion of "typology." Similarly, all four volumes of de Lubac's *Exégèse Médiévale* are in effect a discussion of "allegory." See also Daniélou, *Bible and Liturgy* (Notre Dame, Ind., 1956), and "Origène comme Exégète," 284 ff., as well as Jacques Guillet, "Les Exégèses d'Alexandrie et d'Antioche. Conflit ou malentendu?" *Rech. Sc. Rel.* 34 (1947), 257–302, who uses Daniélou's distinction but in effect supports de Lubac. Wiles, "Origen as Biblical Scholar," 482, rightly points out that "to ask whether Origen's [exegesis] is primarily typological or allegorical . . . is to ask the wrong question." Note that Daniélou himself, in "L'Unité des Deux Testaments," 45 f., *Shadows to Reality*, 277, and *Origen*, 167 ff., shows in effect how Origen's "allegorism" can lead to a deepening of traditional "typology." Because Origen himself seems to use "allegory" more often than "type" and because the former will become the technical medieval term, I myself have used "allegory" in preference to "type."

13. *Com. Joh.* 6.42–48, 151–57; *Hom. Jos.* 6.1, 321 ff. See the discussion by Daniélou, *Shadows to Reality*, 276–86.

levels. Allegorically (in the strict sense of the term)[14] the Fall of Jericho and the sound of the trumpets accompanying its taking represent the fall of the "world" and the joy of the true People of God at the Coming of Christ and at the preaching of His Word through the priests of His Church: the strictly allegorical level has thus both a christological and an ecclesiological dimension. Second, or tropologically, the trumpets represent the joy of the individual Christian, whenever he receives Jesus-Joshua within the city of his soul after the fall of the worldly vices which had previously inhabited it. Anagogically, finally, the whole episode is a type of the Second Coming, of the trumpets of the Last Judgment and of the final overcoming of the forces of this world.[15] As this particularly beautiful example makes clear, the allegorism of Origen need not therefore lead to a distortion of traditional typology through mythographic esotericism and to a consequent dissolution of the "letter" of history. On the contrary, it may, at least as often, deepen the traditional themes of the history of salvation. The three spiritual senses, if properly used, can give a legitimate religious dimension to the literal or historical meaning of the taking of Jericho, while the sequence of the four meanings taken as a whole gives emphasis to the four main stages of the history of salvation: Christ was announced in the Old Testament; He has come into His Kingdom in the New; today He must come again into the soul of each individual Christian; finally, at the end of the world, He will come in glory to judge the quick and the dead.[16]

14. Not only is the terminology confused by the interference of a "typological" with an "allegorical" vocabulary (Daniélou tends to use "allegory" only in *mala parte* as designating a basically non-Christian kind of mythographical esotericism), but in patristic and medieval usage one must distinguish between "allegory" *largo sensu* to refer to the whole of the "spiritual" meaning, and "allegory" *stricto sensu* to refer to the christological and/or ecclesiological meaning as distinguished from the other spiritual senses, i.e., the "moral" (or "tropological") and the "anagogical" meaning. For all this, see de Lubac, *Exégèse Médiévale* 1, passim.

15. *Hom. Jos.* 7 to 11, 327–66; see Daniélou, *Shadows to Reality*, 276–86.

16. This is the order which Daniélou (*Shadows to Reality*, 277; see also *Origen*, 167 ff., and "Origène comme Exégète," 286) calls "the three traditional forms of typology in their proper order." Origen himself, with equal frequency, uses another order, in which the tropological is the first, and the properly allegorical the second of the "spiritual" senses. Moreover, this second or "improper" order is the one which Origen discusses at a theoretical level: see the youthful *De Principiis* 4.2.4–9. This second order—which is apparently Philonic in origin—is based in part on the trichotomous anthropology that is also found in Paul. The literal meaning corresponds to the body and is the only one available to the non-initiates, the "hylics" or materialists. The

Despite his tendency to assume a little too quickly that certain details in the history of the Jewish People could not be literally true, Origen's attitude towards the "letter" of the Old Testament is, on the whole, quite in line with tradition. On one hand, like Saint Paul, Origen undoubtedly feels that "the letter killeth"; like Saint Paul and indeed like Christ Himself, he considers the New Dispensation as in some sense radically opposed to the Old Law. The changeover, the spiritual Passover (*diabasis*) from the Old to the New Dispensation, was for him a radical conversion, a *metanoia*, from letter to spirit.[17] Moses and Jesus are in that sense opposed to each other, "for the precepts of the Law had to do essentially with the external man, the teaching of the Lord with the inner man."[18] Unlike his namesake Joshua, Jesus wrote His legislation, the true Deuteronomy, not "on the stones of the altar" (Joshua 8:32) but "on the living and upright stones" of the hearts of men.[19] Indeed, in the typology of Origen there is a tendency to replace Moses as one of the traditional Christ-types by the figure of Joshua, partly because it was Joshua and not Moses who brought their People into the

---

tropological meaning corresponds to the intermediate part of man, the soul, and is the one available to the "psychic," the ordinary Christian; the properly allegorical, or fully spiritual, meaning corresponds to the spirit, and is available only to the "pneumatics," those who are fully versed in the divine mysteries. (The anagogical meaning may then be tacked on.) The first order deepens traditional typology by making the moral or spiritual progress of the individual Christian (tropology) dependent on the activity of Christ (christology and ecclesiology, i.e., "allegory" in the strict sense of the term). The second order is considered by many as fundamentally non-Christian, or at best as a Christian elaboration of a Greek and Philonic literary device which inevitably leads to a semi-Gnostic form of esotericism. This is the view of Daniélou. It is also that of de Lubac in volume 1 of *Exégèse Médiévale*. By the later volumes, de Lubac is much kinder to this second scheme: under the proper circumstances, this second scheme can be seen as following not the historical order of revelation (in which Christ comes to the soul after He has come into the world), but the journey of the soul back to God. For the soul of the Christian mystic, Christ is perceived phenomenologically within the soul (tropology) before He is theologically conceived (allegory). Hanson, in *Allegory and Event*, ignores the first order and treats the second as purely Philonic and totally foreign to genuine Christianity. Wiles, in "Origen as Biblical Scholar," 467 ff., makes a slightly different distinction. For him, Origen's exegesis is fluid and all the various possibilities can be reduced to a basically twofold exegesis that distinguishes primarily between the literal and the spiritual.

17. For the spiritual Passover, the *diabasis* from Old to New Testament, see Daniélou, "L'Unité des Deux Testaments," 37. For the conversion *(metanoia)* from letter to spirit, see *Com. Mat.* 10.14, 18, cited by de Lubac, *Exégèse Médiévale* 1,311, n. 8.

18. *Frag. Mat.* 329, 143 on Matthew 15:11 cited by Victor Ernst Hasler, *Gesetz und Evangelium in der Alten Kirche bis auf Origenes* (Zürich, 1953), 92 f. See also Wiles, "Origen as Biblical Exegete," 480 ff.

19. *Hom. Jos.* 9.3 , 348. See Hasler, *Gesetz und Evangelium*, 86.

Holy Land and partly because Joshua as the supposed author of Deuteronomy ("which is to say Second Legislation") could be taken to have foreshadowed the replacement of the Law by his namesake, the true Joshua-Jesus, Who by the "Second Law of the Gospel" would fully supersede both Moses and his Law.[20] To be sure, types and figures (such as the Jewish priesthood) wished to survive and thus violently resisted the revelation of the Truth; but with the Coming of the True Priest and True Sacrifice, the sacrifice of blood came to an end and the Temple was destroyed.[21] In the presence of Truth, "types and shadows have their ending";[22] when the Divine Sculptor "has achieved the work for the purpose of which he first fashioned a prototype of clay," the model is destroyed.[23]

On the other hand, for Origen as for Paul and indeed Christ Himself, the Gospel is also a perfecting and thus a continuation and not simply an abolition of the Old Law. As with children who ripen into men, while their form is in no way destroyed but rather becomes more perfect, so is it with the Law: to paraphrase Aquinas, for Origen the New Alliance does not destroy the Law but perfects it. The Covenant of Grace is the Covenant of the Law, enhanced and renewed. Indeed, as Origen emphasizes, it is the duality of spirit and letter that explains both the perfect continuity and the utter opposition between Law and Gospel. Christians must "reject the Law according to the letter,

20. On this whole problem, see Daniélou, *Shadows to Reality*, 229–43.

21. *Com. Joh.* 28.12, 404, cited by Daniélou, "L'Unité des Deux Testaments," 36. See also *Hom. Lev.* 10.1, 441, cited by Daniélou, "L'Unité des Deux Testaments," 33 (not *Hom. Lev.* 11 as is there indicated). Also *Hom. Jos.* 17.1, 400 ff., cited by Daniélou, "L'Unité des Deux Testaments," 35; see below, n. 22.

22. *Hom. Jos.* 17.1, 400 f.: "Cum vero in adventu Salvatoris nostri Dei . . . veritas de terra orta est . . . umbra et exemplaria ceciderunt. Cecidit enim Hierusalem, cecidit templum, altare sublatum est. . . . Sic ergo praesente veritate typus et umbra cessavit; et cum adesset templum illud quod per Spiritum Dei . . . in utero virginis fabricatum est, dirutum est templum ex lapidibus fabricatum. Aderat pontifex futurorum bonorum, cessant pontifices taurorum et hircorum . . . ." See the translation given by Daniélou, "L'Unité des Deux Testaments," 35. My own paraphrase, i.e., "Types and shadows have their ending," comes from the Anglican version of the *Tantum Ergo*.

23. *Hom. Lev.* 10.1, 441: "Est ergo lex et omnia quae in lege sunt . . . sicut hi, quibus artificium est signa ex aere facere et statuas fundere, antequam verum opus aeris producant aut argenti vel auri, figmentum prius luti ad similitudinem futurae imaginis formant—quod figmentum necessarium quidem est, sed usquequo opus quod principale est, expleatur; cum autem fuerit effectum opus illud, propter quod figmentum luti fuerat formatum, usus eius ultra non quaeritur. . . . Venit enim ipse artifex et auctor omnium et legem quae umbram habebat futurorum bonorum transtulit ad ipsam imaginem rerum." See the translation by Daniélou, "L'Unité des Deux Testaments," 31.

but only in order to uphold the Law according to the Spirit."[24] Indeed, for the faithful it is only the spiritual message of the New Dispensation that can give genuine meaning to the Old: "it was the Advent of Christ, which illuminated the Law of Moses with the lightning of Truth, took away from the Law the veil of the letter, and revealed to all believers the good things that were hidden within." In that sense, for Christians, "both Testaments together form a single New Testament, not with respect to time but with respect to the newness of the understanding."[25]

This dialectical outlook on the relationship between the Two Dispensations, which is so strongly Origen's, is particularly apparent in his treatment of the wars of the Old Testament. On the one hand, these acts of violence—though they are recognized as actual facts of history—must be utterly rejected by all Christians.[26] It is the Jews who, resisting the Advent of Truth and wishing these types to survive, give a literal exegesis to the warlike passages of the Old Testament and therefore "become cruel and thirst for human blood"; they mistakenly imagine that, because "the holy men of old massacred the inhabitants" of the cities of Canaan, such deeds are therefore worthy of imitation to the letter.[27] Christians, though, must

24. For the Pauline image of children growing up, see *Frag. Mat.* 97, 55 f. (on Matthew 5:17) cited and translated by Hasler, *Gesetz und Evangelium*, 78. On the Two Laws, the one according to the letter, the other according to the spirit, see *Hom. Lev.* 16.7, 506, cited by Hasler, 75.

25. *De Principiis* 4.1, 6, 302; Butterworth, 265: "Legem ergo Moysi splendor adventus Christi per fulgorem veritatis inluminans, id quod superpositum erat litterae ejus velamen abstraxit, et omnia quae cooperta inibi bona tegebantur, universis in se credentibus reseravit," cited by de Lubac, *Exégèse Médiévale* 1, 324. *Hom. Num.* 9.4, 59: ". . . Illis tantummodo lex vetus efficitur testamentum, qui eam carnaliter intelligere volunt. . . . Nobis autem, qui eam spiritaliter et evangelico sensu intelligimus et exponimus, semper nova est: et utrumque nobis novum testamentum est, non temporis aetate, sed intelligentiae novitate"; see de Lubac, 1, 330.

26. Hanson, *Allegory and Event*, 263, suggests that for Origen some of the atrocities of the Old Testament, such as the massacre of the five kings by Joshua in Joshua 10:12 ff., did not really happen and that the passage has only an allegorical meaning. The references he gives to *Hom. Jos.* 11.1 and 11.5 do not, however, bear him out. On the contrary, *Hom. Jos.* 11.6, 366, suggests that what embarrasses Origen is the thought that Joshua, in including the story in "his" book, intended to teach cruelty to Christians but that it never occurred to Origen to doubt the historicity of the passage: "Sed interim Jesus [Nave] interfecit inimicos, non crudelitatem docens per hoc, sicut haeretici putant, sed futura in his, quae geruntur sacramenta designans, ut, cum interemerit eos reges, qui regnum peccati tenent in nobis, possimus illud implere quod dixit Apostolus [Romans 6:19] . . . ."

27. *Hom. Jos.* 8.7, 343: "Haec cum legunt Iudaei, crudeles efficiuntur et humanum sanguinem sitiunt, putantes quia et sancti percusserunt eos, qui habitabant Gai

reject such literalism. On the other hand, even for Christians the Advent of Truth has by no means put a stop to warfare: it has only intensified that warfare by transposing it to a higher and ultimately more real plane. As has been rightly said, for Origen the whole of the Bible constitutes the Book of the Wars of Jahweh;[28] but Christians must realize that the wars and massacres of the Old Testament should be understood spiritually, as figures and "sacraments" of the wars of the Spirit.[29] Indeed, "unless these carnal wars were meant as types of spiritual warfare, the books of Jewish history, it is my belief," Origen insists, "would never have been handed down by the Apostles to be read in their churches by the disciples of Christ, Who has come, after all, in order to teach peace."[30] At the same time, Christ the Warrior has "come not to bring peace but a sword" (Matthew 10:34). "For the Lord brought peace only to men of good will [Luke 2:14] and His peace is not the peace of this world [John 14:27] for it is the peace of God, which passeth all understanding [Philippians 4:7]."[31]

[Joshua 8:25], . . . non intelligentes in his verbis adumbrari mysteria et hoc nobis magis indicari quod ex his, quorum chaos est habitaculum et qui regnarunt in abysso, daemonibus nullum penitus relinquere debeamus, sed omnes interimere . . . ."

28. De Lubac, *Histoire et Esprit,* 187 and n. 304. De Lubac refers generally to *Hom. Jud.* 6.2, 500. The citation "cum ergo sacra Scriptura tota sit liber bellorum Domini" comes, as de Lubac indicates, from Gerhoch of Reichersberg, *Commentarium in Psalmos,* Ps. 150, *PL* 194.997B; but Gerhoch's expression, though ultimately Origenist, is clearly based on Rupert of Deutz, e.g., *De Victoria Verbi Dei* 2.18 (ed. R. Haacke, *MGH—Quellen zur Geistesgeschichte des Mittelalters,* vol. 5), 66. The *Book of the Wars of the Lord* or *Book of the Wars of Jahweh* is referred to in Numbers 21:14.

29. See above, nn. 26 and 27.

30. *Hom. Jos.* 15.1, 381: "Nisi bella ista carnalia figuram bellorum spiritalium gererent, numquam, opinor, Iudaicarum historiarum libri discipulis Christi, qui venit pacem docere, legendi in ecclesiis fuissent ab Apostolis traditi," referred to by Adolf von Harnack, *Militia Christi, Die christliche Religion und der Soldatenstand in den ersten drei Jahrhunderten* (Tübingen, 1905), 27.

31. *Hom. Lev.* 16.5, 501, *ad Lev.* 26:23: '. . . *dabo pacem super terram vestram*': "Quam pacem dat Deus? Istam quam habet mundus? Negat se istam dare Christus. Dicit enim: 'meam pacem do vobis, meam pacem relinquo vobis; non sicut hic mundus dat pacem et ego do vobis' [John 14:27]. Negat ergo se pacem mundi dare discipulis suis, quia et alibi dicit: 'quid putatis quia veni pacem mittere in terram? Non veni pacem mittere sed gladium' [Matthew 10:34]. Vis ergo videre quam pacem dat Deus super terram nostram? . . . illam pacem [terra] suscipiet a Deo quam dicit Apostolus 'pax autem Dei, quae superat omnem mentem . . . .' [Philippians 4:7]." Also *Hom. Luc.* 13, 79: "Diligens scripturae lector inquirat quomodo Salvator loquatur: 'Non veni pacem mittere super terram sed gladium' [Matthew 10:34] et nunc angeli in sua nativitate decantent 'super terram pax' [Luke 2:14] . . . et in alio loco ex persona ipsius dicitur: 'Pacem meam do vobis . . . non sicut mundus iste dat pacem, ego do pacem' [John 14:27]. . . . Si scriptum esset 'super terram pax,' et hucusque esset finita sententia,

For Origen, therefore, the Pauline theme of spiritual warfare is of fundamental importance.[32] Christians "wrestle not against flesh and blood, but against principalities and powers, against the rulers of the darkness of this world." They must, therefore, put on "the whole armor of God" and stand fast, having their "loins girt about with truth" and armed with "the breastplate of righteousness," "the shield of faith," "the helmet of salvation and the sword of the Spirit, which is the word of God."[33] Indeed, these verses from Ephesians 6:11 ff. are among the biblical passages most frequently cited by Origen, most noticeably in his homilies on Exodus, Numbers, Joshua, and Judges, the main "war books" of the Old Testament.[34] For Origen, moreover, the ascetic, the "true" gnostic, in this fight against sin and temptation, is the Christian warrior above all others. Only he who is continent, only he who has overcome his passions (and Origen questions how many such men there are even among Christians) is worthy to be called a "man of manhood"; he who wants to be a true man must, like the Israelites of old, prove his courage by fighting in battle.[35] The genuinely Christian life is a heroic life; and even among Christians it is already becoming the life of a minority.[36] As has been rightly emphasized, Origen is thus the fountainhead of an ascetic and monastic tradition of spiritual warfare that will culminate in the *Spiritual Exercises* of Ignatius Loyola.[37]

---

recte quaestio nasceretur. Nunc vero id quod additum est, hoc est quod post 'pacem' dicitur in 'in hominibus bonae voluntatis' solvit quaestionem . . . ." CF. also *Hom. Jer.* 2.2, 18. In general, see de Lubac, *Histoire et Esprit,* 186, n. 296, with several references to Origen's use of Matthew 10:34.

32. See Harnack, *Militia Christi,* 26–31; de Lubac, *Histoire et Esprit,* 184–91; and Georg Teichtweiler, *Die Sündenlehre des Origenes* (*Studien zur Geschichte der katholischen Moraltheologie* 7: Passau, 1958), passim, esp. 118–27.

33. Ephesians 6:12–17.

34. See, e.g., the biblical index in *Origenes* 7 (*GCS* 30), 550.

35. *Hom. Num.* 25.5, 240: "Si qui vero pugnare non vult nec militare, si qui non vult habere certamen studiorum divinorum et abstinentiae hic non vult implere illud quod Apostolus dixit [1 Corinthians 9:25]: 'qui autem in agone contendit ab omnibus continens est.' Qui ergo non contendit in agone et ab omnibus non est continens . . . hic etiamsi 'vir' dicatur, 'vir' tamen 'virtutis' non potest appellari. . . . Quis nostrum ita paratus est, ut 'procedat ad bellum' et contra adversarios dimicet, ut et ipse 'vir' possit appellari 'virtutis'? Sicut autem vita continens et abstinentiae labor atque agonum certamina faciunt unumquemque 'virum virtutis' appellari, ita e contrario remissa vita ac negligens et ignava facit virum ignaviae appellari." See Teichtweiler, *Die Sündenlehre,* 119, where the passage is cited.

36. See the remarks by Harnack in *Militia Christi,* 28.

37. De Lubac, *Histoire et Esprit,* 190 f.

At the same time, for Origen as for Paul, this spiritual warfare is by no means merely a shadowy and internalized *psychomachia*, a Hellenistic battle between the virtues and the vices. On the contrary, the spiritual warfare of the Christian has not only an inner, moral or tropological aspect—though that aspect is undoubtedly emphasized—but also a less shadowy and therefore historical, christological, and indeed eschatological dimension: the fight within the Christian takes place against the background of the cosmic struggle between Christ and Devil.[38] There are, Origen asserts, Two Kings and Two Kingdoms: the Kingdom of Sin, whose King is the Devil, and the Kingdom of Righteousness, whose King is Christ. With the Coming of Christ, moreover, the struggle between the two Kings naturally intensified by being transposed onto a higher plane. The Devil knows that Christ has come to dethrone him, and in fear and hatred will do battle even harder than before.[39] Despite the "mildness" and the "gentleness" of the New Dispensation, the Coming of Christ has therefore not abolished the warlike qualities of the God of Hosts (though it has radically transformed the conditions of warfare). It is therefore no accident that, when the Christian first encounters the name of "Jesus," it should be under the guise of Joshua the Warrior: "We meet the name of Jesus for the first time, when we see him as head of an army. From this first acquaintance with the name of Jesus," Origen continues, "I learn the mystery of its never-ending symbolism: Jesus is the leader of an army."[40] Thus, the Book of

38. See the remarks by Teichtweiler, *Die Sündenlehre*, 118, and de Lubac, *Histoire et Esprit*, 186 ff.

39. *Hom. Luc.* 30, 172: "Tam Filio Dei quam Antichristo regnandi studium est. Sed Antichristus regnare desiderat, ut occidat, quos sibi subiecerat; Christus ad hoc regnat ut salvet. . . . Duo igitur reges certatim regnare festinant: peccati rex peccatoribus diabolus, iustitiae rex iustis Christus. Sciensque diabolus ad hoc venisse Christum, ut regnum illius tolleret et hi, qui sub eo erant, inciperent esse sub Christo, ostendit ei omnia regna mundi . . . ." (The story of Christ's Temptation follows.) See the brief discussion in Teichtweiler, *Die Sündenlehre*, 118 f.

40. *Hom. Jos.* 1.1, 288: "Sed 'Iesu' nomen primo invenio in Exodo et volo intueri, quando primum nomen 'Iesu' cognominatur. 'Venit' inquit 'Amalec, et expugnabat Istrahel, et dixit Moyses ad Iesum in Raphidim' [Exodus 17:8–9]. Haec est prima appellatio nominis Iesu. 'Elige' inquit, 'tibi viros potentes ex omnibus filiis Istrahel et egredere, et conflige cum Amalec crastino' [Exodus 17:9]. Moyses confitetur non posse se exercitum ducere, confitetur se non posse obtinere quamvis eum de terra Aegyptii eduxerit. Et ideo, inquit, vocavit Iesum et dixit 'elige tibi viros et egredere.' Vides, cui cesserit bellum gerere adversum Amalec. In hoc primo nomen discimus Iesu, ubi eum videmus ducem exercitus: non cui Moyses iniunxerit principatum, sed cui cesserit

Joshua—to which Origen attaches so much importance—is not primarily about the battles of the son of Nun, it is about the True Leader of the Army of God; it is about the Lord Jesus, "Who has triumphed over the principalities and powers and has nailed them to the Cross in His Person."[41] Finally, as has been seen, if the fall of Jericho is more than a simple act of war, neither is it merely a symbol of internalized moral strife. To be sure, it is both of these, but what gives the episode its basic significance is that it represents the triumph of Jesus, the Divine Commander, over "principalities and powers, over the rulers of the darkness of this world." This triumph, though in principle achieved at the time of the Resurrection (for it is Christ Who has nailed to the Cross the powers and rulers of this world) remains, however, incomplete. Until it shall be made fully visible at the time of the Last Judgment, it has to be perfected within the soul of every individual Christian. The moral or tropological *psychomachia* is thus merely a road-station between the christological triumph of the Lord's First Advent and the final eschatological victory of the Second Coming.[42]

The New Dispensation thus both rejects and intensifies the wars of the Old Testament. If this is true of warfare in general, it is equally true of uses of the sword. Swords, to be sure, need not necessarily be interpreted *in bona parte* in terms of spiritual warfare; sometimes the "swords that transpierce men's souls" are taken to refer to sins and death of the spirit which is their result. Thus, in Luke 2:35, the prophecy of Simeon the Just that a "sword shall pierce through the soul" of the Virgin is curiously enough understood by Origen as foretelling the sin which Mary shall commit when she, like the disciples, will be scandalized by the Crucifixion.[43] Normally, however, Origen

---

primatum. . . . Hic ergo ubi primum disco nomen Iesu, ibi continuo etiam mysterii video sacramentum: ducit enim exercitum Iesus." The passage is referred to by Daniélou, *Shadows to Reality*, 239, and by de Lubac, *Histoire et Esprit*, 187. For Origen's tendency to oppose Joshua-Jesus to Moses, see in general Daniélou, *Shadows to Reality*, 229–86, and above, at n. 20.

41. *Hom. Jos.* 1.3, 290: "Quo igitur nobis haec cuncta prospiciunt? Nempe eo, quod liber hic non tam gesta nobis filii Nave indicet, quam Iesu mei Domini nobis sacramenta depingat. Ipse est enim, . . . qui ducit exercitum et 'confligit adversus Amalec'; et quod ibi adumbrabatur in monte manibus extensis, 'affigit cruci suae triumphans principatus et potestates in semetipso.'" (Cf. Colossians 2:14.) The passage is cited, translated, and discussed by Daniélou in *Shadows to Reality*, 240.

42. See the discussion by Daniélou, *Shadows to Reality*, 284 ff.; also above at nn. 14–16.

43. *Hom. Luc.* 17, 105 f.: "Deinde Simeon ait: 'et tuam ipsius animam pertransibit gladius' [Luke 2:35]. Quis est iste gladius qui non aliorum tantum sed etiam Mariae

will interpret swords in terms of spiritual warfare; this is true whether these swords are on the literal level used for political assassination, for a massacre after victory, for simple warfare, or for wreaking vengeance upon evildoers.

An example of a sword used for a political assassination is provided by Judges 3:12–30. Eglon, the fat king of Midian, we are told in the passage, smote Israel, and the children of Israel served Eglon for eighteen years. But the Lord raised up a deliverer, Ehud, the son of Gera, who was ambidextrous. He made himself a two-edged sword, which he hid on his left thigh, and sought a secret interview with Eglon. When all had gone, Ehud drew forth the dagger with his left hand and thrust it into the fat of the king's belly, so that Eglon's fat closed upon the blade and the sword could not be drawn out. And Ehud escaped to the mountains of Ephraim, where he blew the trumpet and the children of Israel went to him. And Ehud told them: "The Lord has delivered the Midianites into your hands." And they went down after him and slew of Midian about ten thousand, and there escaped not one man.[44]

Every detail of this little vignette is for Origen a source of endless delight. Ehud is ambidextrous, because in him "everything is right: there is nothing left-handed or sinister about him." The chiefs of the Church must therefore take him as their example: they too must be "right" on both sides, in their faith but also in their works.[45] The killing of Eglon was a tyrannicide,

---

cor pertransiit? Aperte scribitur, quod in tempore passionis omnes sint apostoli scandalizati ipso quoque Domino dicente 'omnes vos scandalizabimini in nocte hac' [Mark 14:27]. Ergo scandalizati sunt universi in tantum ut Petrus quoque apostolorum princeps tertio denegarit. Quid putamus, quod scandalizatis apostolis mater Domini a scandalo fuerit immunis? Si scandalum in Domini passione non passa est, non est mortuus Iesus pro peccatis eius . . . ." I reproduce the Latin translation of Jerome, though in this particular case fragments of the Greek original have survived. Note that some manuscripts have replaced this obviously shocking passage with Bede's less controversial exegesis: the sword which shall transpierce Mary's soul stands for the suffering she will undergo at the time of the passion; see ibid., 105, n. 13.

44. Judges 3:12–30. In all these paraphrases I follow as closely as I can the text of the King James version. On occasion, however, when the version used in the Latin Origen is significantly different, I have had to depart from that text. Thus in KJ (as in MT, LXX, Vulg, and all modern versions) Eglon is king of Moab not Midian and the Israelites are fighting the Moabites not the Midianites. But in the version used by Origen-Rufinus, Moab has inexplicably been replaced by Midian. Similarly, while KJ says that Ehud was left-handed, Origen's version (agreeing here with LXX and in content with the Vulgate) says that he was ambidextrous. Since these points are essential to Origen's exegesis, I have kept them in my paraphrase.

45. *Hom. Jud.* 3.5, 485: ". . . 'clamaverunt filii Istrahel ad Dominum et suscitavit iis Dominus salvatorem Aoth filium Gera, filii Gemini, virum ambidextrum' [Judges 3:15]. Ecce qualis est iste, qui suscitatur ad salvandum Istrahel! Nihil habet in se

and Ehud is a figure of the chiefs of the Christian people, for they too must kill the king of the Midianites.[46] The word "Midianite" stands for "violent outpouring" or for "dissolution," and therefore for the words of that philosophy which claims that the highest good consists of pleasure. This philosophy is slain by the words of the Gospel, which, according to Hebrews 4:12, are rightly compared to the sword. The sword, Origen pursues, is justly introduced into the belly of such philosophers so as to destroy the fatness of their evil doctrines. Every ecclesiastical judge who acts in such a fashion and fights by means of the word of God is thus a worthy imitator of the noble Ehud.[47]

Origen's exegetical technique is here quite simple. The sword of Judges 3:16–21 is interpreted by means of the double-edged sword of Hebrews 4:12 and details such as Ehud's ambidexterity, the pseudoetymology of Midian, and the fat of Eglon's belly are efficiently woven into the allegory. Despite the references to pleasure and dissolution, moreover, the interpretation is ecclesiological rather than tropological. Ehud is essentially a type of the Christian prelate who, with the help of the word of God, smites the false doctrines of pleasure-seeking philosophers, such as, presumably, those bugaboos of the Hellenistic intellectual, the followers of Epicure.[48]

Numbers 21:21–25, on the other hand, provides an example of a lengthy exegesis of swords used for simple warfare. Israel,

---

sinistrum, sed utramque manum dextram habet; hoc est enim quod dicitur 'ambidexter.' Dignus vere populi princeps et ecclesiae iudex, qui nihil agat sinistrum . . . in utraque parte dexter est, in fide dexter est, in actibus dexter est . . . ." How the pun on "sinister" would have worked in the original Greek, where the left was of course apophatically called *"aristeros,"* is a little puzzling. Is this an invention of Rufinus? See below, Chapter 2 at nn. 70–74.

46. Ibid., 4.1, 487 f.: "Historia nos edocuit ea, quae de Eglon rege scripta sunt, quomodo sapientissimus hic Aoth arte quadam et, ut ita dicam, callida, sed laudabili usus deceptione interemerit Eglon tyrannum. . . . Oportet ergo tales esse et nostri populi judices, qualis fuit Aoth iste . . . ut omnes volubiles motus et orbitas mali itineris excidant et perimant Madianitarum regem."

47. Ibid., 488: " 'Madianitae' autem interpretantur 'fluxus' vel 'effusio.' Huius igitur fluxae et dissolutae gentis princeps vel dux qui potest videri alius vel intelligi, nisi sermo illius philosophiae, quae summum bonum iudicat voluptatem, quem interficiat et perimat Evangelicus sermo, qui gladio comparatur? Et sermo propheticus ipse in ventre eorum atque in imis praecordiis 'ambidextri' doctoris disputationibus concludatur, ut veritatis eos assertione concludens exstinguat omnem pravi dogmatis et crassae intelligentiae sensum, qui se extollit et erigit adversum spiritalem scientiam Christi; ut haec ita faciens et in verbo Dei dimicans unusquisque ecclesiae iudex fiat etiam ipse laudabilis Aoth."

48. On Origen's attitude towards Epicureanism and on its conformity with that of Hellenistic intellectuals in general, see Daniélou, *Origen*, 82.

we are told, sent messengers to Sihon, king of the Amorites, asking for peaceful transit through his land. They promised not to "turn into the fields, or into the vineyards nor to drink of the waters of the well," but simply "to follow the king's highway" until they were past Sihon's borders. But the king refused and fought against Israel in the wilderness. Israel, however, went out and met him at Jahaz. And "Israel smote him with the edge of the sword and possessed his lands," took over all his cities, "and dwelt in all the cities of the Amorites."[49]

Origen's exegesis is lengthy and fairly complex and is divided into several portions. To begin with, the name "Sihon" has, he contends, a double etymology: it can mean either "barren tree" or "he who is puffed up." At the spiritual level, Sihon is therefore a figure of the Devil, who is both puffed up and barren. Nor is it surprising that he should appear in the form of a king, for the Lord Himself calls the Devil "the prince of this world."[50] "For what good is it," Origen continues, "to claim Christ as our prince, if through our acts we demonstrate that it is the devil, who has power over us?" For is it not clear who is the prince of the lustful, the incestuous and the unrighteous? Christ is indeed the prince of virtue, but it is the Devil who is the prince of unrighteousness.[51]

Next, Origen turns to the Israelites' demand for innocent passage. Christians, too, he notes, are in transit through this world, and would like peaceful passage to the Holy Land.[52] The message to Sihon and the promise not to "turn into the

49. Numbers 21:21–25. In LXX as in the Vulgate and in KJ it is Sihon not Israel that comes out and meets the other, instead of the other way around as Origen (or Rufinus) seems for some reason to have assumed. See also below, n. 57.

50. *Hom. Num.* 12.4, 104: "Historia quidem manifesta est, sed deprecemur Dominum, ut aliquid dignum possimus in interioribus eius sensibus pervidere. Seon duplicem habet interpretationem, sive arbor infructuosa sive elatus. . . . Si secundum spiritalem intelligentiam dixerimus Seon regem figuram tenere diaboli, quia ipse est elatus et infructuosus, puto quod non debeas mirari quod eum dixerim regem, cum audias etiam ipsum Dominum et Salvatorem nostrum in evangeliis de eo dicentem . . .: 'ecce nunc princeps huius mundi mittetur foras' [John 12:31]."

51. Ibid., 104 f.: "Quid enim nobis prodest dicere quia princeps noster Christus est, si rebus et operibus arguamur quia diabolus principatum tenet in nobis? Aut non palam est, sub quo principe agat impudicus, incestus, iniustus. . . ? In quo Christus principatum gerit, nulla ibi immunditia, nulla iniquitas admittitur. . . . Secundum hunc itaque modum recte et Christus virtutum princeps et diabolus malitiae ac totius iniquitatis dicetur."

52. Ibid., 105: "Nos ergo sumus, qui transire volumus per hunc mundum, ut pervenire possimus ad terram sanctam . . . et 'mittimus verbis pacificis ad Seon' promittentes non nos habitaturos in terra eius nec moraturos cum eo, sed 'transituros' tantummodo et 'incessuros via regali nec declinaturos usquam neque in agrum neque in vineam, sed nec de lacu eius aquam bibituros.' "

field or the vineyards" nor to "drink of the waters of the well" foreshadow the renunciation of the Devil and his works which every Christian undertakes at the waters of baptism. There every Christian promises not to make use of the Devil's pomp, nor of his services, nor of any of his pleasures.[53] The Israelites' message to Sihon thus includes a promise not to make use of the Devil's sciences, such as magic or astrology. For Israel has wells of its own and draws its waters from "the wells of salvation."[54] The "king's highway" which the Israelites promise to follow in their passage through the lands of Sihon, the Devil, is without doubt none other than Christ, Who said of Himself that He was the Way, the Truth, and the Life. "To follow the king's highway" and not "to turn into the fields or vineyards" means therefore, Origen avers, that after baptism Christians must take Christ as their way and must no longer turn aside into vineyards filled with the works or thoughts of the Devil.[55] Christians, therefore, would like nothing better than to make peaceful transit through this world; but the very renunciation of this world only incites the anger of its prince. As a result, Sihon refuses Israel's overtures and prepares for war. Israel, however, meets the king at Jahaz. Etymologically, Origen claims, "Jahaz" means "fulfillment of precept."[56] Thus, if Christians go out to this place, to "Fulfillment of Precept," they too will be victorious over Sihon, that puffed-up Devil, even if he confronts them with the whole of his army. Then will be fulfilled the Lord's saying: "Behold I give unto you power to tread

53. Ibid., 105 f.: . . . [as in preceding note] . . . aquam bibituros.' Videamus ergo, quando nos ista promisimus, quando haec verba diabolo denuntiavimus. Recordetur unusquisque fidelium, cum primum venit ad aquas baptismi, cum signacula fidei prima suscepit et ad fontem salutaris accessit, quibus ibi tunc usus sit verbis et quid denuntiaverit diabolo: non se usurum pompis eius neque operibus eius neque ullis omnino servitiis eius ac voluptatibus pariturum."

54. Ibid., 106: "Non enim ultra disciplinae diabolicae, non astrologiae, non magicae, non ullius omnino doctrinae, quae contra Dei pietatem aliquid doceat, poculum sumet fidelis. Habet enim suos fontes et bibit de fontibus Istrahel, bibit de fontibus salutaris; non bibit aquam de lacu Seon . . . ."

55. Ibid.: "Sed et 'via regali incessurum se' profitetur. Quae est 'via regalis'? Illa sine dubio, quae dicit: 'ego sum via et veritas et vita' [John 14:6] . . . 'Via' ergo 'regali' incedendum est nec 'declinandum' usquam 'neque in agrum' eius 'neque in vineam' eius, id est neque ad opera neque ad sensus diabolicos declinare ultra mens fidelium debet."

56. Ibid., 106 f.: "Volumus ergo nos pacifice transire per mundum, sed hoc ipsum magis incitat 'principem mundi' quod dicimus nos nolle permanere cum ipso nec morari nec aliquid eius velle contingere; inde magis exacerbatur . . . et irascitur et commovet nobis persecutiones. . . . Et ideo dicit 'congregavit' inquit 'Seon omnem populum suum et exiit confligere adversum Istrahel.' . . . Sed quid facit Istrahel? 'Venit' inquit 'in Issaar' [: Jahaz]. Issaar interpretatur mandati adimpletio."

unto serpents and scorpions and over all the power of the Enemy."[57]

But what sort of sword, Origen asks, smote Sihon, that barren tree? Surely the sword which Paul has called "the sword of God, which is live and powerful and more penetrating than any two-edged sword" (Hebrews 4:12), the sword which the Apostle elsewhere calls "the sword of the spirit which is the word of God" (Ephesians 6:17).[58] That Israel then "possessed [Sihon's] lands . . . and took all these cities and dwelt in all the cities of the Amorites" means that Christ and His Church now possess all the former land of the Devil, for "the churches of Christ have spread far and wide throughout the world."[59] Moreover, Origen concludes, directly addressing his congregation, "each and every one of us was formerly a city belonging to Sihon, the puffed-up king," for it was the Devil who was king in the kingdom of our stupidity and in the kingdom of our pride. But wherever Sihon was given battle and defeated, "we have all become cities of Israel"; but this is true only if the power has been cut down within us that used to rule us, cut down as is a barren tree.[60]

57. Ibid., 107: ". . . [as in preceding note] . . . mandati adimpletio. Si ergo veniamus et nos ad locum istum, id est ad expletionem mandatorum, etiamsi cum omni exercitu veniat adversum nos Seon iste elatus et superbus diabolus et confligat adversum nos, si omnes suos contra nos daemones concitet, superamus eum, si Dei mandata complemus. Complere enim mandata hoc est diabolum et omnem eius exercitum superare. Et tunc complebitur in nobis . . . quod Dominus ait: 'Ecce, do vobis potestatem calcandi super serpentes et scorpiones et super omnem virtutem inimici, et nihil vobis nocebit' [Luke 10:19]."

58. Ibid., *Hom. Num.* 13.1, 107: "Hesterno die dixeramus, quomodo Seon rex Amorrhaeorum, qui est elatus et arbor infructuosa, congressus cum Istrahel victus fuerit; de quo et observanter Scriptura dicit quia cecidit in 'nece gladii' vel, ut alibi legimus, 'in ore gladii.' Sed si vis diligentius scire quo gladio infructuosus iste et elatus, 'sicut cedrus Libani' [Psalm 36:35] ceciderit, discamus ab Apostolo Paulo dicente 'vivus enim est sermo Dei et efficax et penetrabilior omni gladio' [Hebrews 4:12] et item in aliis 'et gladium' inquit 'spiritus, quod est verbum Dei' [Ephesians 6:17]."

59. Ibid., 107 f.: "Additur post haec 'et dominati sunt' inquit 'filii Istrahel in omni terra eius.' Omnis quidem regio haec terrena terra dicitur Seon, sed Christus et ecclesia eius 'dominatur in omni terra' Seon. . . . 'Et accepit' inquit 'Istrahel omnes civitates istas; et habitavit Istrahel in omnibus civitatibus Amorrhaeorum.' Hic Istrahel, qui in Christo Istrahel est, qui non in carne Istrahel, nec 'in manifesto Iudaeus' [cf. Romans 2:28] est, ipse 'habitat in omnibus civitatibus Amorrhaeorum,' cum in omni orbe terrarum Christi ecclesiae propagantur."

60. Ibid.: ". . . [as in preceding note] . . . propagantur. Sed et unusquisque nostrum prius civitas fuit regis Seon, regis elati: regnabat enim in nobis stultitia, superbia, impietas et omnia quae sunt ex parte diaboli; sed ubi expugnatus et devictus est . . . effecti sumus civitates Istrahel et haereditas sanctorum; si tamen . . . excisa est arbor infructuosa et deiectus est rex elatus et sumus sub eo rege, qui dicit: 'discite a me quia mitis sum et humilis corde' [Matthew 11:29]."

Here Origen quite consciously follows a double exegesis. Every verse is first given an allegorical interpretation, which, in addition to its christological aspect, may also have an ecclesiological or eschatological dimension. But then Christ must live again in each and every Christian and christology is deliberately transformed into tropology. Thus, "Sihon" is first interpreted as the Devil, the puffed-up king, the barren tree, the prince of this world, the Enemy of Our Prince, Who is Christ. But then Origen turns allegory into tropology for the use of his congregation: "For what good is it to claim Christ as our prince, if through our acts we demonstrate" that it is the prince of this world to whom we belong? Second, the Israelites' demand for peaceful transit through the lands of Sihon is interpreted as a figure of the pilgrim Church in transit through the world, the promise "not to turn into the field nor drink of the well" as a type of the renunciation of this world undertaken at baptism, and the promise "to follow the king's highway" as a figure of the engagement to follow Christ. Here the ecclesiological and tropological levels can hardly be separated, but Origen does at any rate remind his congregation what is implied by their baptismal engagement: to renounce the Devil's sciences and his pleasures and follow the straight and narrow path, which is Christ. Third, the battle of Jahaz prefigures the eschatological victory of Christ and His Church over the forces of the Devil: for Christians have received all power over the Enemy. But "Jahaz" means "fulfillment of precept": and individual Christians will be victorious only if they do fulfill the Lord's commandments. Fourth, and finally, the slaying of Sihon foreshadows the destruction of the Devil by "the sword of the spirit, which is the Word of God," while the taking over of the king's cities prefigures the propagation of the churches of Christ. But the individual Christian must still remember that he was once a "city of Sihon"; and that if he wishes to remain a "city of Israel" he must constantly strive to cut down within himself what may remain of the Devil's barren trees.

The episodes of Ehud and of Sihon are good general illustrations of how Origen handles the warlike pericopes of the Old Testament. Of more particular interest, however, because it ends with a more extensive exegesis of an actual sword theme, is his treatment of Joshua 11:1–14, a passage which provides an example of swords used for massacre after victory. The kings of several towns, we are told, including the major city of Hazor, made an alliance against Israel and prepared for battle. But Joshua under instructions from the Lord "hamstrung their horses and burnt their chariots with fire" and was thus able to defeat the kings. Joshua then took Hazor, "smote all the souls that were therein with the edge of the sword, so that there was not any left to breathe" and killed the kings by "death of the sword."[61]

Origen's exegesis of these fourteen verses is almost exclusively concerned with the few phrases that have just been cited. His interpretation, moreover, unlike that of the two previous episodes, is heavily tropological, though a few references to the advent of Joshua-Jesus, to the destruction of sin in every Christian at the time of baptism, and to Origen's own obligations as a preacher of the Word have the effect of giving a christological dimension to his tropology. Horses, Origen notes, stand for "lascivious passions" and a "prideful neck." Indeed, it is no accident that the Israelites seem throughout their history to have preferred asses to horses.[62] "To hamstring their horses" means therefore that Christians, if they "wish to serve in the army of Joshua-Jesus," must "cut off their own vices with the sword of the spirit" and thus "hamstring" the horses of their passions.[63] To "burn their chariots with fire" may allude to the Second Coming, when the Lord shall "send fire on the earth"; primarily, however, it refers to the fire of which the Apostles spoke when they said, "Did not our hearts burn within us, while He opened to us the Scriptures?"[64] To say that in the city of Hazor "there was not any left to breathe" means that no vices must be allowed even to "breathe" within the hearts of the faithful.[65] The Christian must stifle them at once and cut them

61. Joshua 11:1–14.

62. *Hom. Jos.* 15.3, 383: ". . . filii Istrahel numquam equis usi esse referuntur et lex nihil de equis sed de asinis mandat. . . . [Equus] lascivi motus animal et superbae cervicis accipitur. Sunt ergo asini frequenter ab Scriptura in typo gentium positi . . . ." (A long excursus on asses and horses then follows.)

63. Ibid., 386: ". . . nos si recte sub Jesu duce militamus, debemus in nobismet ipsis abscidere vitia et accepto spiritali gladio 'subnerviare' omnem istum equitatum pessimum vitiorum . . . ."

64. Ibid., 385: "Et igni currus exuruntur, cum in nobis completur sermo Domini dicentis 'ignem veni mittere in terram, et quam volo, ut accendatur' [Luke 12:49]. Quo igne iam se illi ardere confessi sunt, qui dicebant 'nonne cor nostrum erat ardens intra nos cum adaperiret nobis scripturas' [Luke 24:32]."

65. Ibid., 386: "Quomodo autem in nobismet ipsis complebimus et hoc quod dicit ut 'non remittatur ullus, qui respiret'? Videndum est, qui sit, qui nec 'respirare' quidem

off before they are permitted to reach maturity. In the words of Psalm 136:9, he must "dash the little ones against the rock."[66] As for the kings who allied against Israel and whom Joshua killed "by death of the sword," they stand for a variety of sins. In the past, everyone of Origen's congregation had within him some particular sin that was king and reigned over him; in some it was avarice, in others pride, in others lust, in still others anger.[67] This kingship of sin, however, prevailed only before they came to believe. For with the coming of Joshua-Jesus, who killed the kings that held everyone in thrall to the kingship of their sins, the members of Origen's congregation were ordered to slay all sins within themselves, so that "none should be left." For if anyone should keep any such "king" alive within him, he cannot possibly serve in the army of Jesus.[68]

Origen spends most of the remainder of the homily on the next verses, Joshua 11:15–23, which deal with some other incidents in the settlement of the Holy Land.[69] He is still, however, concerned with the theme of Christian *psychomachia,* and before concluding comes back to the image of the sword of the spirit. Blessed is he, he tells his congregation, who without ceasing holds the sword of the spirit and smites the foes that

per praeceptum Domini iubetur. Verbi causa, si ira adscenderit in cor meum, potest fieri, ut opera quidem iracundiae non impleam . . . sed non, inquit, hoc sufficit; agendum tibi potius est, quatenus ne ipsa quidem commotio iracundiae locum habeat intra te. . . . Similiter et de concupiscentiae vitio et de tristitiae ceterisque omnibus sententiendum est. De quibus cunctis ita agendum est discipulo Jesu ut nihil omnino horum in eius corde 'respiret,' ne forte, si parvi alicuius vitii aut consuetudo aut cogitatio 'relinquatur' in corde, processu temporis convalescat . . . ."

66. Ibid., 386 f.: "Hoc erat quod et propheta prospiciens in psalmis praemonet dicens: 'beatus qui tenet et allidit parvulos tuos ad petram' [Psalm 136:9], 'Babylonis' scilicet 'parvulos' qui nullii alii intelliguntur nisi 'cogitationes malae'. . . . Quae cogitationes dum adhuc parvulae sunt . . . 'tenendae sunt et allidendae ad petram,' qui est Christus, et ipso iubente iugulandae, ut 'nihil' in nobis 'resideat quod respiret' . . . ."

67. Ibid., 4, 387: " 'Et omnes,' inquit, 'reges eorum interfecit Iesus in morte gladii.' In omnibus nobis 'regnavit peccatum' [Romans 6:12] et in omnibus nobis vitia regnaverunt et fuit in nobis omnibus regnum generale peccati. . . . Unusquisque tamen habuit in se aliquem specialem regem, qui in eo regnabat et dominabatur ei. Verbi causa, in alio regnum tenebat avaritia, in alio superbia . . . libido alii dominabatur et alius regem patiebatur furorem. . . ."

68. Ibid., 387 f.: "Erat ergo regnum peccati in unoquoque nostrum, antequam crederemus. Postea vero quam venit Iesus et occidit omnes reges qui in nobis tenebant regna peccati et praecepit nobis interficere omnes istos reges et 'nullum ex iis relinquere.' Si qui enim aliquem horum in semet ipso servaverit vivum, in exercitu Iesu esse non poterit. Si ergo regnat adhuc in te avaritia, si iactantia, si superbia, si libido, non eris Istraheliticus miles nec imples praeceptum, quod dedit Dominus ad Iesum."

69. Ibid., 4–6, 388–92.

have been described. For, in the words of Jeremiah 48:10: "Cursed be he that doeth the work of the Lord deceitfully, and cursed be he that keepeth back his sword from blood."[70] Of course, it is important to understand this curse in a spiritual sense:

hoc si secundum litteram intelligamus, necesse erit nos indesinenter sanguinem fundere. Quod Iudaei putantes, qui ex integro 'caro' sunt 'et sanguis,' crudeles et implacabiles fiunt dicentes maledictionem positam esse his, qui a sanguine effundendo cessaverint, et ideo 'pedes eorum veloces sunt ad effundendum sanguinem.'[71]

If the curse were literally understood, it would be necessary for Christians to shed blood unceasingly. Indeed, the Jews, who are nothing but "flesh and blood" and have become cruel and merciless, claim that this curse has been put upon those who have ceased from the shedding of blood; and therefore, in the words of Psalm 13:3, "their feet are swift to shed blood."

Perhaps Origen's reference to the Jewish interpretation of Jeremiah 48:10 is more than simply a general condemnation of the "letter that killeth." At least, it is possible to imagine that in Caesarea of Palestine, where those homilies were after all delivered, there was still a memory of the difficulties congregations of Jewish Christians must have faced at the time of the Jewish War and of the rebellion of Bar-Kochba. Perhaps members of the Jewish resistance against Rome had on occasion invoked Jeremiah 48:10 against the absolute pacifism of their Christian compatriots in order to claim "that a curse had been put upon those who have ceased from the shedding of blood." In that case, Origen could well argue that here again was a case where the typological bloodshedding of the Old Dispensation resisted its own demise despite the Advent of Truth.[72] For him, in any event, such a literal interpretation is of concern only to the Jews:

mihi autem praestet Dominus numquam negligere opera Domini nec auferre spiritalem gladium verbi Dei a sanguine contrariarum virtutum et mortificare eas in unoquoque auditorum. Interficiuntur autem in vobis ita demum, si his auditis earum opera non agatis.[73]

70. Ibid., 6, 392: "Beatus ergo est, qui indesinenter spiritalem machaeram tenens non aufert eam a cervicibus horum hostium, de quibus superius memoravimus, sicut et Hieremias propheta dicit: 'Maledictus homo qui facit opera Domini negligenter et aufert machaeram suam a sanguine inimicorum.' "

71. Ibid.

72. See above at nn. 21 and 22.

73. *Hom. Jos.* 15.6, 392, loc. cit.

As for Origen, may God lend him strength never "to do the work of the Lord deceitfully or keep back the sword" of the spirit from the blood of contrary powers, so that he may kill these powers in everyone of those listening to him. As for the members of his congregation, may these vices be slain within them, so that after listening to Origen's words they may no longer practice the works of these powers.

Origen's interpretation of the episode as a whole is thus essentially tropological. Christians must use the sword of Ephesians to hamstring their lascivious passions. They must allow none of their vices even to breathe and they must be sure to slay them when still young. The kings, moreover, stand each for an individual vice, and reign as in their kingdoms in the souls of men. Origen's reference to the "advent of Joshua-Jesus," however, as well as the contrast which he draws between the condition of men before and after their conversion, gives a christological and an ecclesiological slant to his tropology. The same applies to Origen's use of Jeremiah 48:10. The curse is first used tropologically in order to call on members of his flock to fight and slay the vices within them. Tropology then insensibly passes into ecclesiology and christology, for Origen is reminded that it is his special duty as a preacher, by means of the sword of the Spirit (which is the Word of God), to slay these "kings" who may still rule within his congregation. In this ecclesiological use of Jeremiah 48:10, Origen thus anticipates none other than Gregory VII.[74] Finally, ecclesiology passes once more into tropology, as Origen asks his congregation to give effect to the words which they have heard. Here, too, the tropology of Origen is not simply a Hellenistic *psychomachia* with virtues and vices attempting to slay one another in an abstract setting: it is an eschatological struggle between Jesus-Joshua and the devil-kings for the allegiance of the souls of men.

The most interesting of all these examples of Origen's treatment of swords within an Old Testament context is furnished by a commentary on a passage from the Book of Numbers, in which the sword is used to wreak vengeance on evildoers. Though Origen's exegesis is brief and relatively simple, it almost surely contains a reference to the sword pericope and to the Lord's rebuke of Peter in Matthew 26:52. Moreover, it con-

74. Cf. Gregory VII, *Registrum* (*MGH—Epistolae Selectae* 2.1, ed. E. Caspar; Berlin, 1920) 15.10, 23.30, 28.25, 131.15, 221.30, 249.5, 291.30, 500.25, 563.20.

sciously opposes the "corporeal sword" to the "sword of the spirit." The episode in Numbers 25:1–15 tells the story of the children of Israel who went whoring after the daughters of Midian. And a certain Zimri, the son of Salu, a prince of the tribe of Simeon, went in before his brethren to a harlot of Midian. But Phineas, the son of Eleazar, the son of Aaron the Priest, took a spear and, going after them into the chamber, rammed it right through the Israelitish man and the Midianitish woman through her womb. And because of the zeal of Phineas, the zeal of the Lord was appeased against the children of Israel and He made a covenant that the priesthood should remain forever with Phineas and his seed.[75]

Because of the way in which the episode is linked with the establishment of the Jewish priesthood, the figure of Phineas looms relatively large in later Jewish history. Thus, in the great anamnesis of Ben Sirach, "let us now praise famous men," Phineas is one of the twenty-four heroes of Israel and in its celebration of the Exodus he is called "third in glory" after Moses and Aaron.[76] Again in the little anamnesis of 1 Maccabees 2:50 ff., Phineas is listed among the "Fathers" of old—even though Moses himself is not included. Finally, in the commemoration of the Exodus of Psalm 105, Phineas is again mentioned together with Moses and Aaron. In all those anamneses there is emphasis on Phineas's "zeal, which was accounted unto him for righteousness."[77] This zeal of Phineas probably became famous in Maccabean times; and the zeal for the Law

75. Numbers 25:1–15. Numbers 25:7–8: "And Phineas, the son of Eleazar, the son of Aaron the priest . . . took a spear in his hand and went in after the Israelitish man into the chamber and pierced them both through, both the Israelitish man and the woman through her womb" (LXX). The Bible-text in Rufinus' translation, Origen, *Hom. Num.* 20.5, 198 (see below, n. 80), is less sexist and closer to the Vulgate; Phineas seems to have pierced through the genitals of both. Yet, as is clear from the remainder of Rufinus' own translation (which emphasizes the *vulva* alone) (see below, n. 83), Origen must have followed a text close to the Septuagint: Rufinus, one may assume, was simply following the text of the Old Latin Version (see below, n. 80). If we can trust Heinrich Heine (which oddly enough we can, if only in part), Phineas managed to miss Zimri and instead hit an innocent bystander, a certain Schlemihl ben Zuri Schaddai—whence the origin of the word "shlemihl"; see Heine, "Jehuda ben Halevy," sec. 4, 11.180–204 ("Hebräische Melodien" in Heine, *Sämtliche Werke*, ed. Rudolf Frank; Munich, 1923), vol. 1, 367. In very early Jewish tradition, Zimri was for some reason identified with the Shelumiel ben Zurishaddai of Numbers 1:5; see Louis Ginsberg, *The Legends of the Jews* (Philadelphia, 1909–38), vol. 6, 137 f., n. 799, and *Sanhedrin* 82b.

76. See Ecclesiasticus 44–50 for the great anamnesis "Let us now praise famous men"; Ecclesiasticus 45:28 for the reference to Phineas "third in glory."

77. 1 Macchabees 2:54: "Phineas our father by being zealous in the zeal [of God] received the covenant of an everlasting priesthood." Psalm 105:30 f: "Then Phineas

demonstrated by Mattathias (father of Judas Maccabee and his brethren) through his slaying of the apostate Jew upon the idolatrous altar at Modin is consciously compared to Phineas's killing of Zimri.[78]

Later Church Fathers will seize on this theme; and by the fourth and fifth centuries Phineas the priest will become a figure of Peter, and the zeal shown by Phineas in his slaying of the unfortunate Zimri compared to the zeal shown by Peter in his defense of the Lord and his amputation of the ear of Malchus.[79] Origen will not yet go that far; but the seeds of the later comparison are clearly contained in his exegesis of the passage. Phineas, he reminds his congregation, took up his spear and with it transpierced through the genitals both the Israelite and the Midianitish whore:

> Haec aedificaverint priorem populum. Tibi autem qui a Christo redemptus es et cui de manibus gladius corporalis ablatus est et datus est gladius spiritus, arripe hunc gladium![80]

---

stood up and made atonement and the slaughter ceased; and it was reckoned unto him as righteousness from generation to generation for evermore."

78. 1 Macchabees 2:24–26: ". . . and Mattathias saw and was inflamed with zeal . . . wherefore he ran and slew him upon the altar . . . and he showed zeal for the Law as Phineas did by Zimri the son of Salu."

79. See, for instance, Ambrose, *Expositio Evangelii secundum Lucam* 10.66, *CC* 14, 364: "Denique Petrus eruditus in lege, promtus adfectu, qui sciret Fineae reputatum ad justitiam quod sacrilegos peremisset, percussit principis servum." See Jerome, *Epistola* 109.3, *CSEL* 55, 354, ll.13 ff. (the deed of Phineas compared to Peter's slaying of Ananias and Sapphira in Acts 5:3 ff.); see also below, n. 87.

80. *Hom. Num.* 20.5, 198: "Post haec refertur quia, 'cum vidisset Finees filius Eleazar filii Aaron sacerdotis' Istrahelitem quendam introisse ad mulierem Madianiten, 'rapto siromaste in manu sua ingressus sit prostibulum, et utrumque per ipsa pudenda transfoderit.' Et pro hoc, inquit, 'dixit Dominus ad Moysen: Finees filius Eleazar filii Aaron sedavit iracundiam meam.' Haec aedificaverint . . . [as in text] . . . arripe hunc gladium." *Siromastēs* (*seiromastēs* in the LXX) is an extremely rare word in ordinary (that is outside Judaeo-Christian) Greek, where it is for all practical purposes a *hapax* and means a "probing-stick" used by the defenders of a fortress to discourage mines (cf. Liddell and Scott, ad loc.). In the Septuagint, however, it is together with *logchē* (lance) and *doru* (javelin) one of the three words that translate the Hebrew *romah*, apparently a rather heavy kind of spear, in contrast to the lighter *hanit* (almost always *doru* in the Septuagint); see E. Hatch and H. A. Redpath, *Concordance to the Septuagint*, ad vv. cit. The curious choice of *seiromastēs* may be due to assonance with Hebrew *romaḥ*. Rufinus, in the Origen passage just given, is almost certainly citing some version of the *Vetus Latina: prostibulum* means brothel as Vulg. *lupanar* and in contrast to LXX *kaminon* (nonsensical "furnace" or "chimney"), while the use of the septuagintism *siromastes* in VL for the present passage seems also attested by Jerome, *Epistola* 109.3 (see preceding note), and *Epistola* 147.9, *CSEL* 56, 325 f.; see Robert Murray, "The Lance Which Re-opened Paradise, a Mysterious Reading in the Early Syriac Fathers," *Orientalia Christiana Periodica* 39 (1973) 228, n. 7. See below, n. 82, for the transformation of LXX *seiromastēs* ("spear") into "sword."

Such deeds might have edified[81] God's former people! As for the Christian, who has been redeemed by Christ, from whose hands the corporeal sword has been taken, and who has received in its stead "the sword of the spirit," that is the sword which he should brandish, that and no other![82]

Should the Christian, therefore, Origen pursues, perceive within himself any "Israelite sense" whoring after Midianitish

81. That *aedificaverint* means "might have edified" or "could/would have edified" and not "might have built up" is shown by Rufinus' frequent use of *aedificare* in its pious sense in his translation of these Homilies. See also the French rendering by André Méhat, *Origène, Homélies sur Nombres* (Paris, 1951), 412.

82. What makes Origen pass without further ado from the *seiromastēs* of his text (which he must have understood as "spear") to a sword of some sort? From Rufinus' translation, it is of course impossible to tell whether Origen used the classical *xiphos*, the almost exclusively septuagintal *rhomphaia*, or *machaira*, a term common to both the Septuagint and the *koinē* of his time. The clear reference to Ephesians 6:17 and the highly probable reference to Matthew 26:52 (passages in which *machaira* is used) suggest that it is the latter term that was actually employed by Origen. On the other hand, as Father Murray has shown, Semitic *rmḥ* (Hebrew *romaḥ*, Syriac *rûmḥâ*) and Greek *rhomphaia* "show . . . a repeated semantic influence in both directions" through which spears (or lances) become swords and swords in turn may turn into spears (Murray, "The Lance Which Re-opened Paradise," 229). Though the influence is heaviest in Syriac literature, there is on the Greek side—and specifically for the rendering of the Phineas episode—the use of *rhomphaia* instead of *seiromastēs* by Josephus in *Antiquitates Judaeorum* IV.6.12 (Loeb Classics), 153, and apparently the same rendering by Pseudo-Philo in his *Antiquitates Biblicae* (ed. G. Kisch; Notre Dame, Ind., 1949), 236 (preserved here only as *rhomphea* in the Latin translation); see Murray, art. cit., 228, n. 6. The evidence from Origen here presented should be added to that collected by Father Murray. So should the fact that Philo, though fully aware of the "probing" meaning of *seiromastēs* and quite willing to make use of it in some of his interpretations of the Phineas episode (see, e.g., *De Posteritate Cain* 183 and *De Ebrietate* 1.73), can in the same breath equate that "probing-stick" of Phineas with "the sharp-edged Word" (*De Mutatione* 5.108; cf. also *De Confusione* 5.57), the same Word which he often conceives as the Word-as-Cutter (*Logos-Tomeus*) and can therefore be said to have been "whetted to an edge of utmost sharpness" (*Quis est Heres* 7.130 ff.). For Philo the *Logos* can be equated with the *rhomphaia* that stands between the Cherubim in Genesis 3:24 (*De Cherubim* 1.27) as well as with the *machaira* used by Abraham in the sacrifice of Isaac (ibid., 2.31). Finally, it is just possible that St. Ephrem the Syrian, in *Carmina Nisibena* 39.12, makes a reference to Matthew 26:52 (to suggest this seems in any case to have been the intention of the translator Edmund Beck: "Da nun aber die Gerechtigkeit ihr *Schwert in die Scheide gesteckt* hat," [emphasis added] *CSCO* 241 [*SS* 103], 20, 11.3 f.; though Father Michael Guinan of the Franciscan Seminary in Berkeley and the Graduate Theological Union informs me that the Syriac original is actually much vaguer). Since the swords of the Zealots and the lance or spear of Phineas the Zealot play a large role in the remainder of the poem (e.g., *Carmina Nisibena* 39.5, 7, 15, 16), it is just possible that for Ephrem as for Origen the rebuke of Peter is ultimately a rebuke of Phineas (and with Phineas of all Zealots). For St. Ephrem and Syriac literature in general, see the excellent book by Father Murray, *Symbols of Church and Kingdom. A Study of Early Syriac Tradition* (Cambridge University Press, 1975), and on sword imagery the article by the same author, "The Exhortation to Candidates for Ascetical Vows at Baptism in the Ancient Syriac Church," *New Testament Studies* 21 (1974/75), 59 ff., esp. 64.

harlots, that is to say, any wallowing in devilish thought, let him show neither mercy nor toleration, let him strike and kill on the spot. Moreover, let him strike the womb itself, and by thus penetrating the secrets of nature, let him destroy the seat of sin so that there be no further conception and no further progeny to pollute the encampments of Israel. If this is the way the Christian acts, he shall indeed appease the Lord; he shall avoid the day of judgment, the day that is called "the day of wrath."[83] With this exhortation, Origen can now conclude his homily:

> Et ideo surgentes, oremus, ut inveniamus paratum semper istum gladium spiritus, per quem exterminentur et semina ipsa et conceptacula peccatorum ac propitius nobis fiat Deus per verum Fineem ipsum Dominum nostrum Iesum Christum, cui gloria et imperium in saecula saeculorum. Amen.[84]

"And therefore," Origen tells his flock, "as we rise, let us pray that we may always have ready at hand that sword of the spirit, by which sin is destroyed in both seed and womb, so that God may be gracious to us, through the True Phineas, Our Lord Jesus Christ Himself, to Whom belongs the Glory and the Power, world without end. Amen."

On first impression, with, to be sure, the notable exception of the doxology, Origen's exegesis may seem purely tropological. The Christian must imitate the example of Phineas and take up the sword of the spirit to strike out mercilessly at his "Israelite senses" if he catches them whoring after any devilish thoughts. As in his exegesis of the sacking of Hazor, Origen emphasizes that they must be caught when they are young,

83. *Hom. Num.*, loc. cit., 198: ". . . [as in text at n. 80] . . . arripe hunc gladium; et si videris Istraheliticum sensum cum Madianiticis scortantem meretricibus, id est cum diabolicis se cogitationibus volutantem, nolo parcas, nolo dissimules, sed statim percute, statim perime. Ipsam quoque vulvam, id est secreta naturae discutiens et penetrans illum ipsum peccandi fomitem deseca, ne ultra concipiat, ne ultra generet et maledicta peccatorum suboles Istrahelitica castra contaminet. Hoc enim si facias, continuo sedabis iracundiam Domini; praevenisti enim iudicii diem, qui 'dies irae' [cf. Romans 2:5] dicitur et . . . securus venies ad iudicii diem." The emphasis on the female sexual parts—and those alone, as in the Septuagint—reinforces the assumption that in citing the biblical text ("*et utrumque* per ipsa pudenda transfoderit," above at n. 80), Rufinus is not following the Septuagint but the *Vetus Latina*; see above, nn. 75 and 80. As for Origen's text, note a marked Philonic influence, not only through the medium of *Legum Allegoriae* III.242 (noted by Baehrens in his edition in the *GCS*, ibid., 198, n. at ll.12 ff.), where the influence is limited to *ne ultra generet et maledicta peccatorum*, but also through that of *De Ebrietate* 1.73 and *De Posteritate Cain* 183, where the emphasis is on the *seiromastēs* probing into the secrets of nature.

84. Ibid.

indeed before they are even born. Let the Christian "dash the little ones against the stones," let him, like Phineas, use his sword to strike at the genitals of both, so as to exterminate sin "in both seed and womb." The carefully rephrased doxology, however, makes it clear that when the Christian does all this he becomes an antitype not so much of the fleshly Phineas as of the Phineas of the Spirit; or, rather, that he becomes the former only through the mediation of the True Phineas, Who is none other than the Lord Jesus Christ.

This particular piece of exegesis makes especially clear the dialectical relationship between the Two Dispensations. On the one hand, Phineas's slaying of Zimri and his whore must be imitated by the individual Christian, just as Eglon's tyrannicide should be an example to the Christian prelate. On the other, to say that "such things might have edified God's former people" strikes a negative and indeed rather ironical note. But then the Jews have been rendered "cruel and bloodthirsty" by their literal reading of the Old Testament. Christians, on the other hand, realize that "types and shadows have had their ending" and that they must not push their imitation of Old Testament types to the point of resisting the Advent of Truth. Phineas's example should be imitated, yet it should also be rejected: in other words, there must be a transfiguration, or a conversion (*metanoia*), from the carnal to the spiritual level. In the present context, moreover, Origen saw the main symbol of this spiritual passover (*diabasis*) from the Old to the New Dispensation in a sort of transmutation of swords: because of his redemption by the True Phineas, the Lord Jesus Christ, the Christian has exchanged the corporeal sword of Phineas for "the sword of the Spirit, which is the Word of God"—that is to say, the sword of Ephesians 6:17.[85]

Finally, it is highly possible that when Origen says that "the corporeal sword has been taken away" from Christians he is actually alluding to the sword pericope and to the Lord's rebuke of Peter in Matthew 26:52. Tertullian had already interpreted that rebuke as an *ablatio* or taking away of the material sword; and, as will be seen, Origen's own exegesis of Matthew 26:52 involves a "deposition of the sword of war" and an exchange of that sword for "the sword of the spirit."[86] It thus

85. Above at nn. 80, 71, 17, 21 and 22.

86. See Tertullian, *De Idolatria* 19.2–3 (*CC* 2), 1120: "Et virgam portavit Moyses; fibulam et Aaron, cingitur loro et Iohannes; agmen agit et Iesu Nave; bellavit et

seems likely that in his commentary on Phineas, Origen was also referring to the sword pericope. In any case, whatever his conscious intent, when later generations made the comparison between Phineas and Peter and between the slaying of Zimri and the abscission of Malchus's ear, they only rendered explicit what was already implied in the exegesis of Origen.[87]

Undoubtedly, the most interesting aspect of Origen's interpretation of the deed of Phineas lies, however, in the contrast which he consciously draws between the *gladius corporalis,* the corporeal sword, the sword of the letter, and the *gladius spiritus,* the allegorical sword, the sword of the Spirit, which is the Word of God. To be sure, Tertullian's whole argument in *Adversus Marcionem* 3.14 already presupposes such an opposition: if the Lord in Matthew 10:34 speaks of an "allegorical" or "figurative" sword, such a sword is by implication contrasted with a "literal," "historical," or simply "corporeal" sword.[88] However, it is only with Origen that the contrast between the two swords has become an explicit symbol for three major and interrelated themes of his theology: the allegorization of Old Testament violence, its transfiguration into spiritual warfare, and in effect the whole of the dialectical relationship between the Two Dispensations. If "Jesus was the leader of an army," if the whole of the Bible is "the Book of the Wars of Jahweh," it is fitting that the sword should be the symbol for all of Holy Writ; and indeed it is no accident that Paul in Ephesians should

---

populus, si placet ludere. Quomodo autem bellabit, immo quomodo etiam in pace militabit sine gladio quem dominus abstulit? Nam etsi adierant milites ad Iohannem et formam observationis acceperant, si etiam centurio crediderat, omnem postea militem dominus in Petro exarmando discinxit." For a more "moderate" position on the part of Tertullian, see *De Corona* 11.1–4 (*CC* 2), 1056 f. In general, see W. Rordorf, "Tertullians Beurteilung des Soldatenstandes," *Vigiliae Christianae* 23 (1969) 105 ff. For Origen, see below, chapter 2 at nn. 118 to 135, at n. 133 in particular. For the whole problem of Early Christian Pacifism, see below, chapter 2, n. 151, and chapter 4, n. 6.

87. See above, n. 79; Bede, *In Marci Evangelium Expositio* IV (14.47), *CC* 120, 618 f., and *In Lucae Evangelium Expositio* VI (22.51), *CC* 120, 388 f., closely follows Ambrose. Gregory the Great, *Homiliae in Ezechielem Prophetam* I.7.11 (*CC* 142), 90 f.: "Certe si legentis animum spiritus vitae in zeli fervore tetigerit, protinus in sacris eloquiis videt quod Moyses ad castra rediens et populum per idola peccasse cognoscens hunc per fervorem spiritus gladiis stravit. Quod Phinees persequendo luxuriam, iram Domini gladio placavit. Quod Petrus sibimet mentientes verbo perculit et occidit" (cf. Acts 5:3 ff.). See also Nicholas I, *Epistola* 6, *MGH—Epistolae* VI, p. 327.

88. Tertullian, *Ad Marcionem* 3, 13–14 (*CC* 1), 524–27. See, in particular, ibid., 14.5, 526: "Hanc et dominus ipse machaeram venit mittere in terram non pacem [Matthew 10:34]. Si tuus Christus est, ergo et ipse bellator est. Si bellator non est, machaeram intentans allegoricam, licuit ergo et Christo Creatoris in psalmo sine bellicis rebus ense sermonis praecingi figurato . . ." (Psalm 44:4).

speak of "the sword of the spirit, which is the Word of God." But if the word of God is radically one, it speaks through two radically distinct Dispensations. The Book of the Wars of Jahweh is one, yet it falls into two parts: the book of corporeal warfare is succeeded by the book of the wars of the spirit. The spiritual sword is both identical with and yet radically opposed to the sword according to the flesh. The sword of Peter both is and is not the same as the spear of Phineas.

CHAPTER II

THE SWORD AND THE SPIRIT

Transfiguration of the "corporeal sword" into the "sword of the spirit" becomes a symbol for the *metanoia* or conversion from the Old to the New Dispensation. The emergence of this symbol in the context of Origen's discussion of the Phineas episode in the Homilies on Numbers was apparently brought about by the confrontation of Origen's normal spiritualization of the acts of violence of the Old Dispensation with the sword pericope of the New Testament. Indeed, Origen's other references to the sword pericope—which will be discussed in this chapter—make clear that for him the essential meaning of that episode lies precisely in that same conversion. Origen arrives at that interpretation by emphasizing the seeming contradiction between the first and last moments of the sword pericope, between the Lord's charge to the disciples to buy themselves a sword and His rebuke of Peter for having used the same. With the substitution of the New for the Old Dispensation, the Lord wanted Christians to give up the corporeal sword and instead buy themselves a sword of the spirit; but the disciples misunderstood and interpreted the Lord's injunction literally, as is demonstrated by their replying "Lo! Lord! Here are two swords," as well as by Peter's abscission of Malchus' ear; this is why Christ found it necessary to rebuke Peter for this use of the literal sword.

This interpretation of the sword pericope is not found in any single passage; for in the extant works of Origen there is unfortunately no full discussion of the pericope as a whole. There is, to be sure, a lengthy exegesis of the later moments of the pericope in the Commentary on Matthew (or, rather, in the anonymous Latin translation of the *Commentariorum Series*); and the same, basically Matthean, material is also commented upon more briefly in a *catena*-fragment, as well as in Origen's great apologetic work, the so-called *Contra Celsum.*[1] The early moments of the sword pericope (which are found only in Luke) are not, however, discussed in this Matthean context. Origen's Homilies on Luke have been preserved in only incomplete fashion, and what is extant stops before the narrative of the Passion and therefore the sword episode; and the same is true of the enormous Commentary on John, which, because of its length, might otherwise have included some discussion of the Lucan material.[2] The early moments of the sword pericope are therefore nowhere taken up *in situ,* in their proper exegetical framework. They are commented upon, albeit a little briefly and not always in the expected exegetical context, at three separate places in Origen's works: in the Homilies on Leviticus, in a passage which deals with the food legislation of the Old Testament; in the Commentary on Matthew, in a passage that comments on "those who make themselves eunuchs for the sake of the Kingdom of Heaven"; and finally in another brief (and incomplete) *catena*-fragment.[3] Origen's interpretation of the pericope as a whole has therefore to be reconstituted from these scattered pieces (as well as from the rather allusive remarks in his exegesis of the Phineas episode in the Homilies on Numbers, which has just beendiscussed).

This chapter will thus naturally fall into two main parts. The second will consist of a fairly straightforward exposition of Origen's lengthy exegesis of the latter moments of the sword pericope in *Contra Celsum,* the *Commentariorum Series,* and one brief, though complete, *catena*-fragment. The first part will of necessity have to be more complex. To be sure, Origen's exegesis of the first moments of the pericope consists also of

1. Below at nn. 113–34.

2. The Commentary on John (*Origenes* 4, *GCS* 10) stops with John 13:33, towards the beginning of the Last Discourses. The Homilies on Luke (*Origenes* 9, *GCS* 49) stop with Luke 20:21–40 before the Passion Narrative has even begun. Above, chapter 1, n. 2.

3. *Hom. Lev.,* below at nn. 5 to 13; *Com. Mat.,* below at nn. 46 to 53; *catena*-fragment, below at nn. 109–11.

three passages (and in this case rather brief passages at that): in the Homilies on Leviticus, the Commentary on Matthew, and a brief and incomplete *catena*-fragment. Yet, the exposition of these three passages will have to be interrupted here and there by material that will deal more generally with Origen's exegetical method: for, as will appear, Origen's exegesis of the first moments of the sword pericope is intimately associated with an exegetical problem of fundamental importance.

So far, only Origen's exegesis of the Old Testament has been examined; and that exegesis, though often lavishly complex in its details, is really very simple in its basic structure. Almost every passage in the Old Testament has a literal (legal or historical) sense; over and above that meaning there is a second, allegorical (christological or ecclesiological) level; over and above that there is then a third, tropological, sense which adds a personal dimension to the literal and allegorical levels. Finally, a fourth, anagogical or eschatological, meaning may or may not be present. But what about the New Testament? How can there be a spiritual meaning beyond its letter? After all, the very function of allegory in the Old Testament was to point to the message of the New. The New Testament *is* the revelation of the Old; once the veil of the Temple has been rent in twain, what further need is there for the veil of allegory? Yet Origen dares to state without hesitation: "even in the Gospel, there is 'a letter that killeth.'" And in both the Homilies on Leviticus and the Commentary on Matthew that statement is closely associated with the first moment of the sword pericope, that is to say with the Lord's command that the Apostles should buy themselves a sword.[4]

Because of the difficulties that have just been alluded to, the passage from the Homilies on Leviticus will at first glance appear far stranger than any of the examples of Old Testament exegesis that have been discussed. Yet, behind that apparent strangeness there lies a key to Origen's exegesis of the New Testament, and of the sword pericope in particular. The strangeness begins with the context. The reference to the first moment of the sword pericope actually occurs in margin of some eucharistic reflections on John 6:53: "unless ye eat the flesh of the Son of Man and drink his blood, ye shall not have life." These reflections are in turn the product of a commentary on the

4. Below at nn. 9 and 10, and n. 48.

Mosaic legislation on clean and unclean foods in Leviticus 11:2 ff. In his exegesis of that legislation, Origen begins by noting that all men may be said to offer themselves as "food" to one another simply in daily intercourse: through gesture or through word they "offer" themselves to their neighbors and are thus "tasted" by them.[5] In that sense, if a man is "clean," others through him partake of "clean food"; if he is "unclean," of "unclean food." This is why the Lord could say in John 6:53: "unless ye eat the flesh of the Son of Man and drink his blood, ye shall not have life."[6] Because Jesus is absolutely "clean" (for all He does is holy and all He says is true), "his flesh is food and his blood is drink indeed": and with that flesh and blood he refreshes all mankind. Below Christ, Peter, Paul, the Apostles and all the disciples of Christ can also be called "clean food": for everyone in proportion to his merits has the capacity of offering himself as "clean food" unto his neighbors.[7] To be sure, Origen pursues, some may turn a deaf ear to this truth or attempt to distort it, as did the Jews, when they asked in John 6:52: "how can this man give us his flesh to eat?" True Christians, however, if they are genuine sons of the Church, "if they are filled with the spiritual mysteries of the Gospel so that 'the Word made Flesh dwelleth within them' will recognize" that this exegesis of Origen's comes directly from the Lord. Let them acknowledge that what has been written in the books of Holy Writ consists of *figurae* and that they have a duty to understand

5. *Hom. Lev.* 7.5, 386: "Omnis homo habet aliquem in se cibum quem accedenti ad se proximo praebeat. Non enim potest fieri, ut, cum accesserimus ad invicem nos homines et conserverimus sermonem, non aliquem vel ex responsione . . . vel ex aliquo gestu aut capiamus inter nos gustum aut praebeamus."

6. Ibid., 386: ". . . [as in preceding note] . . . praebeamus. Et si quidem mundus homo est et bonae mentis is, de quo gustum capimus, mundum sumimus cibum; si vero immundus sit, quem contingimus, immundum cibum, secundum ea, quae supra dicta sunt, sumimus. . . . Verum ut evidentius tibi patescant ad intellectum, quae dicimus, de maioribus sumamus exemplum, ut inde paulatim descendentes usque ad inferiora veniamus. Dominus et Salvator noster dicit: 'nisi manducaveritis carnem meam et biberitis sanguinem meum, non habebitis vitam in vobis ipsis. Caro enim mea vere cibus est, et sanguis meus vere potus est'." See Daniélou, *Origen*, 66.

7. Ibid., 386 f.: ". . . [as in preceding note] . . . 'potus est'. Iesus ergo quia totus ex toto mundus est, tota eius 'caro cibus est' et totus 'sanguis' eius 'potus est,' quia omne opus eius sanctum est et omnis sermo eius verus est. Propterea ergo et 'caro' eius 'verus est cibus et sanguis' eius 'verus est potus.' Carnibus enim et sanguine verbi sui tamquam mundo cibo ac potu potat et reficit omne hominum genus. Secundo in loco post illius carnem mundus cibus est Petrus et Paulus omnesque Apostoli; tertio loco discipuli eorum. Et sic unusquisque pro quantitate meritorum vel sensuum puritate proximo suo mundus efficitur cibus." I have made use of Daniélou's translation, *Origen*, loc. cit.

such things not as "carnal" but as "spiritual men." For if they receive such "food" in the fashion of "carnal men," it will harm rather than "feed" them:[8]

Est enim et in Evangeliis 'littera' quae 'occidit.' Non solum in Veteri Testamento 'occidens littera' deprehenditur: est et in Novo Testamento 'littera' quae occidat eum qui non spiritaliter, quae dicuntur, adverterit. Si enim secundum litteram sequaris hoc ipsum quod dictum est: 'nisi manducaveritis carnem meam et biberitis sanguinem meum,' occidit haec littera.[9]

For even in the Gospels there is a "letter that killeth". Not only in the Old Testament is "the letter that killeth" found: in the New Testament too there is a "letter" that will "kill" him who will not spiritually perceive what is said therein. For suppose one were to follow the aforesaid saying, "unless ye eat of my flesh and drink of my blood": here surely is a "letter that killeth"!

The repetitions are not particularly elegant but they make clear how much importance Origen attaches to the matter. Moreover, he will not leave the theme alone: for besides John 6:53 another example comes to his mind:

Vis tibi et aliam de evangelio proferam 'litteram quae occidit'? 'Qui non habet,' inquit, 'gladium, vendat tunicam et emat gladium.' Ecce et haec littera evangelii est, sed 'occidit.' Si vero spiritaliter eam suscipias, non 'occidit,' sed est in ea 'spiritus vivificans.' Et ideo sive in lege sive in evangeliis, quae dicuntur, spiritaliter suscipe, quia 'spiritalis diiudicat omnia, ipse vero a nemine diiudicatur.[10]

Does the reader wish another instance of a "letter that killeth" from the Gospels? There is Luke 22:36: "he that hath no sword let him sell his tunic and buy one." Behold! this too is the letter of the Gospel, but it is a "letter that killeth." Yet if it is spiritually received, it does not kill; for there is within that letter a

8. Ibid., 387: ". . . [as in preceding note] . . . efficitur cibus. Haec qui audire nescit, detorqueat fortassis et avertat auditum secundum illos, qui dicebant: 'quomodo dabit nobis hic carnem suam manducare? . . .' Sed vos si filii estis ecclesiae, si evangelicis imbuti mysteriis, si 'verbum caro factum habitat in vobis,' agnoscite quae dicimus quia Domini sunt. . . . Agnoscite, quia figurae sunt, quae in divinis voluminibus scripta sunt, et ideo tamquam spiritales et non tamquam carnales examinate et intelligite quae dicuntur. Si enim quasi carnales ista suscipitis laedunt vos et non alunt." See Daniélou, *Origen*, loc. cit.

9. Ibid.: ". . . [as in preceding note] . . . et non alunt. Est enim . . . [as in text] . . . occidit haec littera."

10. Ibid.: ". . . [as in preceding note] . . . occidit haec littera. Vis tibi . . . [as in text] . . . a nemine diiudicatur."

"spirit that giveth life." What is said therefore in either the Law or the Gospel must be received by the Christian in a spiritual manner: for, in the words of 1 Corinthians 2:15, "the spiritual man judgeth all things and is himself judged by no man."

With this alluring but all too brief reference to the first moment of the sword pericope, Origen can now return to the subject of the clean and unclean foods of Leviticus 11:2 ff. As already explained, the food legislation of the Old Testament must be "received in a spiritual manner." Through participation first in the example of Christ, then in that of the Apostles and of their disciples, every good Christian is filled with "clean food," which he must in turn feed unto his neighbors.[11] On the other hand, Origen pursues, evil men are receptacles of "unclean food." Everyone therefore offers himself as "food": some innocently and with a righteous heart like a clean animal, as lambs; others, in the guise of animals that are unclean.[12] It is clear, moreover, Origen concludes, that only such a "spiritual" interpretation of the Mosaic food code is consonant with the Divine Majesty. For at the purely literal level, merely human laws such as those of the Lacedemonians, the Athenians, and the Romans are unquestionably far more elegant and rational than the Torah! Indeed, if he followed the letter (as do the Jews and the "simpler folk" among the Christians), Origen would have to be ashamed of confessing that such legislation as this could possibly be the Law of God! On the contrary, if the Law is understood "in accordance with the spiritual intelligence taught by the Church," then it will be seen to tower over every human enactment. With these remarks, Origen leaves the general subject and turns to specific items in the Mosaic code.[13]

11. See above, n. 6: ". . . de maioribus sumamus exemplum, ut inde paulatim descendentes usque ad inferiora veniamus. Dominus et Salvator noster . . . [etc.] . . . ." Then above, n. 7: ". . . Secundo in loco post illius carnem mundus cibus . . . [sunt] Apostoli; tertio loco discipuli eorum . . . ."

12. *Hom. Lev.*, loc. cit., 387 f.: ". . . [as in n. 10] . . . 'a nemine diiudicatur.' Ut ergo diximus omnis homo habet aliquem in se cibum, ex quo qui sumpserit, si quidem bonus est . . . mundum cibum praebet proximo suo. Si vero malus et profert mala, immundum cibum praebet proximo suo. Potest enim quis innocens et rectus corde mundum animal ovis videri et praebere audienti se cibum mundum tamquam ovis, quae est animal mundum. Similiter et in ceteris. Et ideo omnis homo, ut diximus, cum loquitur proximo suo et sive prodest ei ex sermonibus suis sive nocet, mundum ei aut immundum efficitur animal . . . ."

13. Ibid., 388: "Si secundum hanc intelligentiam dicamus Deum summum leges hominibus promulgasse, puto quod digna videbitur divina maiestate legislatio. Si vero adsideamus litterae et secundum hoc, vel quod Iudaeis vel vulgo videtur, accipiamus

The strange association of Luke 22:36 (the first moment of the sword pericope) with the eucharistic saying of John 6:53 and the food legislation of Leviticus 11:2 ff. is explained in part by Origen's exegetical assumptions. Two of these are clearly enounced in the passage that has just been cited and paraphrased. First, Origen—as a cultivated Greek—is ashamed of the Torah when it is literally interpreted: civilized legislation does not deal with little owls, lapwings, and cloven-hooved animals—whether or not they chew the cud. By including such laughable material into His writings, God must have intended to give the attentive hearer a clue to the spiritual meaning which He intended over and above the Law.[14] Second, the same principle applies in a sense even to the Gospels. But in what sense? When Origen says that "the letter" of Luke 22:36 and John 6:53 is a "letter that killeth," precisely what does he intend to say? No doubt, that a literal interpretation will involve the Christian in the spiritual death of sin. But what kind of sin? And does the letter of Luke 22:36 kill in precisely the same way as the letter of John 6:53?

Take first the eucharistic saying of John 6:53. Does Origen really intend to reduce its meaning to the moralistic platitude that Christians have an influence on one another? Does he really wish to deny the sacramental value of drinking the blood and eating the flesh of Christ? What he says elsewhere about the Eucharist suggests that the case is more complex. On the one hand, Origen undoubtedly emphasizes that the Eucharist is "true food and drink" and that Christians must receive the Lord's Body "with all veneration and caution, in fear lest they drop some small parcel thereof."[15] On the other hand, he stresses that God's Word is, in the end, more important than

---

quae in lege scripta sunt, erubesco dicere et confiteri quia tales leges dederit Deus. Videbuntur enim magis elegantes et rationabiles hominum leges, verbi gratia, vel Romanorum vel Atheniensium vel Lacedaemoniorum. Si vero secundum hanc intelligentiam, quam docet ecclesia, accipiatur Dei lex, tunc plane omnes humanas supereminet leges et vere Dei lex esse credetur. Itaque his ita praemissis spiritali, ut commonuimus, intelligentia de mundis et immundis animalibus aliqua perstringamus."

14. Above, preceding note; see also below at nn. 19 and 127.

15. See the brief and excellent remarks by Daniélou, *Origen*, 61–68. For Origen's recognition of the Eucharist as "true food and drink," see below, nn. 28 and 32; also Daniélou, loc. cit., 66. For the veneration with which Christians rightly receive the Eucharist, see *Hom. Ex.* 13.3, 274: ". . . nostis qui divinis mysteriis interesse consuestis, quomodo, cum suscipitis corpus Domini, cum omni cautela et veneratione servatis, ne ex eo parum quid decidat, ne consecrati muneris aliquid dilabatur. Reos enim vos creditis, et recte creditis, si quid inde per negligentiam decidat." Text cited in part by Daniélou, loc. cit.

His Flesh; or at least that the sacrament properly understood consists of "the word spoken over the bread" more than of the bread itself.[16] Jewish Christians (such as Christ's own Jewish followers) are, Origen points out, scandalized by the words of the Lord in John 6:51 ff. and therefore ask in John 6:52: "how can this man give us his flesh to eat?" But the genuine Christians, the true people of God, understand the Lord's *logion,* for they know that they "are said to drink Christ's blood not only in the sacramental rite, but whenever they receive His words"; for it is in this Word that Life resides.[17] The sweeping statement in the Homilies on Leviticus does not mean that Origen rejects the eucharistic meaning of John 6:53. What then does he intend by the statement that "the letter killeth even in the Gospel"?

In his theology of the Old Testament, Origen believes, of course—with Saint Paul—that every letter is a "letter that killeth." Yet, as has been seen, this does not mean that he denies its literal meaning. He may, to be sure, have had some doubts about the historicity of some of the events in the opening chapters of Genesis; and he undoubtedly believed that a few of the

16. *Hom. Ex.*, loc. cit.: ". . . [as in preceding note] . . . decidat. Quod si circa corpus eius conservandum tanta utimini cautela et merito utimini, quomodo putatis minoris esse piaculi verbum Dei neglexisse quam corpus?" *Com. Mat.* 11.14, 58: "The material bread is of no benefit. . . . What is of benefit is the word spoken over the bread" (translation from the Greek by Daniélou, *Origen,* 64).

17. *Hom. Num.* 16.9, 151 f. (Origen is commenting on Numbers 23:24): "He shall not sleep until he eat of the prey and drink of the blood of the wounded." See below, n. 36. The meaning must be allegorical: "Quomodo enim iste populus . . . in hoc veniet ut 'sanguinem vulneratorum bibat,' cum tam validis praeceptis cibus sanguinis interdicatur a Deo, ut etiam nos qui ex gentibus vocati sumus, necessario iubeamur 'abstinere nos' sicut 'ab his quae idolis immolantur' ita 'et a sanguine' [Acts 15:29]. . . . Haec erant, quae et in evangelio audientes ii, qui ex Iudaeis Dominum sequebantur, scandalizati sunt et dixerunt: quis potest 'manducare carnes et sanguinem bibere'? [John 6:52] Sed populus Christianus, populus fidelis, audit haec et amplectitur et sequitur eum qui dicit: 'Nisi manducaveritis carnem meam et biberitis sanguinem meum non habebitis vitam in vobis ipsis: quia caro mea vere cibus est et sanguis . . . vere potus est.' . . . 'Bibere' autem dicimur 'sanguinem Christi' non solum sacramentorum ritu, sed et cum sermones eius recipimus in quibus vita consistit. . . ." Daniélou, *Origen,* 66, gives a translation which, because of its incompleteness, is perhaps just a little misleading. On the observance by Christians of the Apostolic Decree and blood-avoidance, see Arnold Ehrhardt, "Der Sonntagsbraten der christlichen Hausfrau" in "Soziale Fragen in der Alten Kirche," *Existenz und Ordnung. Festschrift für Erik Wolf* (Frankfurt, 1962), 156–67; Tertullian, *Apologeticum* 9.13–14 (*CC* 1), 104; below, nn. 135, 137, and 151, and chapter 4, n. 6, for the whole problem of Early Christian pacifism. For Origen, see below, chapter 4 at nn. 5, 7, and 54. It seems clear to me that in the text from the Homilies on Numbers just quoted Origen contrasts *nos qui ex gentibus vocati sunt,* i.e., Gentile Christians, with *ii qui ex Iudaeis Dominum sequebantur,* i.e., the Jewish followers of Christ.

precepts of the Mosaic Law (such as the prohibition against carrying a burden on the sabbath) are literally absurd. As has been seen, for Origen such "stumbling-blocks" have been deliberately "woven into" Holy Writ by the Holy Spirit as a clue to a "higher" meaning over and above the literal.[18] Apart from these few exceptions, however, Origen believes that every narrative verse of the Old Testament is historically correct; and that every precept of the Old Law had been literally incumbent upon the Jews. To "smite all the souls" in the city of Hazor "so that there were not any left to breathe" was no doubt a barbarous act typical of the bloodthirsty Jews;[19] to include in one's religious rites the slicing off of foreskins and sacrifices of blood, at least as horrendous; and to have legislation about cloven hooves and chewing the cud, ridiculous and unworthy of a civilized people. Such acts could not lead to salvation, but they were nevertheless incumbent upon the Jews and had all equally been ordained by God. Only those few patriarchs and prophets who saw behind "the letter" of these deliberately bloodthirsty and scandalous precepts the messianic and christological light that shone through them despite their absurdity (indeed their very absurdity was a clue to the hidden spiritual meaning) could hope for salvation. In that sense, every letter of the Law could be said to kill.

As might be expected, the New Testament is both radically different and yet fundamentally the same. On rare occasions, the Holy Ghost is still busy "weaving stumbling-blocks" and obstacles. Though he was later to repent of these doubts, the young Origen seems to have questioned—on the grounds of historical verisimilitude—the actuality of the story of the Cleansing of the Temple:[20] and, as will be seen, he undoubtedly believed that some precepts of Christ (including the first

18. See above, chapter 1, n. 10.

19. Above, chapter 1 at nn. 61–71.

20. On Origen and New Testament exegesis, see Harl, *Fonction Révélatrice*, 146–57, and R. M. Grant, *The Earliest Lives of Jesus*, 62–70 and 84–88. For Origen's doubts on the historicity of certain Gospel events and the necessity of a spiritual interpretation, see Harl, *Fonction Révélatrice*, 147, 149, 152 ff. For the Cleansing of the Temple, see *Com. Joh.* 10.4–25, 174–98. The passage is long and complex, and de Lubac in *Histoire et Esprit*, 210 f., maintains that Origen never in fact doubted the historicity of the episode. In *Com. Mat.* 16.20, 544 (Greek only), however, Origen seems to admit his former doubts and insist that they were due to his still "slaving after the letter": he had put too much emphasis on minor discrepancies in the text. See Grant, *Earliest Lives*, 67.

moment of the sword pericope) were never intended to be carried out to the letter.[21] For the remainder, however, every verse of the Gospel was either historically true or consisted of a precept that was literally incumbent upon Christians.[22] As for the exceptions, the apparent absurdity of certain episodes or precepts was intended by the Holy Spirit as a signpost to the fact that over and above this literal faith in the historical Jesus and over and above that literal obedience to the precepts of the Lord there was even in the New Testament a higher and more spiritual meaning.

So far, the situation seems exactly the same as in the Old Testament. An important distinction which Origen draws *within* the New Dispensation is, moreover, in many ways analogous to the basic distinction *between* the letter of the Old and the spirit of the New. This is the distinction between "simpler folk" and "the many" (*hoi polloi*), "the mob," or "the psychic," those who understand only the letter of the New Testament, on the one hand, and the true "gnostic," the "pneumatic," the "spiritual man" or mystic who is able to transform the Gospel of the Senses (*to aisthēton euaggelion*) into the Gospel of the Mind and Spirit (*to euaggelion noēton kai pneumatikon*), on the other.[23] In a sense, that Gospel of the Senses, just like the Old Testament, can be a "letter that killeth." Insofar as the "simpler folk" are not simply at a lower state of perfection but use the letter of the Gospel as an excuse stubbornly to refuse to look beyond that letter, one may be sure that Christ's warning to "the scribes and Pharisees" of the Old Law applies to those whom Origen on occasion rather tellingly refers to as "the scribes of the Gospel."[24]

At this point, however, the parallelism breaks down: for "letter" and "spirit" do not, after all, function in the New Dispensation in quite the same fashion as in the Old. The Old Testament *was* the letter, of which the New Testament was to be the spirit. Every letter of the Old Testament was therefore a "letter that killeth": that is to say, faith in the historicity of

21. See above at nn. 9 and 10; below at nn. 46–50, 69–78, 84–86, and 92–97.

22. See below, nn. 25–28.

23. On the "simpler folk" (*hoi akeraioteroi, simpliciores*), "the mob" (*hoi haplousteroi*), or "the many" (*hoi polloi*), see Daniélou, "L'Unité des Deux Testaments," 29. For the transforming (*metalabein*) of the *aisthēton euaggelion* into an *euaggelion noēton kai pneumatikon*, see *Com. Joh.* 1.8.10, 13.

24. For "the scribes of the Gospel," see below, next notes.

the Old Testament and faithful obedience to its commandments were radically insufficient for salvation. But in a New Testament context, that "the letter killeth" only means that literalism *can* kill even now. Thus, while Origen warns in the Homilies on Leviticus and the Commentary on Matthew that "the letter killeth even in the Gospels," in two important passages of the *Commentariorum Series* he joyfully proclaims the opposite. In one, he insists that "every letter of the Gospel, even as letter, giveth life to 'the scribes of the Gospel' (if one may call them so)"; even though over and above the salvation which is given even unto the many, "the Spirit, which goes beyond the nature of the letter, illuminates those for whom the Gospel is not veiled."[25] In the other, he sharply contrasts "the unfortunate scribes of the Law" with "the scribes sent by Christ in accordance with the Gospel." For "the spirit of the Gospel," Origen pursues, "giveth life and its letter doth not kill unlike the letter of the Law: those who follow the letter of the Law fall into superstition, while those who follow the letter of the Gospel (that is to say the plain narrative) are saved, because that simple history is itself sufficient for the salvation of simpler folk."[26]

Nothing could be plainer. The simple faith of simple folk in the historical Jesus *can* save; while the belief of Jews in the historical narrative of the Old Testament could only damn. Similarly, literal obedience to the precepts of the Lord *can* save; while obeying the letter of the Law could only bring death. Indeed, Origen can inveigh against those who, because of their "exaggerated regard for human infirmity," consider some of the Lord's precepts as impossible of fulfillment, and without respect for the literal meaning "turn to allegory and thus despise the words" of Christ. Consider, for instance, Matthew 19:21: "if thou wilt be perfect, sell what thou hast and give to the poor." Though the saying has no doubt a higher and more "spiritual"

25. *Commentariorum Series* 139, 289: ". . . omnis quidem littera evangelii quasi littera vivificat evangelicos (ut ita eos appelem) scribas; spiritus autem, qui supergreditur litterarum naturam, divinioribus motibus magis eos inluminat quibus evangelium non est velatum . . . ."

26. Ibid., 27, 47 f.: "Alii enim sunt scribae infelices legis, alii autem sunt scribae qui mittuntur a Christo secundum evangelium, cuius et spiritus vivificat et littera non occidit, sicut littera legis; quoniam litteram legis sequentes in infidelitatem et in vanas superstitiones incurrunt, litteram autem evangelii qui sequuntur (id est simplicem narrationem ipsius) salvantur, quoniam et ipsa sola . . . narratio simplex sufficit simplicioribus ad salutem." Hasler, *Gesetz und Evangelium*, 74, refers to this text, but he ignores those of the *est et in evangeliis littera quae occidit* type.

interpretation, Origen insists that it must not therefore be assumed that it cannot or should not be literally implemented: indeed, it has been fulfilled to the letter not only by Christian ascetics, but even by a few pagan philosophers.[27] Similarly, in the case of the eucharistic saying of John 6:53, Origen has, in fact, no intention of denying that participation in the rites of communion may be sufficient for salvation. "It is enough," he admits in the Commentary on John, "if the bread and the cup are understood by the simple as being the Eucharist, as is the common interpretation: but those capable of going deeper should take it as referring to the Word of Truth, which is divinely promised us as our food."[28]

Despite appearances, "letter" and "spirit" are thus not normally opposed in Origen's New Testament exegesis as death is to life. He explicitly states that "the scribes of the Gospel," the literalists of the New Dispensation, can be saved; they are not necessarily subject to spiritual death. Letter and spirit are rather opposed as a lower stage of spiritual perfection is to a higher. Clearly, this is because the letter of the Gospel, unlike the letter of the Law, is already spirit, at least to some extent, and "even as letter" is capable of being spiritually understood. Even if implemented at its most literal level, the precept of the Lord "sell what thou hast and give to the poor" involves for the Christian (when properly comprehended) an imitation of the Son of God, Who emptied Himself in order to take on the form of a servant. Even at the most literal level, eucharistic participation in the Body and Blood of Christ involves a participation in the sacrifice of Jesus. What underlies Origen's reasoning is a theologically unimpeachable assumption: the Christ-dimension, which was only foreshadowed in the Old Testament, is in the New Testament part of the very letter of the text.

Nevertheless, Origen is obviously worried about an overly

27. *Com. Mat.* 15.15–18, 391–403; see 397 f. for the literal interpretation according to the *simplicitatem verborum*, and 399 f. for the *subtilior expositio moralis;* but see in particular 391 f.: "Si quis autem aspiciens humanam infirmitatem et difficile hoc putans hominem posse inplere, despiciat verba et ad allegoricum se intellectum convertat, audiat . . . historiam quorundam gentilium . . . . Si ergo propter sapientiam gentium [the Greek text has *di' Hellēnikēn sophian*] . . . hoc facere potuit homo gentilis, quomodo non facilius potest facere, qui concupiscit in se suscipere Christi perfectionem? Si autem et de divinis scripturis placari quis vult, quoniam possibile est quod praecipit Christus, audiat historiam de Actibus Apostolorum."

28. *Com. Joh.* 13.30, 468. I have used the translation in Daniélou, *Origen*, 65. In general, see Daniélou, *Origen*, 61–68.

literal interpretation of the eucharistic saying in John 6:53, and indeed of the whole of the New Testament. Those who are incapable of "transforming the Gospel of the Senses into the Gospel of the Mind and Spirit" *may* be saved, but they run a great risk. "Simple history," "the plain narrative of the Gospels," may be "sufficient for the salvation of simple folk"; but only the more perfect pneumatic, "the spiritual man, who judgeth all things"[29] will fully understand that "the physical acts which the Evangelists relate were intended by the Savior to become symbols of His spiritual activities" within the very souls of the faithful.[30] Christ and the Spirit may be present even in the letter of the Gospels. But to stop with "the plain narrative of the Gospels" involves the risk that the Christian will not heed the divinity incarnate in the Jesus of history; the risk that the letter, which "even as letter"[31] is intended to initiate a spiritual transformation, will instead be degraded into a merely historical and sentimental reminiscence or an empty rite. What worries Origen, in his comments on the eucharistic saying of John 6:53, is clearly a sort of sacramental mechanism. To believe that the eucharist (or, for that matter, baptism) can save without a genuine turning-around, a *metanoia*, or conversion of the spirit, is to fall back into the literal ceremonialism of "the scribes and Pharisees"; though it is also an actual misreading of the literal intent of the historical Jesus. For "the scribes of the Gospel," to understand the bread and cup of the Last Supper, as simply prefiguring the eucharistic rite rather than primarily the Word of God in a more "spiritual" sense is indeed sufficient;[32] but only so long as this limited understanding does not lead back to the deadening ritualism of the Pharisees, so long as it does not actually keep the Word of God from being listened to and the Spirit of Life from quickening the soul. For when limited understanding turns into ritualistic mechanism, the letter of the New Testament will kill "the scribes of the Gospel" just as surely as the letter of the Law killed the scribes and Pharisees of the Old Dispensation. If all Christians looked at the eucharist in this not only limited but empty and

29. For these expressions, see above, nn. 23, 26, and n. 10 in the text.

30. *Com. Mat.* 16.20, 545: ". . . in mysterio spiritalium actuum suorum. Et tunc fecit visibiliter quod semper invisibiliter agit." (Latin here adds to the Greek.) See de Lubac, *Histoire et Esprit*, 206.

31. See above at n. 29.

32. See above at n. 28.

deadening fashion, the Jews would have been quite right to be scandalized at this sort of spiritual cannibalism and to ask as they did in John 6:52: "how can this man give us his flesh to eat?"[33] In that sense the dialectic which operates between the Two Testaments functions also within the Gospel. To reject the letter of the Gospel is to reject the flesh of Christ; but to remain content with that letter and that flesh is to risk cutting off the Word of Life.

All of this is theologically unimpeachable. At the same time, in order fully to understand Origen's exegetical method, it is necessary to recognize that the danger of a mechanical literalism, which through limited understanding may deaden the soul by refusing to open itself to the Spirit, looms so large in Origen's mind that it obscures for him the opposite yet equally threatening danger: the danger of a sometimes overweening intellectualism that may confuse its own perhaps equally mechanical subtleties with a quickening of the Spirit, and through that confusion dissolve the flesh of history (and with it the flesh of Christ and the body of His Church) into a spirituality that need not be that of the Spirit but may instead be that of the ghostly wisdom of this world, the disembodied spiritualism of Platonists and Gnostics.[34] The simpler folk need not necessarily be damned, but for Origen the only Christian who can be sure that he will be "judged by no one" remains "the spiritual man"; and for Origen "the spiritual man" mentioned by Saint Paul is the pneumatic, that odd mixture of the ascetic, the intellectual, and the saint which was the peculiar product of the school of Alexandria.[35] Commenting on a particularly bloodthirsty passage of the Old Testament, Origen once noted that "here even the most contentious defender of 'history' will rush for refuge to the sweetness of allegory."[36] In a peculiar way, the same kind of rushing applies to Origen's own exegesis of the Gospels. Origen does tend to glide over the liturgical

33. See above at n. 17.

34. The reader is reminded that "Gnostic" with a capital *G* refers to heretical sects; while "gnostic" or "true gnostic" with a small *g* is, in accordance with common usage, used to distinguish these heretics from those "gnostics" whom Origen identifies with the "pneumatics."

35. See above at n. 23.

36. *Hom. Num.* 16.9, 151: " 'Non dormiet, donec comedat praedam et sanguinem vulneratorum bibat' [Numbers 23:24]. In his verbis quis ita erit historicae narrationis contentiosus adsertor, immo quis ita brutus invenietur, qui non horrescens sonum litterae ad allegoriae dulcedinem ipsa necessitate confugiat? Quomodo enim iste populus . . . [see above, n. 17] . . . ."

and institutional Eucharist as he tends to glide over the historical Jesus. He rushes for refuge to the sweetness of the pneumatic Eucharist, the Eucharist according to the Spirit. He does not deny that the liturgy plays a fundamental role; but like many a mystic after him he is in a hurry to leave the fundaments and climb to the heights. As a result he glides not only over the commemorative and liturgical, but even over the ecclesiological and christological dimensions of the Eucharist: for him these aspects are in a sense part of "the letter" of the Gospel. What Origen does therefore in his exegesis of the Gospels is to rush from the harshness of the letter not so much to the sweetness of allegory as to the (to him much greater) sweetness of a purely inward-looking, purely spiritual, tropology.[37] The Greek intellectual in Origen is so ashamed of the Torah that on occasion he will fall into the temptation of being ashamed of the more historical and liturgical aspects of the Gospel, and indeed even of those theological truths that are more particularly rooted in the flesh of Christ. For him these aspects of the Gospel are in danger of constituting a sort of Gospel of the Flesh, in contrast to the true Gospel of the Spirit, the *evangelium aeternum*, the Everlasting Gospel.[38] He is not quite at home with the scandal of the Cross.

It is these theological (and exegetical) premises which explain the otherwise strange association between the first moment of the sword pericope, the eucharistic saying of John 6:53, and the food legislation of Leviticus. Origen wishes to give a tropological exegesis of the Leviticus text: what underlies the letter of the Law is the spiritual truth that men must keep themselves "clean" for altruistic reasons, since in daily intercourse they become "food" for one another. To prepare for this interpretation, he begins by citing John 6:53. In a hurry "to rush to the sweetness" of tropology, he glides over the more obvious eucharistic meaning. It then occurs to him that "the simpler folk," "the scribes of the Gospel," may object to such an "allegorizing" of the letter, to what he himself calls "turning to allegory and thus despising the words" of the Lord. He therefore deliberately

37. Daniélou, *Origen*, 28 ff. and 61 ff.; de Lubac, *Exégèse Médiévale* 1.2, 558 and 592; above, preceding note.

38. For the contrast between the Gospel of the Flesh and the Gospel of the Mind or Spirit, see above, n. 23. For Origen's development of the concept of the *evangelium aeternum*, the Everlasting Gospel (taken from the Apocalypse), see *De Principiis* 4.3.13, 343 f., and *Com. Rom.* 1.4, 847; cf. de Lubac, *Histoire et Esprit*, 221, n. 154.

stresses only one side of the question. He does not say (as he does elsewhere) that "the letter of the Gospel does not kill, for simple history is itself sufficient for the salvation of simpler folk"; on the contrary, here he stresses that "even in the Gospels, there is a 'letter that killeth'; it is not only in the Old Testament that the letter is found." Besides John 6:53, another example comes to his mind: Luke 22:36, the first moment of the sword pericope.[39]

The allusion to Luke 22:36 is tantalizing in its brevity, yet the context, together with Origen's other references to the sword pericope, make possible a first approximation of his meaning. The saying, "he that hath no sword, let him sell his tunic and buy one," if taken literally, will lead to mortal sin: it therefore demonstrates that the letter may kill even in the Gospel. Yet hidden beneath that very letter, there is "the spirit that giveth life."[40] This last point must be understood in the light of the remainder of Origen's interpretation of the sword pericope as a whole. As has been seen in the context of the Phineas episode, Origen envisages the transfiguration of the Old into the New Dispensation as symbolized by a sort of interchange of swords: the corporeal sword of the Old Testament has been taken away by the Lord, and the Christian has received in its stead the sword of the Spirit, which is the Word of Life.[41] As will be seen, Origen interprets Peter's abscission of Malchus's ear as a witness to the disciples' lack of spiritual understanding: they misunderstood the Lord's injunction and instead of the spiritual sword of the Gospel took up the corporeal sword of the Old Dispensation, the sword of physical violence, of armed resistance, and of war.[42] Yet "the spiritual man, who judgeth all things"[43] will understand that concealed beneath the "letter" of the corporeal sword—the sword of the Old Testament—there is the spiritual sword, of which the letter is only the figure, that is to say the Word of God and the Spirit of Life.

The question still remains, in what sense is Luke 22:36 an example of a "letter that killeth"? As is clear from what precedes, the statement that "the letter killeth even in the Gospels" can have at least two meanings for Origen. First, it can be taken quite generally as applying to everything in the New Testament.

39. See above at nn. 5–10.
40. Above at n. 10.
41. Above, chapter 1, pp. 37ff., and this chapter, p. 40.
42. See below at nn. 118 and 133.
43. Above at n. 10 [I Cor. 2:15].

In that sense, however, it only means that the letter *can* kill: an overly restrictive literalism may prevent the Christian from actually living the Gospel; for only life can save, and not the merely historical faith in a dead and not resurrected past or the mechanics of a merely external rite. Second, it can be taken more specifically as applying to a very few passages, which, according to Origen, were not intended to have any literal meaning at all, but were "stumbling-blocks and obstacles" deliberately "woven into" the texture of Scripture by the Holy Spirit, so that Christians should be forced to seek out a more "spiritual" meaning.[44] As has already been suggested, the first moment of the sword pericope belongs, in fact, to this second and rather exceptional category.[45] This is made explicit, however, not by Origen's brief treatment of Luke 22:36 in the Homilies on Leviticus, but by the longer exegesis of the same passage in the Commentary on Matthew.

In the exegesis of that Lucan material in the Commentary on Matthew, the context of the first moment of the sword pericope is, on first reading, just as strange as in the Homilies on Leviticus. Here the immediate occasion is not the interpretation of the food legislation of Leviticus, but the exegesis of Matthew 19:12: "There are some eunuchs, which were so born from their mother's womb; and there are some eunuchs, which were made eunuchs of men; and there be eunuchs, which have made themselves eunuchs for the kingdom of heaven's sake." So far, Origen points out, there have been two schools of interpretation for this saying of the Lord's. The exegetes of the first school have had the audacity to assert that all three types of eunuchs must be understood in purely carnal fashion. Yet those who out of an imagined fear of the Lord and an "impure lust for purity," an immoderate desire for moderation, practice castration on themselves will only succeed in being subjected to shame and obloquy not only among those who are strangers to the faith but even among those who normally forgive the ignorance of men (that is to say, even among Christians).[46] The exegetes

44. Above at nn. 18–21, and chapter 1 at nn. 5–10.

45. Above at n. 10 and n. 21.

46. *Com. Mat.* 15.1, 348 f.: "Priusquam exponamus, quae nobis videntur in loco, notum facimus duas esse expositiones loci istius: quorundam quidem [qui] duas eunuchizationes carnales aspicientes quasi consequenter dicere aestimantes, ausi sunt etiam tertiam eunuchizationem dicere corporalem, utputa, qui propter timorem dei corporaliter se eunuchizant et obiecerunt se opprobriis et confusionibus non solum apud alienos fidei sed etiam apud eos qui ignorantiae omni hominum ignoscere solent." This section of the Commentary on Matthew has been preserved in Greek; yet as

of the second and far more numerous school acknowledge that the third type of eunuch must be interpreted in purely spiritual terms, but like the first school they assume that the first two types are to be understood on a literal level. Origen, however, cannot agree with either school. To be sure, unlike the first school, the exegetes of the majority view are not morally reprehensible; yet their exegesis is mistaken because they fail to understand a simple rule of style. In a rhetorical sequence, such as that of Matthew 19:12, all elements in the enumeration, Origen asserts, must be at the same level of meaning. Suddenly to leap from the literal to the figurative level would be to offend against the most elementary rules of rhetorical "similitude" (something which the Lord presumably would not dream of doing). Since, however, it is morally and theologically certain that the third type of eunuch must be given not a carnal but a spiritual interpretation, it follows—Origen insists against both exegetical schools—that even the first two types cannot be understood at a literal level.[47]

Before proceeding, however, with his own purely allegorical exegesis, Origen must first deal with a possible objection:

Cui autem displicet, quoniam est et evangelica littera occidens, audiat, exempli gratia, quod dixit ad apostolos suos: '. . . qui habet sacculum accipiat, similiter et peram, et qui non habet vendat vestimentum suum et emat gladium.' Si quis ergo litteram volens aspicere et non

---

usual I give the ancient Latin translation, since it is that version that is influential in the West. When necessary in my paraphrase I also make use of the Greek version, acknowledging this in the notes. Here, for instance, the Greek says that those who castrate themselves are moved *phantasiā[i] phobou theou kai sōphrosunēs ametrō[i] erōti* "by a phantasy of the fear of God and an unmeasured lust for temperance." On this passage and the problem of Origen's own act (or alleged act) of self-castration, see below at nn. 54–60.

47. Ibid., 15.1, 349 ff.: "Alii autem et plerique sic intellexerunt, non discutientes modum consequentiae verborum: duas quidem eunuchizationes priores similiter prioribus expositoribus carnales esse dixerunt et nihil spiritaliter intellegendum in eis; tertiam autem eunuchizationem dixerunt ex verbo non corporalem, quando spe regni caelestis [a] severissimo verbo praecidunt concupiscentiae passionem. Et primi quidem facti amatores evangelicae litterae et non intellegentes quod etiam haec in parabolis locutus est Iesus, consequenter prioribus eunuchizationibus duabus corporalibus intellexerunt et tertiam. . . . Secundi autem interpretatores tertiam quidem eunuchizationem salubriter exposuerunt fieri verbi praecisione, non autem consideraverunt quoniam talis expositio conveniens erat etiam in prioribus eunuchizationibus duabus secundum similitudinem illius tertiae." Grant, *Earliest Lives,* 107, mistakenly believes that Origen includes himself among the second group of exegetes. Walter Bauer, "Matth. 19, 12 und die alten Christen," *Neutestamentliche Studien. Georg Heinrici zu seinem 70. Geburtstag* (*Untersuchungen zum Neuen Testament* 6; Leipzig, 1914), 235 ff. (: W. Bauer, *Aufsätze und Kleine Schriften. Tübingen,* 1967, 253 ff.), had given the correct interpretation.

intellegens voluntatem verborum vendiderit vestimentum suum corporale et 'emerit gladium' [homicidialem, quasi accipiens gladium] talem, contra voluntatem Christi [faciens et prave] suscipiens verbum eius 'peribit,' forsitan et 'in gladio peribit.' De quo autem gladio dicat, non est loci huius exponere.[48]

If anyone, however, is displeased by the idea of a Gospel "letter that killeth," let him hear, for example, what the Lord said to His apostles in the first moment of the sword pericope: "he that hath a purse, let him take it, and likewise his scrip, and he that hath no sword, let him sell his garment and buy one" (Luke 22:36). Now suppose, Origen pursues, that someone pays attention to this "letter" without understanding the intention of the words: he will sell his corporeal and perceptible garment and buy himself the sword of homicide. Yet by taking up this kind of sword he will have acted wrongfully and taken up the word of Christ against the very will of Christ. He will therefore surely "perish"; perhaps (in the words of Matthew 26:52 and the last moment of the sword pericope) he will even "perish by the sword." The present context, Origen remarks, is not, however, the proper place for commenting at length on what kind of sword Christ had actually in mind.

In addition, Origen pursues, let the hypothetical objector consider Luke 10:4: "Salute no man by the way." If someone were to attempt to fulfill this precept without regard for Jesus' actual intention, he would simply manage to appear moronic and inhuman in the eyes of all. Indeed, he would make it seem as if Christ had taught men to be savage and barbaric and thus only succeed in having men hate the very words of Jesus. In the end he might even die having incurred the hatred of all: in effect, he will have subjected himself to "the death of the letter."[49] The same is true, Origen adds, of Matthew 5:29: "If

48. Ibid. 15.2, 351 f. Except for the passages in brackets, which are Klostermann's emendations from the Greek, the Latin is an almost word for word translation; whence its awkwardness. As usual, *corporalis* in the Latin Origen translates *aisthētos*, the term which in Platonic philosophy is opposed to *noētos* (*intelligibilis*), and should really be translated by "perceptible"; see above at n. 23. As for the last sentence, it is often Origen's custom to refuse to reveal a "mystery" when the audience or context is not right. Often this is done with reference to Hebrews 9:5; see Crouzel, *Théologie de L'Image*, 153 ff. See also below, n. 133, and at nn. 146–149.

49. Ibid., 15.2, 352 f.: "Sed et illud aspiciat, 'neminem in via salutaveritis' [Luke 10:4], si quis non discutiens, quid volens Iesus hoc [loco] praecepit, quasi zelans vitam apostolorum 'neminem' salutaverit 'in via,' quasi inhumanus et stultus videbitur omnibus et sic docebit odire omnes verba Christi quasi agrestes et inhumanos docentia homines esse. Forsitan autem et morietur in odium cunctorum deductus,

thy right eye offend thee, pluck it out," and of Matthew 5:30: "If thy right hand offend thee, cut it off." To pluck out one's eye because one blames it for one's bad sight, to cut off one's right hand or foot according to the flesh, will only accomplish that one will bear the stigma of insanity and that in the end one will die a fruitless death.[50]

Having dealt with the objection that in the Gospel there is no "letter that killeth," Origen can now return to the problem at hand: the allegorical interpretation of all three of the forms of castration in Matthew 19:12. All previous interpretations must be rejected. The true pneumatic, "the spiritual man" in the true sense of the term, must "spiritually interpret the words of the spirit." It will therefore be Origen's task to give a tropological interpretation of the whole of the Lord's saying.[51] The first type of castration refers not to those who are genuinely "eunuchs by birth" but simply to those who "by nature are colder than other men." The second type refers not to men who castrate themselves but to those "who cut off their sexuality, that is to say restrict their concupiscence not because of the Word of God but because of the words of men": such as, for instance, some of the philosophers among the Greeks, or some of the heretics who, in the words of 1 Timothy 4:3, even "forbid to marry."[52] The third form of castration refers to those who, in the words of Hebrews 4:12, take up "the word of God, which is quick and powerful and sharper than any two-edged sword" (this is the same sword, Origen adds, which Paul in Ephesians 6:17 calls "the sword of the spirit"). By means of that sword, Origen can finally conclude, these eunuchs of the third sort cut off

littera se occidente." The Greek speaks of "the death of the letter." See below, n. 71, for the very similar comments on the same saying in *De Principiis* 4.3.3, 327 f.

50. Ibid., 353: "Si autem et dextrum quis oculum eiciat aut manum, aut pedem, post opprobrium insaniae infructuosum patietur interitum." The Greek is mutilated but adds a few details (for instance, about "the right foot according to the flesh") which have been incorporated into my paraphrase.

51. Ibid., 15.4, 357: "Nos autem (si spiritales sumus) verba spiritus spiritaliter accipiamus et de tribus istis eunuchizationibus aedificationem introducentes moralem [Gr.: *tropologia*]. Eunuchi nunc moraliter [Gr.: *tropikōs*] abstinentes se a venereis sunt appellandi."

52. Ibid., 357 f.: "Eorum autem qui se continent differentiae tres sunt: et quidam quidem sunt natura frigidiores prae ceteris viris, de quibus recte dicitur 'sunt quidam eunuchi, qui de utero matris suae nascuntur sic.' Quidam autem continentes sunt propter verba hominum, quorum concupiscentiam virilem praecidit non verbum divinum, sed verba humana, utputa qui philosophati sunt apud antiquos in gentibus [Gr.: simply *par' Hellēsin*] aut apud eos 'qui prohibent nubere' . . . [1 Timothy 4:3] apud haereses, isti 'sunt eunuchi qui ab hominibus fiunt.'"

their sexual concupiscence, without in any way touching their own body; they do this, moreover, not against their will nor because they fear men or wish to be praised, but only for the sake of the Kingdom of Heaven.[53]

In the Homilies on Leviticus the first moment of the sword pericope was associated with the food code of Leviticus 11:2 ff. and the Lord's eucharistic saying in John 6:53. Here in the Commentary on Matthew it is associated with three other *logia:* Matthew 19:12, the enigma about the three types of eunuchs; Luke 10:4, the rude injunction about saluting no one; and Matthew 5:29 f., the offensive saying about plucking out one's eye and cutting off one's hand. Here Origen is obviously presenting the reader with a list of four "impossible" sayings on the part of the Lord. But in what sense are they "impossible," in what sense does their letter kill? Before returning to the first moment of the sword pericope, it will be best to have a look at Origen's treatment of the accompanying sayings (and of some others which he treats in similar fashion) not only in the Commentary on Matthew but also in the remainder of his works and indeed his life.

Origen's treatment of the enigma of the three types of eunuchs presents one immediate problem which may have puzzled the reader: how to reconcile this strong condemnation of self-emasculation with the statement in Eusebius' *Historia Ecclesiastica* that the young Origen had castrated himself only later to repent his rashness. Eusebius of Caesarea came from the city in which Origen spent the last years of his life; he was a follower of Origen's theology and early in his career (though, to be sure, some fifty years after Origen's death) had collaborated with one of Origen's last surviving disciples in composing the so-called *Apologia* in defense of the master. His account of the life of Origen is therefore usually regarded as one of the more reliable sections of the *Historia Ecclesiastica.* In addition, Eusebius strongly disapproves of Origen's alleged act of mutilation; because of his great admiration for the master it is therefore not the sort of story he would have invented or even rashly

53. Ibid., 357 f.: ". . . [as preceding note] 'qui ab hominibus fiunt.' Qui autem suscipit 'verbum vivum et efficax et acutius super omnem gladium bis acutum' [Hebrews 4:12] et 'gladium spiritus'—sicut ait Apostolus [Ephesians 6:17]—et praeciderit concupiscentiam suam corpus suum non tangens, et hoc fecerit non invitus propter timorem hominum neque propter laudem humanam sed propter solam spem regni caelestis, isti 'sunt qui eunuchizaverunt seipsos propter regnum dei.' "

reported, unless it was supported by what he must have regarded as strong evidence. Most scholars therefore accept the account of Eusebius.[54] Yet the silence of Origen in the Commentary on Matthew remains extremely puzzling. Were he really a repentant *castratus*, is he likely to have missed the opportunity for personal confession on the dangers of an exaggerated literalism, which the exegesis of Matthew 19:12 so conveniently afforded? Personal reticence, after all, is not a virtue of the period: in Early Christian times the repentant sinner was not one likely to be misled by a sense of false shame. Perhaps Eusebius was misled by his sources; there is some evidence that he found the story in letters that originated with Origen's enemies.[55] Perhaps he mistook a rumor for a fact and simply took the passage in the Commentary on Matthew as evidence for Origen's repentance. On the other hand, is it possible that Origen's reference to those who mutilate themselves out of "an imagined fear of the Lord and an immoderate lust for temperance" and are afterwards scorned even by Christians "who normally forgive human ignorance"[56] was actually meant as an allusion to his own misadventure? The point will presumably never be solved.

Whatever may have been the case for Origen himself, such acts of self-mutilation did occur among heretics and even on occasion on the fringes of orthodox communities. The so-called Encratites held intercourse illegitimate even in marriage (it is to that group of heretics that Origen presumably refers in his exegesis of the second type of eunuch); but there were also isolated examples of extreme ascetics who had taken the next logical step—on occasion apparently even among Catholics. Thus for the second century the perfectly orthodox Justin Martyr records such an instance (for Alexandria, it should be noted) without

54. Eusebius, *Historia Ecclesiastica* 6.8.1 (*GCS* 9.2), 534 ff. On the problem, see W. Bauer, "Matth. 19, 12 und die alten Christen," 236 ff. (: *Aufsätze*, 255 ff.), and R. P. C. Hanson, "A Note on Origen's Self-Mutilation," *Vigiliae Christianae* 20 (1966) 81 f. Both authors accept the story as well founded but report that because of Origen's remarks in the Commentary on Matthew "some doubts have been raised" on the subject; see, e.g., Adolf von Harnack, "Der Kirchengeschichtliche Ertrag der Exegetischen Arbeit des Origenes," *TU* 42.4 (1919) 122, n. 1. For the general reliability of Eusebius' account, see, e.g., Daniélou, *Origen*, 1; see *Origen*, 13, for Daniélou's acceptance of the castration story. See also, for instance, Altaner, *Patrology*, 223.

55. Eusebius, *Historia Ecclesiastica* 6.8.1 (*GCS* 9.2), 536 f.; it seems as if Eusebius is here making use of a letter or letters by Demetrius, the Bishop of Alexandria, who had forced Origen to seek refuge in Caesarea.

56. See above, n. 46.

any sign of disapproval.[57] In the third century the Pseudo-Cyprianic *De Singularitate Clericorum* seems to refer, albeit disapprovingly, to the custom of cutting off one's genitals for fear of masturbation;[58] and in the fourth century instances of self-mutilation persisted among monks in both Egypt and Syria, while the Councils of Arles and Nicea found it necessary to proclaim that voluntary castration, because it was a sign of the inability to repulse the vices of the flesh, formed an impediment for promotion to the ranks of the clergy.[59] Origen's polemic against the literal interpretation of Matthew 19:12 must therefore be taken as more than merely academic. There was a real danger that the simpler folk, those "scribes of the Gospel," should be deceived into taking their imagined or phantasmagoric fears for the genuine fear of the Lord and allow themselves to be driven by an exaggerated asceticism, which because it was immoderate and indeed without measure was actually a form of lust. The only result of their rash act will be the scorn of their fellow citizens; and what is worse, they will in the process have exposed to ridicule the very words of Christ. On the contrary, Christians must remember that they are "spiritual eunuchs" and that it is in that sense—and in that sense only—

57. Justin Martyr, *Apology* 1.29, 2–3, cited by Bauer, "Matth. 19, 12," 238 (: *Aufsätze*, 257), and Hanson, "Self-Mutilation," 81. The "eunuchs" mentioned by Athenagoras, *Libellus*, 34.1–2, and the "spadones voluntarii" mentioned by Tertullian, *De Resurrectione Mortuorum* 61.6 and *De Virginibus Velandis* 10.1, do not seem to me to support Hanson's contention that "self-castration was, on the whole, [an] approved custom in the Christian Church of Origen's time." Both Athenagoras and Tertullian surely refer to "spiritual" (metaphorical) eunuchs; in Tertullian, at least, it is clear that these *many* (*quot* or *tot*) "spadones voluntarii" are simply male parallels to the *virgines*, i.e., not voluntary castrates but voluntary (male) virgins. See also below, next note.

58. Pseudo-Cyprian, *De Singularitate Clericorum* 33 (*CSEL* 3.3), 208 ff. Hanson, "Self-Mutilation," 81, seems to suggest that Pseudo-Cyprian approves of these "spadones" who "amputatis genitalibus semet ipsos abscidunt." The Latin of Pseudo-Cyprian is a little obscure, but it seems to me fairly clear that he strongly disapproves of them. The passage is almost two full pages long and cannot be quoted or even meaningfully excerpted. Note, however, that the author speaks of a "confusio spadonum," apostrophizes these castrates with deliberate irony as "spirituales eunuchi," compares them to the castrate priests of Attis (*Galli*) and the Jews (circumcision being for the purposes of the argument equated with castration) and in the end contrasts all these bloody acts with the merely spiritual continence which he believes is required of the clergy: "clerici vero pro dignitate sacerdotii caelestis non sanguinem fundunt, non tolerant ferrum, non est aliquod vulnus . . . sed solus eos contra Dominum feminae torret aspectus."

59. Athanasius, *Historia Arianorum* 28; Cyrillus Scythopolitanus, *Vita Sabae* 41 (Cotelerius, *Ecclesia Graecae Monumenta* 3 [1686] 284 f.); Epiphanius, *Expositio Fidei* 13.1095; Nicea, canon 1; Arles, canon 7: "hos qui se carnali vitio repugnare nescientes abscidunt, ad clerum pervenire non posse." All these citations come from Bauer, "Matth. 19, 12," 239 (: *Aufsätze*, 257).

that they must subject themselves to castration "for the sake of the Kingdom of Heaven."[60] Thus, it is in a very concrete sense that the "letter" of Matthew 19:12 is "a letter that killeth."

At the same time, as Origen himself emphasizes, it is clear that this "allegorical" treatment of the third type of eunuch does not distinguish Origen's exegesis from that of the majority of his contemporaries. What he considers his own peculiar contribution is, on the contrary, the "allegorization" of the first two types: because the rules of rhetoric forbid sudden leaps from one level of meaning to another, the metaphorical nature of the third type of eunuch means that the first two types must be equally "tropological."[61] Origen here uses "letter" and "allegory" (or "tropology") in a somewhat peculiar fashion. In Old Testament times, God quite literally wanted the Jews to massacre all the inhabitants of Hazor, to practice the bloody and barbarous rite of circumcision, and to worry about such absurdities as cloven hooves and cud-chewing; though in order to be saved the Jews had to see beyond the "letter" of the Law to the "allegory," that is to say to the intimations of Christ, which alone could give life.[62] Again in the New Testament, Christ intended most of His precepts to be literally obeyed; even though He no doubt expected "those for whom the Gospel is not veiled" to go beyond the "plain narrative" to the more perfect Gospel of the Spirit, the Everlasting Gospel hidden beneath the Gospel of the Senses.[63] In the case of Matthew 19:12, however, Origen sharply distinguishes between the "letter" and the actual intent of the words (*voluntas verborum*) or the will of Christ (*voluntas Christi*). Christ did not intend His disciples to commit self-mutilation. The New Dispensation remains part of the "Book of the Wars of Jahweh." But the sword Christ wanted His disciples to use is not the sword of war or of self-mutilation, but "the sword of the spirit, which is the Word of God," that same "word of God, which is quick and powerful and faster than any two-edged sword."[64] Christ's actual intent must therefore be distinguished from the "letter." What Origen here calls "literal" interpretation is actually a misconstruction of the text; what he calls "tropology" merely a metaphor.

As will be seen, the same is essentially the case with the three

60. Above, nn. 46, 53, and (for the phrase "spiritual eunuchs"), 58.
61. Above, n. 47.
62. Above at nn. 14 and 19.
63. Above, nn. 25, 38, and 23.
64. Above, n. 53.

"difficult" *logia* that accompany Matthew 19:12. The rude saying about saluting no one, the offensive saying about plucking out one's eye, and the first moment of the sword pericope are essentially metaphorical.[65] "Literalism" here as in the case of the three types of eunuchs does not merely mean that one ignores or does not understand the spiritual meaning that shines through the literal sense, but rather that because of excess of literalism one actually misconstrues the literal intent. In all four cases the result will be self-mutilation, killing, maiming, or at least being rude to others; such a misconstruction, moreover, will bring shame to these "scribes of the Gospel" and hold up to ridicule the very words of Christ.[66]

Before looking more specifically at Origen's interpretation of the three sayings that have not yet been discussed—and therefore before returning to the text of Luke—it will be well to look a little more closely at this fusion or confusion between allegory (or tropology) and metaphor. Only thus will it be possible to understand the complexity and subtlety of Origen's exegesis. Origen's handling of the metaphors and figures of speech of the Bible, and of the New Testament in particular, is rather remarkable and indeed, for moderns, perhaps, distinctly odd. His exegesis of such figures of speech begins with the obvious consideration that metaphors and the like should by definition not be subjected to a "literal" interpretation: for at the level of "the letter" they seem to involve inaccuracies of language. The next point is the one that may seem a little strange: for Origen insists that in the case of Holy Writ these "inaccuracies" are directly inspired by the Holy Ghost. Thus, the command to forgive one's brother "until seventy-seven times" in Matthew 18:22 cannot possibly be taken to mean that one must forgive that number of times and no more. Such harshness would be unworthy of the Lord. The choice of this particular figure by Christ and the Holy Spirit must mean, therefore, that a "deeper significance" is hidden in that number: in this case a tropology or allegory of forgiveness by both man (seven) and God (seventy).[67] This does not mean, however, that Origen was

65. Below at nn. 92 to 105; see also at nn. 75 to 82. Hanson, *Allegory and Event*, 246 f., has pointed out this curious treatment of metaphors on Origen's part, but his interpretation is quite different from mine. See below at n. 87.

66. Above, nn. 46, 49, 50; below at nn. 92–105.

67. *Com. Mat.* 14.5, 281–84. The passage is too long to cite. Note, however, the following (ibid., 282): "Proximi in se peccata non solum septem dimittere oportere sed etiam septuaginta septem, post septuaginta autem septem iam neque fratri

perversely unaware of what the Lord's figure of speech was plainly intended to convey. To be sure, as de Lubac has rightly stressed, Origen's interest in the "subtler" or "deeper" interpretation may easily mislead the modern reader. On occasion, he finds the "simpler" meaning so boringly obvious that he will allude to it only implicitly or in haste.[68] This is true, for instance, of his discussion of this particular saying. Yet it seems plain that he recognizes the literal meaning of the metaphor: it is precisely because he assumes that the Lord cannot have intended Christians to stop forgiving at any particular number that he is led into his numerological investigation. Here, Origen recognizes three levels: the "letter" of the text—forgive your brethren seventy-seven times; the meaning of the metaphor—forgive your brethren any number of times; and the allegorical (or tropological) meaning suggested by the "inaccurate" figure of speech—the forgiveness of sin by both God and man.

Elsewhere Origen will assert in one context that a figurative or metaphorical saying has "no" literal meaning, only to make it clear in another that he really intended no such thing. This is true, for instance, of his interpretation of two of the *logia* in the famous list of "impossible" sayings in *De Principiis* 4.3.3. Like the list of the Commentary on Matthew, this is a list of four, and includes the saying about saluting no man, as well as the one about plucking out one's eye; instead of the riddle about the three kinds of eunuchs and the first moment of the sword pericope, it lists Matthew 5:39, "whosoever shall smite thee on thy right cheek, turn to him the other also," and Matthew 10:10, where the Lord forbids the disciples to possess two tunics.[69] On the surface, all four sayings seem treated on a par. In *De Principiis* 4.2, Origen had formulated his general theory that "there are certain passages of scripture, which have no literal meaning at all" and had been "woven in" by the Holy Ghost as deliberate "stumbling-blocks and obstacles" so that the hearer might be brought "to a higher and loftier road."[70] *De Principiis* 4.3.3 proceeds with actual examples and specific

---

dimittere, satis mihi videtur contemptibile et indignum . . . ." (The text which Origen used seems to have read "seventy-seven"—*hebdomēkonta kai hepta,* a misreading for *hebdomēkontakis hepta,* or "seventy times seven.") Hanson, *Allegory and Event,* 24, interprets this exegesis of Origen's as an instance of the fact that Origen totally denies the literal meaning.

68. De Lubac, *Histoire et Esprit,* 30 ff. and 113 ff.

69. *De Principiis* 4.3.3, 327 f.; Butterworth, 292 f.

70. Ibid., 4.2.5, 314 f. and 4.2.9, 321 ff.; Butterworth, 277 f. and 285.

instances of such precepts in the Gospels. All four of the sayings there listed are treated in great haste. The command "salute no man by the way" is simply condemned as "irrational" or "absurd." The saying about the right cheek is called "most incredible, for every striker unless he suffers from some abnormality (i.e., left-handedness) strikes the left cheek" and not the right. The saying about the two tunics (this is attested only in the Latin version) is called "impossible," because it cannot be observed "in countries where the bitterness of winter is accentuated by icy frosts." The command about plucking out one's eye is called "impossible" or not "logical," for "how can the blame be attributed to the right eye, when there are two eyes that see?," while the Latin version adds that thus "to lay hands upon oneself would be a most serious crime."[71] If one confines oneself to the sketchy treatment in *De Principiis,* one is left with the impression that all four sayings are equally examples of passages in the Gospel "that have no literal meaning at all."[72]

Elsewhere, however, Origen makes it perfectly clear that two of the four sayings have what moderns would call a "literal meaning"; and that once more in fact if not in vocabulary he is making not only the double distinction between "letter" and "spirit," but a triple distinction between "letter" (misconstrued meaning out of exaggerated literalism), "metaphorical meaning" (actual intent of the words), and "allegory" or "tropology" (over and above that intent). The "quaintness" of Origen's apparent refusal to recognize the literal (that is to say metaphorical) meaning of the saying about turning the other cheek has raised many eyebrows.[73] Yet in a little-known *catena*-fragment he demonstrates his full acceptance of that meaning. The Lord's saying, he argues there, was not *only* meant to curb anger and impatience; it was *also* meant to indicate that the Christian when attacked in his faith should offer to his opponent not just the "right cheek" of his "right" beliefs but also "the other cheek" of his way of life.[74] The "left-handed" exegesis in *De Principiis* must thus be seen in perspective as far less perverse than it first appears. The saying "whosoever shall smite thee on thy right cheek, turn to him the other also" means

71. Ibid., 4.3.3, 327 f.; Butterworth, 292 f.
72. Above at n. 70.
73. Hanson, *Allegory and Event,* 240; even de Lubac, *Histoire et Esprit,* 115 f.
74. *Frag. Mat.* 108, 60. The passage is ignored by Hanson, *Allegory and Event,* 240.

that Christ wanted his disciples to be peace-loving, "curb their anger and impatience," and practice nonresistance. Beyond this plain meaning, obvious even to "simpler folk," the pneumatic, because of his very respect for the words uttered by Truth, will note that in a right-handed world the figure of speech used by Christ is technically inaccurate; for him the letter of the metaphor is a guide to a subtler tropology as well as to the plainer meaning.

The same is essentially the case for Matthew 10:10, where the Lord forbids the use of two tunics. Here too to say that the saying has "no literal meaning at all" because it cannot be applied to those unfortunate countries where the temperature drops below freezing in winter is simply Origen's way of pointing out that, where Truth itself is speaking, such "inaccurate" figures of speech are clues for a subtler meaning over and above the obvious one. Despite the bald statement in *De Principiis,* Origen offers in fact a double exegesis: though in this case that double exegesis takes two slightly different forms, one in the Homilies on Luke, another in the Homilies on Leviticus. In the Homilies on Luke, Origen equates the saying about the two tunics with the one about not serving God and Mammon. Christ did not want his disciples to wear two tunics, because once they have taken on the New Man they must shed and no longer wear the clothing of the Old.[75] In the words of Luke 3:11, Origen pursues, "he that hath two coats, let him impart to him that hath none." By this saying (which is directed to the disciples rather than to the common people),[76] the Lord wished to indicate that those who have truly put on Christ have a special responsibility to pass on that "tunic" to those who are still "naked," that is to say to those who are still covered by the garment of their flesh.[77] Nevertheless, Origen

75. *Hom. Luc.* 23, 142: "Vult enim nos Salvator, quomodo non debemus, 'duobus dominis servire,' sic nec duas habere tunicas nec duplici veste circumdari, ne sit unum indumentum veteris hominis et alterum novi. E contrario autem cupit ut 'exspoliemus nos veterem hominem et induamus novum.' Hucusque facilis expositio est."

76. Ibid., 141 f.: " 'Qui habet duas tunicas, det ei, qui non habet . . .' [Luke 3:11], quod quidem nescio si turbae conveniat praecipi. Magis enim apostolis quam vulgo congruit, ut qui duas tunicas habet unam tribuat non habenti. Et ut scias magis hoc apostolis convenire quam populis, audi quid a Salvatore dicatur ad eos: 'neque duas tunicas tollatis in via' [Matthew 10:10]. Duplex itaque vestimentum quo unusquisque vestitur et praecipitur, ut alterum tribuat 'non habenti,' aliam intellegentiam sonat. Vult enim . . . [as preceding note] . . . facilis expositio est."

77. Ibid., 142 f.: ". . . [as above, n. 75] . . . Porro quaeritur, quomodo iuxta hanc interpretationem iubeatur nobis 'non habenti' tribuere vestimentum. Quisnam est ille,

emphasizes, this is not to say that by that precept Christ did not wish to teach *by a sort of hyperbole* the importance of generosity and mercy to the poor; but "the passage should *also* receive a deeper meaning."[78]

At a literal level, Origen thus equates Matthew 10:10 and Luke 3:11: Christians should give to the poor whatever is superfluous and not necessary for survival. And as far as his own person is concerned, Origen himself (if one believes Eusebius) "thought it particularly important to observe the gospel precepts according to which one should not possess two tunics"; in *Contra Celsum*, moreover, he states that while passages of this sort "can be taken in a deeper sense, they may also be understood more plainly to mean that one's soul should not encumber itself with cares about food and clothing."[79] Yet the pneumatic should note that in His sayings about the two tunics, the Lord is using what is technically known as hyperbole. In Egypt (and perhaps in most regions where Christianity had spread) literal obedience to commands of this sort was possible and indeed commendable, at least for pneumatics or ascetics; but in those "countries, where the bitterness of winter is accentuated by icy frosts" it could not possibly be observed. The hyperbole is therefore a signal for the presence of a deeper meaning.

In the Homilies on Leviticus, Origen's double exegesis has a slightly differing shape. Here he begins by opposing Matthew 10:10 to the precept of Leviticus 8:7 according to which the liturgical vestments of the priests of the Old Dispensation were to include both an inner and an outer tunic. The opinion (apparently held by others) according to which the Lord in Matthew 10:10 wished to "perfect" the Law by restricting the liturgical vestments of the priests of the New Dispensation to a single garment is, Origen admits, quite a "probable" one.[80]

---

qui ne unum quidem super carnem suam indumentum habet, qui nudus est, qui omnino nulla veste coopertus? Neque vero hoc dico . . . [below, next note] . . . qui omnino non habeat. Quis est ergo iste, qui tunicam non habet? Nempe ille, qui penitus Deum non habet. Debemus igitur exuere nos et ei dare, qui nudus est . . . ."

78. Ibid.: "Neque vero hoc dico, quo non praecipiatur liberalitas et in pauperes misericordia et hyperbolica clementia [Gr.: *kath' hyperbolēn*], ut etiam nudos altera tunica protegamus. Sed hoc aio, quod et profundiorem locus iste recipiat intellectum et oporteat nos dare ei tunicam qui omnino non habeat." For this and the remainder of the paragraph, cf. de Lubac, *Histoire et Esprit*, 198.

79. Eusebius, *Historia Ecclesiastica* 6.3.10 (*GCS* 9.2), 528 f.; *Contra Celsum* 7.24, 4, 70 f.; *GCS* 3, 176; Chadwick, 414; de Lubac, *Histoire et Esprit*, 198.

80. *Hom. Lev.* 6.3, 363 f.: ". . . 'Tunica' inquit 'et praecinxit eum zona et iterum

Personally, however, Origen prefers not to limit his interpretation to the narrow confines of such a liturgical interpretation. In a larger sense, the two tunics of the Old Dispensation must be taken to symbolize that priests of the Old Law practiced both carnal and spiritual sacrifices; the priests of the New Dispensation, however, have shed the "outer tunic," that of the carnal ministry, and kept only the "inner tunic" of the Spirit.[81] Here, the "literal" exegesis, which Origen rather grudgingly grants to be a "probable one," is liturgical; while the "spiritual" interpretation gives an explanation for the liturgical symbolism that is itself based on the relation between "letter" and "spirit."[82]

If one wishes, the double exegesis in the Homilies on Leviticus can be made to interlock with that in the Homilies on Luke. One thus arrives for Matthew 10:10 at four related meanings arranged in a progressive series from the simplest to the subtlest. At the lowest level, the hyperbolic figure about the two tunics is merely meant to convey the importance of generosity and of not encumbering oneself with cares about externals. At a somewhat higher level, Matthew 10:10 becomes a liturgical precept. The poverty and simplicity of the Christian life, its deliberate shedding of all externals, has become symbolized in a "perfecting" by Christ of the liturgical vestments of the priests of the Old Dispensation. From that point of view, this second level is both literal and allegorical: literal, because Christ (if one follows this particular interpretation) really did command the new priesthood to wear a single liturgical vestment; allegorical,

---

vestivit eum tunicam talarem,' vel ut alibi legimus 'interiorem' [cf. Leviticus 8:7]. Duabus, ut video, tunicis per Moysen induitur pontifex. Sed, quid facimus, quod Iesus sacerdotes suos, Apostolos nostros, prohibuit uti duabus tunicis? . . . Posset fortasse dicere aliquis quia, quod praecepit Iesus duas tunicas non habendas, non est contrarium legi, sed perfectius lege, sicut et cum lex homicidium vetat, Iesus autem etiam iracundiam resecat. . . . Sic ergo videbitur et duabus ibi tunicis pontificem, hic una Apostolos induisse. Sit quidem etiam iste sensus probabilis, si videtur . . . ."

81. Ibid., 363 f.: ". . . [as in preceding note] . . . sensus probabilis, si videtur; ego tamen non intra huius intelligentiae angustiam pontificalia sacramenta concludo. Amplius mihi aliquid ex ista forma videtur ostendi: pontifex est qui . . . legem et secundum spiritum et secundum litteram novit. Sciebat ergo pontifex ille, quem tunc ordinabat Moyses, quia esset circumcisio spiritalis, servabat tamen et circumcisionem carnis. . . . Habebat ergo iste duas tunicas: unam ministerii carnalis et aliam intelligentiae spiritalis. Sciebat quia et sacrificia spiritalia offeri debent Deo, offerebat tamen nihilominus et carnalia. . . . Apostoli vero . . . ut huiusmodi secundum litteram legis observantias penitus repudiarent . . . merito duas tunicas habere prohibentur, sed sufficit iis una, et haec 'interior' . . . ."

82. Hanson, *Allegory and Event*, 241 f., criticizes the "allegorism" of this interpretation; yet it seems to me that for Origen this liturgical meaning is primarily "literal"—this is why he is not satisfied with it. But see below, next paragraph.

because the liturgy expresses a higher symbolism. The third level, on the contrary, is purely allegorical: the still "carnal" emphasis of the liturgy is forgotten and the precept forbidding the use of two tunics seen directly as an allegory of the dialectic between "letter" and "spirit" and between the Old and the New Dispensation. At that level, therefore, the two tunics of Matthew have become the exact equivalent of the sword pericope; for, as will be recalled, that pericope allegorically expresses the transmutation of the corporeal "sword" of Phineas into "the sword of the spirit, which is the word of God." Finally, the saying about the two tunics can be seen from a tropological perspective: for the allegory of "letter" and "spirit" must be allowed to enter the soul of the Christian. At that level the command not to wear two tunics means that once the Christian has "put on the New Man" he must resolutely shed the wearing of the Old. To the extent that he has become pure spirit, he must discard his garments of flesh.

This highest and most "spiritual" level is here exactly the same as the lowest and most "literal": for the Christian to "put on the New Man" means that in his actual life he will no longer encumber himself with cares about externals, and will shed the superfluities of his former life. From the outside, the life of the Christian is seen as mere "letter," the sign of a higher "spiritual" reality; but from the inside the Christian life is itself the reality of the spirit. The linear and hierarchical structure of Origen's exegesis thus suddenly ends in a circle. This feat becomes possible because the underlying structure is itself circular: in Christian thought letter is to spirit as the Old is to the New Dispensation, as the Old Man is to the New, as superfluities and externals are to the inner life, as letter is to spirit, and so on *ad infinitum.* This sort of circular structure, composed of a series of dialectical opposites, each of which corresponds at one and the same time to each of the others, is the structure that underlies much of the exegetical history of the sword pericope.[83] It may be argued that these two complex and interlocking structures go beyond the letter of Origen's exegesis, whether in the Homilies on Leviticus or in the Homilies on Luke; but one cannot, I think, legitimately claim that they betray its spirit. In any event, Origen acknowledges the existence of a literal meaning in the proper sense of the term, in the case of

83. See below, chapter 3, at nn. 6–17.

the two tunics, as in that of the right cheek, or in that of the seventy-seven times one must forgive one's brother. That these sayings, "have no literal meaning at all," is merely supposed to convey that they are metaphorical and, in addition, that the metaphor points to a higher meaning over and above the obvious, or plainer meaning which Origen does not, however, intend to deny.

Before going back to the two swords, it is well to have a brief look at Origen's treatment of one last category of *logia* with "no literal meaning at all": those that contain not simply figures of speech but what might be called figures of theological thought. Here Origen's exegesis is not particularly startling and can be dealt with very rapidly. The most prevalent of these theological metaphors are those that attribute human passions to God, particularly objectionable passions such as anger or vengeance. While such "figures" are particularly abundant in the Old Testament, they exist also in the New: for instance, John 9:39, "for judgment I am come into the world, that they which see not might see and they which see might be made blind," a saying which suggests that God deliberately blinds to spiritual truth and is thus capable of cruelty. In such cases, Origen's treatment is essentially twofold. On the one hand, the presence of such "allegories" in the New Testament provides him with the stock argument against Gnostics and Marcionites: if they themselves must "rush to take refuge in tropologies" in their exegeses of the Gospels, why do they not accept that method when it is applied to the Old Testament?[84] On the other, it helps him to argue (again against dualists of various stripes) that the God of the Gospel is the same as the God of the Law: He is the God of Love, but insofar as He still destroys

84. *Hom. Luc.* 16, 97: "Est autem . . . intelligendum adversus eos . . . qui contra conditorem latrant et hinc inde de veteri testamento, quae non intellegunt testimonia congregantes 'simplicium corda decipiunt.' . . . 'Ego' inquit [Deus] 'occidam et ego vivificabo . . .' [Deut. 32:39]. Audiunt 'occidam' et non audiunt 'vivificabo.' . . . Istiusmodi occasionibus Creatorem calumniantur. Igitur . . . opponam eis testimonium evangelii dicamque adversus haereticos—innumerabiles quippe haereses sunt, quae evangelium secundum Lucam recipiunt—. . . . Quid respondebunt? Utrumne recedent a cultu eius an quaerent aliquam interpretationem et ad tropologias confugient . . .? Et quomodo iustum erit, quando quid in evangelio tale reperitur, ad allegorias et novas intellegentias confugere, quando vero in veteri instrumento, statim accusare et nullam explanationem, quamvis probabilis sit, recipere . . .?" The argument is directed against the Marcionites, who accept only the Gospel of Luke; see Adolf von Harnack, *Marcion: Das Evangelium vom Fremden Gott*, *TU* 45 (Leipzig, 1921), 38 and Beilage IV, 221* f.

and punishes the "old man," He is still the God of Wrath.[85] The many parables of the Kingdom in which Christ compares God to a jealous father or a strict husband are also usually treated in this fashion.[86] The danger of the "letter" here is an exaggerated anthropomorphism; "the spiritual man" will realize that what is involved are "allegories," that is to say in this case analogies that for a theological purpose speak of God in human terms.

Two conclusions emerge from this catalogue. On the one hand, the whole wide range of *logia* discussed in the last pages belongs, for Origen, to the category of sayings that "have no literal meaning at all." What they have in common is that in each case the Holy Ghost has woven into the text of the Gospels a "letter" that is in some sense "impossible." In every case, moreover, the "letter" consists of some sort of hyperbole, metaphor, analogy, or other figure of speech. Even in profane usage, moreover, metaphors and figures of speech are significant, for they exemplify the necessarily dialectical relationship between letter and spirit: since in their case the letter is "impossible" by definition, it both does and does not convey the spirit or inner meaning which it is intended to express. In Holy Writ, however, the spirit conveyed by the letter is necessarily a facet of the Spirit: any discrepancy between the two is therefore worthy of particular notice. Indeed, these discrepancies are signposts, which the Logos, as Divine Pedagogue, has put into the text of Scripture in order to educate the faithful: so that they might learn the better to understand the relationship between letter and spirit, and through that relationship, that between flesh and spirit, the human and the divine, this world and the next. This process of education—or Divine *Paideia*—is, moreover, progressive. In the Old Dispensation, the dialectic between "letter" and "spirit" is carried, so to speak, by the facts themselves: the bloody atrocities of the history of the Jewish People and the scandalous barbarity of its Law. In the

85. Ibid., 97 f.: "Ego vero, qui opto esse ecclesiasticus et non ab haeresiarchae aliquo, sed a Christi vocabulo nuncupari et habere nomen . . . aequalem et in veteri et in nova lege quaero rationem. Loquitur Deus 'ego interficiam'; libenter habeo ut interficiat Deus. Quando enim vetus in me homo est . . . cupio ut occidat in me Deus veterem hominem. . . ."

86. See, for instance, *Com. Mat.* 17.18, 636. For the whole of this paragraph and for Origen's treatment of similar sayings, see Daniélou, "L'Unité des Deux Testaments," 29.

Gospels, on the other hand, the dialectic must needs be expressed by language alone: the parables, the enigmas and the metaphors deliberately uttered by the Lord. For Origen, to be sure, the unity of the process is more important than its stages: under both Dispensations the Divine Pedagogue wishes to point up the discrepancies between "letter" and "spirit." Origen does not therefore so much confuse the allegory of the Old Testament with the metaphor of the New as deliberately fuse the two procedures. From the point of view, moreover, of this Divine *Paideia,* the various types of metaphorical sayings are legitimately considered as one: in each case there is enough of a discrepancy between letter and spirit for Origen to say that "they have no literal meaning at all."[87]

On the other hand, it is equally clear that on closer investigation these metaphorical sayings may be said to fall into two classes of which the second may in turn be divided into two subcategories. The three sayings about the other cheek, the two tunics, and the seventy-seven times one must forgive one's brother form one small but distinctive grouping. In the case of these *logia,* the metaphorical meaning is not in fact fused with the allegorical or tropological meaning. In Origen's terminology, both senses are simply degrees of the tropological level: the one simpler or plainer, the other subtler or deeper. Because of the double content of their "spirit," their "letter" may be said to "kill" in a twofold manner. At a lower level, there is the danger of misconstruing "the intention of the words" through exaggerated literalism: for instance, a Christian may refuse to forgive his brother the seventy-eighth time around, hit back if hit on the left instead of the right cheek, or commit suicide by freezing to death in the forests of Germany. This is a danger these sayings share with the other categories of metaphorical sayings. At a higher level, there is however also the danger of a "literalism" of a different kind. To be sure, the lower level of the tropological meaning (i.e., the metaphorical)

87. For the importance of the concept of the Logos as Divine Pedagogue and for that of Divine *Paideia* in the thought of Origen, see the brief but cogent remarks by Werner Jaeger, *Early Christianity and Greek Paideia* (Cambridge, Mass., 1965), 66 f. and 135 f., and the whole first half of Hal Koch, *Pronoia und Paideusis.* Koch, however, exaggerates the lack of importance of the Incarnation for Origen and does not see the progressive nature of the Divine Paideia (Jaeger in this tends to follow Koch). For Origen's treatment of metaphors, see the quite different interpretation by Hanson, *Allegory and Event,* 246 f.

is sufficient for the salvation of simpler folk. To practice asceticism, nonviolence, and forgiveness is in itself an imitation of the historical Jesus: no higher spirituality is absolutely required. But if "the scribes of the Gospel" practice these virtues mechanically and, as it were, ritualistically, without a genuine quickening of the spirit, they will fall once more under the curse of the letter. This is a danger this group of sayings shares with Christ's nonmetaphorical sayings.[88]

All the other *logia* discussed in the last few pages belong to a second grouping of metaphorical sayings: in them there is only one meaning, which is both metaphorical and allegorical at one and the same time. This much larger category can in turn be subdivided. One subdivision is represented by such sayings as "for judgment I am come into the world, that they which see might be made blind," and more broadly by such parables as that of the strict husbandman. Here the metaphor-allegory deals directly with God or with Christ. The danger is that because the letter must needs use human analogies, the simpler folk may misconstrue the intent of the words and thus fall into the temptation of thinking of the divine mysteries in too anthropomorphous a fashion.[89] The second subdivision consists essentially of the list of four sayings in the Commentary on Matthew: the riddle about the three types of eunuchs, the *logia* about casting out one's eye and saluting no one on the way, and the first moment of the sword pericope. Here it is tropology and metaphor which are fused into one: and the metaphor-tropology has to do not with the relationship between God and Christ but with the life of the Christian. Misconstruction here will not lead to anthropomorphous thinking but to rash and scandalous behavior in the name of Christ.[90]

This analytical scheme is no more than a helpful tool for the understanding of Origen. Nowhere explicitly is it found in his works; it should therefore be used with some flexibility. Thus, the eucharistic saying of John 6:53 is perhaps best thought of as both nonmetaphorical and metaphorical; and insofar as it is metaphorical, as fitting into all three of the categories or subdivisions that have just been outlined. When discussed at the beginning of this section it was presented as essentially a nonmetaphorical saying: Origen admits that a literal interpretation

88. See above at nn. 67, 70, 72, 75–77.
89. See above at nn. 84–86.
90. See above at nn. 46–53, 65 and 66, and below at nn. 98–101.

of the words of institution is sufficient for the salvation of simpler folk. From that point of view the eucharistic sayings are like ordinary, nonmetaphorical *logia:* their letter kills only if it is used to deaden the spirit. On the other hand, the discussion of Origen's treatment of metaphors has made apparent that from Origen's point of view these eucharistic sayings may also be classified as metaphorical: for sacraments by definition are symbolic. In his discussion of John 6:53 it seems that Origen is not simply worried by the danger of ritualistic mechanism. There is also a hint that he fears actual misconstruction of the *voluntas verborum:* that he is worried by the scandal of a sort of eucharistic cannibalism. Eucharistic sayings (and perhaps all sacramental *logia*) are peculiar in that they fit in all the possible categories and subdivisions of metaphors. First, they deal with both Christian behavior and the nature of Christ: sacramental mechanism and a "cannibalism" not too different from self-mutilation and castration are here linked with a too exclusively anthropomorphic conception of Christ. Second, the meaning of such sayings is both twofold and univocal. Their meaning is twofold insofar as Origen does distinguish a lower metaphorical (in this case sacramental) meaning from the higher (in this case both allegorical and tropological) meaning: what Christians partake in is not only the Flesh of Christ but also the Word of God. Yet insofar as it is the function of sacraments (and particularly of this sacrament) to unite these two levels, the two meanings must be seen as ultimately one. When metaphor becomes sacrament it is hard to distinguish from spiritual reality.[91]

Only now that the crucial role played by metaphor and its relationship to allegory and tropology in Origen's exegesis of the New Testament has been clarified is it possible meaningfully to return to the first moment of the sword pericope. Unlike the similar list in *De Principiis,* the list in the Commentary on Matthew is apparently homogeneous: all four of its *logia* should be considered as belonging to the class of metaphorical sayings in which the metaphorical and tropological meanings are fused into one. In the case of Luke 10:4, the saying about saluting no man, this cannot be proven with absolute certainty. Origen here limits his exegesis to the brief remarks that have been paraphrased above, and does not seem to have alluded to the *logion* elsewhere in his works. All one can say, therefore, is that for Origen the literal execution of this precept would be

91. See above at nn. 6–8, 11–13, 15–17, and 27–33.

absurd: for it would make it appear that Christ had taught men to be savage and barbaric. What is then the meaning of the saying? Origen nowhere seems to say. He clearly states, however, that the problem stems from "disregarding the actual intent of Jesus": as in the associated sayings, what is involved is the misconstruction of a metaphor.[92] The case of the riddle of the three types of eunuchs has already been discussed at length: here too what is involved is the misconstruing of a metaphor, a metaphor which in this case is about the ascetic life required of the Christian, or at least the pneumatic, and which is therefore tropological.[93] The same is true basically of the third saying in the list, namely, Matthew 5:29: "if thy right eye offend thee, pluck it out." Here Origen says remarkably little either in the context of the list in the Commentary on Matthew or in that of the list in *De Principiis:* one is only told that he who would attempt to carry out the precept in a literal fashion would be insane (or even guilty of "a most serious crime") for what Christ meant are not eyes or hands "according to the flesh."[94] Elsewhere, however, in the Commentary on Matthew, Origen gives a whole series of allegorical and tropological interpretations. At the ecclesiological (and therefore allegorical) level, the "eye" may be interpreted as the priests or bishops of the Church, the "hand" as deacons and other ministers, the "foot" as the simple faithful: if any of these cause scandal they must be "plucked out" or "cut off" from the Church.[95] "Plucking out" or "cutting off" thus becomes an allegory for excommunication, or anathema. At a somewhat more internalized or tropological level, the "eye," "hand," and "foot" may be interpreted as referring to one's parents or spouse and to other members of one's household: if contact with them becomes a cause of sin, they too must be cast off by the Christian.[96] Finally, at a still more internalized level, the hand may be taken to stand for the actual act of (the foot for the ingress into, and the eye for the contemplation or intentionality of)

92. See above at n. 49.

93. Above at nn. 46–47 and 51–52.

94. Above at nn. 50 and 71.

95. *Com. Mat.* 13.24, 244 ff. The passage is much too long to cite in its entirety, but see, for instance, ibid., 246 f.: "Sacerdotes autem rationabiliter possunt dici ecclesiae oculus, quoniam et speculatores habentur; diaconi autem ceterique ministri manus, quoniam per eos opera spiritalia universa geruntur; populum autem esse pedes ecclesiae: quibus omnibus parcere non oportet si scandalum ecclesiae fuerint facti." (Note that this particular passage does not exist in the Greek version.)

96. Ibid., 13.25, 247 f. Here too the passage is too long for citation.

sin: all these "members" of the complex of sin must be cast out or cut off by the good Christian. For, as Origen notes, in biblical rhetoric, "the members often designate the work of these members."[97] Here too what Origen is worried about is clearly the misconstruction of metaphors and rhetorical rules. Here too, moreover, metaphor is fused with allegory or tropology; though in this case Origen's exegesis is again architectonic and carefully proceeds from the more external allegory of excommunication to the more inward tropology of the struggle against sin.

Origen obviously means to interpret the fourth of the sayings in the list of the Commentary on Matthew, the first moment of the sword pericope, in the same fashion. "He who sells his corporeal and perceptible garment," Origen insists, and in its stead "buys himself the sword of homicide" has only "paid attention to the letter, without understanding the intention of the words."[98] Here too what is involved is the misconstruction of a metaphor. And here too the danger is behavioral, indeed almost physical: presumably it is no accident that three of the four sayings in the list involve swords, or at least the act of cutting, while the fourth involves "savage and barbaric" behavior.[99] In all four cases, Origen is worried about aggressiveness in the name of Christ, whether against others or against the self. He is worried about misconstruction of "the sword of the spirit" of Ephesians and "the word of God, sharper than any two-edged sword" of Hebrews. In the specific case of the first moment of the sword pericope, he may be worried about Christian soldiers in the Roman armies (such as those attacked by Tertullian) who might use Luke 22:36 as an excuse for killing in wartime.[100] More likely, he is troubled by the possibility

97. Ibid., 248: "Potest autem et sic intellegi, ut actus animae peccans *manus* intellegatur, et incessus animae peccans *pes* et visus animae peccans *oculus:* quos oportet praecidere si scandalum faciunt. Frequenter enim ipsa opera membrorum pro membris in scriptura ponuntur, quale est illud: 'et tuli manus meas ad mandata tua' [Psalm 118:48], non ipsas manus sed opera manuum . . . ." (The last sentence, again, is not in the Greek version.)

98. Above, n. 48.

99. Above at nn. 46, 49, and 50.

100. Tertullian, *De Idolatria* 19.1 (*CC* 2.1120): "At nunc de isto quaeritur, an fidelis ad militiam converti possit, et an militia ad fidem admitti etiam caligata vel inferior quaequae, cui non sit necessitas immolationum vel capitalium judiciorum. Non convenit sacramento divino et humano, signo Christi et signo diaboli, castris lucis et castris tenebrarum: non potest una anima duobus deberi, deo et Caesari. Et virgam portavit Aaron . . . [as above, chapter 1, n. 86] . . . exarmando discinxit. Nullus habitus licitus est apud nos illicito actui adscriptus." See Rordorf, "Beurteilung" (cited

that Christian Zealots might offer armed resistance in the face of persecution, as will be the case here and there within a few decades of Origen's death; Jewish Zealots at the time of the Jewish War and the rebellion of Bar Kochba may well have used the curse of Jeremiah 48:10 against the radical pacifism of their Christian compatriots.[101] The persistence of the dialectic between "letter" and "spirit" even within the New Dispensation means that there is always a danger of relapsing into Jewish literalism. The fact that the "Book of the Wars of Jahweh" operates under two radically distinct Dispensations may be forgotten; the sword of the spirit may once more be confused with the sword of Phineas.

This is why in his exegesis Origen directly connects Luke 22:36 with the rebuke of Peter in Matthew 26:52. "Those who have taken up a sword of this kind," namely, a corporeal and perceptible sword, "have acted wrongfully and against the will of Christ": they have misconstrued the metaphor. They "will therefore surely perish," Origen insists; perhaps they will (in the words of Matthew 26:52) "even 'perish by the sword.'" The exegesis of the riddle of the three types of eunuchs is not, however, Origen remarks, the proper context "for commenting at length on what 'sword' the Lord had actually in mind."[102] Nevertheless, Origen's meaning is reasonably clear. An overly literal interpretation of the first moment of the sword pericope will have the same results as the misconstruction of the three other sayings in the list of the Commentary on Matthew. To castrate oneself, practice self-mutilation, or indeed simply refuse to salute anyone on the way will only result in subjecting oneself to shame and obloquy, "make men hate the very words of Jesus," and "in the end perhaps" bring about a "fruitless death" having "incurred the hatred of all."[103] Similarly, "those who take up the sword will surely perish, perhaps even perish by means of the sword."[104] In the words of Psalm 7:16 (which

above, chapter 1, n. 86), 107, and 107 n. 4; however one does translate *at nunc* it is clear that in this passage Tertullian is attacking "laxists" who would allow at least certain types of Christians to engage in certain forms of military activity (a position which, with certain restrictions, Tertullian himself accepts in *De Corona* 11.1-4 [*CC* 2], 1056 f.). See below, n. 151, and chapter 4, n. 6, for a more general bibliography on Early Christian pacifism.

101. See above, chapter 1 at nn. 71 and 72.

102. Above at n. 48: "De quo autem gladio dicat, non est loci huius exponere."

103. Above at nn. 46, 49, and 50.

104. Above, n. 48: "Si quis . . . 'emerit gladium' homicidialem, quasi 'accipiens' gladium talem . . . 'peribit,' forsitan et 'in gladio peribit.' "

Origen cites in his commentary on the last moments of the sword pericope): "he who has dug a pit, shall himself fall into that hole."[105] Those who take up the sword may die in battle. As in the case of "carnal" eunuchs or of those who mutilate themselves, moreover, their death is quite useless: for it will damn them and not achieve salvation. As will be seen, however, Origen's commentary on these latter moments makes it clear he does not believe that "all those who take up the sword of homicide" necessarily die by the sword of homicide. Here too the danger is that of an exaggerated literalism. The sword by which they will die may be the sword of eternal punishment; it may be the sword of sin itself.[106]

One thing alone remains unexplained: Origen emphasizes that the tunic which must be sold so that a sword may be bought must not be interpreted as a "corporeal and perceptible garment"; but he nowhere seems to have gone into the hidden symbolism of that tunic. From his exegesis of the pericope as a whole, however, in his interpretation of the Phineas episode and elsewhere, it is clear that the sword which must be bought is "the sword of the Spirit, which is the word of God," that is to say the sword of the New Dispensation. Surely the tunic which must be sold is therefore the tunic of the Old Dispensation. In one passage the passover or conversion from the Old to the New Dispensation was symbolized by the exchange of the sword of Phineas for the sword of the Spirit; in another by the shedding of the outer tunic, the garment of flesh of the Old Man, and the putting on of the inner tunic of the New;[107] here, it is symbolized by the selling of the tunic and the acquisition of the sword. The contents of the metaphor, the contents

105. See below at n. 133.

106. See below at nn. 133 and 134. The problem is only adumbrated by Origen. It is carried a little further by Hilary of Poitiers, *Commentarius in Matthaeum* 32.2, *PL* 9, 1071: "nam plures aut febris aut alius accedens casus absumit qui gladio aut judicii officio aut resistendi latronibus necessitate sint usi"; still further by Saint Jerome, *Commentariorum in Mattheum Libri* IV (26.52), *CC* 77, 258: "Etsi non frustra portat gladium qui ultor Dominicae irae positus est in eum qui malum operatur attamen quicumque gladium sumpserit gladio peribit: quo gladio? illo nempe qui igneus vertitur ante paradisum et gladio spiritus qui in Dei describitur armatura." It is finally fully exploited in the ninth century by Paschasius Radbertus, *Expositio in Matthaeum* 12.26, *PL* 120.916–19, who clearly suggests that one may be transpierced not only by the sword by which disobedience is avenged and by means of which one is cut off from the Body of Christ, but also by the sword of the spirit, which is the Word of God and striketh so as to give life. (I hope to exploit some of this material in a forthcoming work on the medieval doctrine of the two swords of Luke.)

107. Above, chapter 1 at nn. 80–84; and above, this chapter at nn. 75, 77, and 81.

of the "letter," are thus actually an allegory of the dialectical contrast between the Two Dispensations, of the dialectical contrast between "letter" and "spirit." As Origen stresses in the Homilies on Leviticus, the first moment of the sword pericope is a "letter that killeth," yet "there is within that letter a 'spirit that giveth life.'"[108] And the "spirit" of that "letter" is in fact simply that: "the letter killeth but the spirit giveth life."

The same point is made by Origen in his Homilies on Numbers in the interpretation of the Phineas episode; in his exegesis of the food legislation of Leviticus; and in the Commentary on Matthew in the context of the riddle of the three types of eunuchs. It is made perhaps most succinctly in an incomplete *catena*-fragment on Matthew 26:52 in which Origen may well be referring not only to the last moment of the sword pericope but also to its first two moments. Commenting on the verse that "all they that take the sword shall perish with the sword," Origen explains that "there are perceptible swords and then there is an intelligible sword [*eisin aisthētai kai esti noētē machaira*]; some, on the one hand, perish by means of the two [*kai hoi men dia tōn duo apolluntai*] . . . ." Here the fragment unfortunately breaks off.[109]

What are these "two"? There seem to be only two possibilities. Origen may simply be referring to the distinction between perceptible and intelligible swords which he has just adumbrated. The completed fragment would then presumably have been something as follows: of those who take up the perceptible sword, some perish by means of both the perceptible and the intelligible sword (that is, they will first be killed by means of the perceptible and then be subjected to eternal punishment by means of the intelligible sword), but others will perish only by means of the latter and will not necessarily be executed or die in battle. As far as one can tell from the incomplete fragment, such a reconstitution would, however, assume a somewhat faulty grammar. Origen distinguishes not simply between *an* intelligible and *a* perceptible sword, but between an intelligible sword in the singular (*noētē*) and perceptible swords in the plural (*aisthētai*). To make that plural and that singular into the common antecedent of "the two" is, to say the least, a rather odd construction.

108. Above, n. 10.

109. *Frag. Mat.* 536, 219. The editors do not indicate that the fragment is grammatically incomplete. But surely the *hoi men* calls for completion by a *hoi de*?

A second interpretation may therefore be preferred. Perhaps "the two" with which the fragment breaks off should be taken to refer not to the distinction between perceptible and intelligible swords but instead to the two swords of Luke. In that case the fragment would have continued more or less as follows: of those who take up the perceptible sword, some perish by means of the two swords, others by means of the one. For Origen, it should be stressed, the number "two" is normally a symbol of the carnal or merely perceptible; the number "one" in true Platonic fashion, of the divine, the spiritual or the intelligible. If this reconstitution is allowed, Origen's point becomes both more interesting and more complex than under the first hypothesis. What he would be claiming is that it was no accident that the Lord asked the disciples to buy themselves *a* sword in the singular, while they responded in the plural and came up with two. Christ wanted His disciples to acquire the *one* sword, the single intelligible sword of spiritual warfare;[110] but as so often before the Resurrection, the disciples misunderstood the Lord. They did not yet (as Origen will emphasize in the full-scale commentary on the last moments of the sword pericope) fully understand the gospel patience handed unto them by Christ but were still acting in accordance with the Law.[111] They therefore brought forth not the *one* sword of the spirit, but *two* perceptible swords. Of those who take up these two swords of Luke, some no doubt will perish by means of such swords: they will die in battle or by the sword of the executioner. Their death, however, will avail them nothing; it will be a fruitless death, for they will not have merited the crown of the martyr. Others who have taken up the two perceptible swords of Luke will not die in this fashion: they too will be subject to eternal death by means of the one sword, but by means of the sword of the spirit. The greater attractiveness of the second interpretation does not mean, of course, that it is the one Origen had

110. *Commentariorum Series* 66, 155: " 'duo' enim videtur carnalis numerus esse." On the symbolism of "one" and "two" in Origen's writings, see Harnack, "Kirchengeschichtliche Ertrag," *TU* 4 (1919) 110. It may seem curious that the first part of the fragment does not speak of *mia noētē machaira* (*one* intelligible sword) but simply opposes *an* intelligible sword (*noētē machaira*) to perceptible swords (*aisthētai* [*machairai*]). But the Lord's instruction in Luke 22:36 is simply *agorasatō machairan* "buy *a* sword"—not "buy *one* sword." Numbers only occur with the disciples' answer in Luke 22:38, "*Kurie, idou machairai hōde duo*" ("Lo, Lord, here are *two* swords!"). The assumption would then be that *mia* would have occurred in parallel construction to *duo*, that is, in the missing part of the fragment.

111. Below, n. 118.

in mind. I think it is fair to say, however, that any patristic or early medieval exegete who was familiar with the fragment (or its echo) could easily have read it in this light.

There are thus numerous references to the first and one probable allusion to the second moment of the sword pericope. The third moment, the Lord's "it is enough," does not seem to be discussed anywhere in Origen's extant works. But if the interpretation of the second moment that has just been given is indeed Origen's, the third moment does not need an exegesis: *hikanon estin*, "that's enough," the Lord said, in simple impatience at the disciples' misunderstanding. And, this is indeed the interpretation favored in the fifth century by Origen's fellow townsman, the great Cyril of Alexandria.[112] Scattered references to the latter moments of the sword pericope have already been alluded to here and there. For a fuller understanding of Origen's exegesis of this essentially Matthean material it will, however, be necessary to look at three main passages: a rather brief one in Book Two of *Contra Celsum;* a rather lengthy commentary on Matthew 26:51 ff. in the *Commentariorum Series;* and another short *catena*-fragment.

The passage in *Contra Celsum* is the simplest of all; yet it is rather typical of the surprisingly literal way in which Origen deals with some of the last moments of the sword pericope. As is well known, *Contra Celsum* is not an exegetical but an apologetic work. The whole of Book Two (as indeed much of Book One) attempts to refute an argument which Celsus in his now lost *True Word* had put in the mouth of a Jew. This fictional opponent of Christianity had apparently begun his polemic with a number of Talmudic stories about Jesus' illegitimate birth and the like. He then proceeded, in rather Hellenistic fashion, to accuse the followers of Christ of having abandoned the customs of their forefathers, the Jews. This argument Origen refutes by pointing out that those Christians who had come to the faith from Judaism (such as the Ebionites) were still in fact following these customs.[113] Celsus' Jew then

112. Cyril of Alexandria, *Explanatio in Lucae Evangelium* 22.38, *PG* 72.917 f. Two swords should be plenty against the Jewish War that is approaching! The Lord's "it is enough" is thus said while "gently laughing" (*mononouchi diagelā*[*i*]). See the eleventh-century exegete Theophylactus of Ochrida, *Enarratio in Evangelium Lucae, PG* 123, 1079 f., who states that the Lord's "it is enough" is said *kat' eirōneian* (in the ironical mode).

113. *Contra Celsum* 1.28–2.79, 1, 150–447; *GCS* 2, 120–379; Chadwick, 27–128. (For the fourfold method I have used in citing *Contra Celsum*, see the second note to

continued his speech with a general indictment of the powerlessness of Christ: "how could we [Jews]," he says, "regard him as God, when he did not implement anything which he had professed to achieve, for when we had convicted him he was caught hiding and indeed was betrayed by those whom he called his disciples?"[114] To disprove this charge, Origen emphasizes that "if he was caught" it was not against his will. This is clear from John 18:4 ff., where it is said that "knowing therefore all that was coming upon him, [Christ] went out and said, 'Whom do you seek?' " This is equally clear from the latter moments of the sword pericope: "to the man who wanted to come to his aid and struck the servant of the high priest and cut off his ear," Jesus said, "put up your sword into its place, for all they that take the sword shall perish with the sword; or do you think that I cannot now beseech my Father and He will send me here more than twelve legions of angels? But how then should the scriptures be fulfilled that thus it must be?"[115] Thus, Origen concludes, Christ went to His death willingly, as had been the case even of the Greek Socrates; for Christ "had been made 'the Lamb of God' so that He might 'bear away the sins of the world.' "[116]

In *Contra Celsum* Origen's exegesis is thus both literal and limited. It simply brings out the apologetic intent that is already plainly implicit in the Lord's own *logion* in the fifth moment of the sword pericope. Christ went to His death willingly, for He could easily have asked His Father to intervene on His behalf. Considering "the twelve legions of angels" on whom the Lord could count, Peter's use of the corporeal sword was simply silly and implied a lack of faith in Christ's divine powers. Celsus' Jew makes, in fact, the same mistake as the Apostles: they do not understand a Son of God Who willingly goes unto His death; and yet had this not been the case even of a mere man, Celsus' fellow Greek, the Athenian Socrates? The Son of God had to die, for how else "should the scriptures be fulfilled,"

the Abbreviations, above, p. xiv; for some of the reasons for giving pride of place to the *SC* rather than to the *GCS* edition, see above, chapter 1, n. 3. For the Ebionites see *Contra Celsum* 2.1, 1, 266 f.; *GCS* 2, 126 f.; Chadwick, 66; also *Contra Celsum* 5.61, 3, 166; *GCS* 3, 65; Chadwick, 311 f.)

114. *Contra Celsum* 2.9, 1, 300; *GCS* 2, 135; Chadwick, 73. In the text, for this passage as well as in the few that follow, I have felt free to use the excellent translation by Chadwick.

115. Ibid., 2.10, 1, 308; *GCS* 2, 137 f.; Chadwick, 75.

116. Ibid. and *Contra Celsum*, 2.17, 1, 330; *GCS* 2, 146; Chadwick, 83.

how else could the Lamb of God bear away the sins of the world? Origen here avoids his more usual allegorical method and is on the whole content with letting the Lord speak in His own words. In addition, he concentrates strictly on the fourth and fifth, and makes no allusion to the other, moments of the sword pericope. But despite its simplicity, the apologetic argument is worthy of notice. Indeed the assumption that Christ and His disciples could have resisted but did not choose to do so, that they had the power but not the will to make use of the material sword, will in the Middle Ages become an essential part of the classical argument of the two swords of Luke.[117]

In the *Commentariorum Series,* on the other hand, Origen's exegesis of Matthew 26:51 ff. is positively lavish. Allegory, though playing a much smaller role than in his interpretation of the first moments of the pericope, is by no means excluded from the discussion; and there are definite cross-references to these first moments as well as to the meaning of the pericope as a whole. Most of these elements are already apparent in Origen's treatment of Matthew 26:51, the fourth moment of the pericope, Peter's abscission of the ear of Malchus. For Origen, that act demonstrates that the Prince of the Apostles was still entangled in the meshes of the Old Testament. He cut off the ear of Malchus

> nondum manifeste concipiens apud se evangelicam patientiam illam traditam sibi a Christo nec pacem quam dedit discipulis suis, sed secundum potestatem datam Iudaeis per legem de inimicis, 'extendens manum' accepit gladium et percussit 'servum principis sacerdotum' et 'amputavit auriculam eius.'[118]

117. Ambrosiaster argues that the disciples were allowed to strike by the Lord and then stopped midway "*ut et* vindicare se *posse* viderentur sed *nolle et ut* virtus ostenderetur in eo [i.e., in Christo] manere in quo fuerat, *ut in utroque* vindicare se *posse* non ambigerentur" [emphasis mine]. (*Quaestio 104.4 de Evangelio Lucae,* in *Quaestiones Veteris et Novi Testamenti, CSEL* 50, 229.) Ambrose has the same opposition between *posse* and *velle:* "Cur emere jubes qui ferire me prohibes? nisi forte ut sit parata defensio non ultio necessaria: ut videar *potuisse* vindicare sed *noluisse*" [emphasis mine]. (*Expositio Evangelii Secundum Lucam* 10.53, *CC* 14, 361.) Bede then applies this distinction to the two swords of Luke: "Duo gladii sufficiunt ad testimonium sponte passi Salvatoris. Unus qui . . . apostolis audaciam pro Domino certandi . . . inesse doceret; alter qui nequaquam vagina exemptus ostenderet eos nec totum quod potuere pro ejus defensione facere permissos." (*Commentarium in Lucam* VI, 22.38, *CC* 120, 384.) This tradition underlies, I believe, the famous distinction between *nutus* and *manus* made by Saint Bernard in *De Consideratione* 4.3.7, *Sancti Bernardi Opera,* ed. J. Leclerq and H. M. Rochais, Editiones Cistercienses (Rome 1957–74) vol. 3, 454.

118. *Commentariorum Series* 101, 220 f.: " 'Et ecce unus ex his qui erant cum Iesu extendens manum exemit gladium suum et percutiens servum principis sacerdotum

Peter did not yet clearly entertain within himself the gospel patience handed unto him by Christ, nor the peace which the Lord had left to His disciples. Instead, he still acted in accordance with the power of defense against enemies given unto the Jews by the Law. Therefore, he stretched forth his hand, took up the sword, smote the servant of the High Priest, and cut off his ear.

Up to this point, Origen's treatment of the fourth moment has remained literal, though the connection with his allegorical interpretation of the first moments of the pericope is obvious. Basically, he simply provides a psychological and historical explanation for Peter's act, an explanation that will be endlessly repeated in the future. The disciples did not free themselves fully from their carnal, overly literal, and, in short, Jewish understanding of the message of Jesus until after the Resurrection. Until then they were not yet perfected, and in many ways the equivalent of the Christian literalists, "the scribes of the Gospel" of Origen's own day.[119] Because of the still-powerful attraction of the Old Dispensation, they did not yet fully grasp the gospel patience, the long-suffering and nonresistance, which was such an essential part of the teaching of Jesus. Indeed, this is why in the first moments of the sword pericope they had misconstrued Christ's reference to the sword of the spirit, and instead of the one intelligible sword had presented him with two corporeal or perceptible weapons.[120] What they did not as yet understand was that with the passover from the Old to the New Dispensation, the corporeal sword (which might have edified God's former people) had been taken away and replaced with the sword of the spirit.[121] But then it was only with the Resurrection that that Passover would be fully accomplished.

Having given a literal interpretation that is itself anchored in the allegory of the passing from letter to spirit, Origen then proceeds with a more specifically allegorical exegesis. Despite the lack of understanding shown by the Prince of the Apostles, Peter's deed, Origen suggests in an exegesis that was to become famous, may nevertheless have been a "sacramental" act full of

---

amputavit auriculam eius.' 'Unus' autem eorum 'qui erant cum Iesu' nondum manifeste concipiens . . . [as in text] . . . et 'amputavit auriculam eius.' "

119. See, for instance, *Contra Celsum* 2.2, 1, 290; *GCS* 2, 128; Chadwick, 67 f.: because the Apostles were Jews it was difficult for them to overcome the literalism of types and shadows. It was only after the Apostles had received the Spirit at Pentecost that they became fully capable of understanding the Truth.

120. See above, n. 48, and at nn. 109 and 110.

121. See above, chapter 1, pp. 34–39.

hidden allegorical meaning: for it is surely not without a purpose that the Gospel of John should point out that it was the right ear of Malchus that was cut off.[122] It may indeed be argued that

Iudaici populi dextra auditio fuerat amputanda propter malitiam eorum demonstratam in Iesum. Nam etsi videntur audire legem, modo cum sinistro auditu audiunt umbram traditionis de lege non veritatem.[123]

It was the "right" understanding, the understanding of the right ear, which was cut off from the Jewish People, because of the wickedness which they had shown towards Jesus. From now on, even though they might appear to be hearing the Law, they would, in fact, be hearing only with the sinister hearing, the hearing of the left ear; for the Law to which they would listen would be the shadow of tradition, not the Truth.

Like Malchus, who was a slave of the High Priest, Origen pursues his exegesis, the Jews have become "the slave of words"; they claim to be servants of God, but in truth they do not serve Him. Indeed, this is the mysterious sacramental meaning behind the words of the pericope: this is why Malchus is said to be the slave of Caiaphas, the enemy of the True High Priest, Who is none other than Jesus.[124] (As Origen asserts in

122. *Commentariorum Series* 101, 221: ". . . [as above, n. 118] . . . 'amputavit auriculam eius.' Sicut autem dicit Iohannes [John 18:10,' *** [LACUNA]*** et dextram auriculam amputavit' apud quem [i.e., Johannem] et nomen servi dicitur, quia 'Malchus' vocabatur. Et forsitan quod agebat Petrus mysterium erat, quoniam Iudaici populi . . . [as below, next note] . . . non veritatem . . . [see below, n. 124] . . . ." As Klostermann (the editor of this volume of the *GCS*) points out, the lacuna here is simply the missing first half of John 18:10. Note that Origen, though pointing out that the name Malchus is found only in John, unlike his successors does not comment on the meaning of that name. But see below, n. 124.

123. Ibid.

124. Ibid.: ". . . [as above in text at n. 123] . . . non veritatem, cum sint servi sermonis profitentis servitium dei, non autem servientis in veritate. Huius sermonis mysterium erat adversus Christum ***[LACUNA]*** adversarius Christi princeps sacerdotum Caiphas." As Klostermann notes, the lacuna should probably include some form of *militare;* he points to the parallelism with *Commentariorum Series* 105 (see below, next note). Like the Latin exegetes, such as Hilary and Jerome, who depend here on Origen, the original Greek text probably played on the relationship between Malchus' status as a slave and Jewish slavery to the letter, as I have suggested in my paraphrase in the text. For Hilary, see *Commentarius in Matthaeum* 32.2, *PL* 9.1071: "Igitur ab apostolo servo principis sacerdotum auricula desecatur: populo videlicet sacerdotio servienti per Christi discipulum inoboediens auditus exciditur et ad capacitatem veritatis hoc quod erat inaudiens amputatur." For Jerome, *Commentariorum in Mattheum Libri* IV (26.51), *CC* 77.257: "Servus quoque principis sacerdotum Malchus appellatur; auricula quae amputata dextra est. Transitorie dicendum quod Malchus, id est rex, quondam populus Iudaeorum, servus factus sit impietatis et devorationis sacer-

another context, types and shadows always resist the Advent of Truth.)[125] As is clear from the Epistle to the Romans, Origen continues, the reason that this "ear of right understanding" was taken away from the Jews is precisely so that all those who came to Christ from the Gentiles might constitute one people. In the words of the prophecy of Isaiah 6:10: "Blind the hearts of this people and make their ears heavy: lest they see with their eyes and hear with their ears and understand with their hearts and be converted and I heal them!"[126]

Origen, to be sure, tends to falsify the message of Saint Paul and the Epistle to the Romans. For Paul, some of the Jews have been blinded for a time so that the fullness of the Gentiles might come in; but Christians form one people precisely because they have been foregathered from both Jews and Gentiles. The very Jewish Apostle to the Gentiles boasted of being a "Hebrew of the Hebrews" and a "Pharisee, the son of a Pharisee." Origen is self-consciously a Gentile Christian, who is ashamed of a Torah so obviously inferior to the laws of the Athenians, the Lacedemonians, and the Romans.[127] He condemns both groups of Jewish Christians (heretics and orthodox alike): both are called Ebionites or "Poor Men" because of the

---

dotum, dextramque perdiderit auriculam ut totam litterae vilitatem audiat in sinistra, sed Dominus in his qui ex Iudaeis credere voluerunt reddidit aurem dextram et fecit servum genus regale et sacerdotale." Augustine, *In Iohannis Evangelium Tractatus* 112.5, *CC* 36.635, gives the same etymology of Malchus as Jerome ("Malchus autem interpretatur 'regnaturus' "), but for him there is no historical reference to Jews but simply to those who before baptism were "slaves to the letter," but after conversion will become kings through the spirit of grace. Bede, *In Lucae Evangelio Expositio, CC* 120.388 f. (and most of the subsequent tradition will follow), gives both Jerome's and Augustine's interpretation of the name "Malchus." Origen, on the other hand, seems not to have dealt with the etymology of Malchus but to have emphasized instead the status of Caiaphas as Priest of Shadows (see below, next note) because of that same Jewish slavery to the letter.

125. Ibid., 105, 225 [ad Matt. 26:57]: ". . . Caiphas est, qui adversus veritatem militat Iesu qui dicitur princeps sacerdotum. Iesus autem secundum veritatem sacerdos est. . . . Ubi autem Caiphas est princeps sacerdotum, illic congregantur 'scribae' id est litterati qui praesunt litterae occidenti . . . qui non in veritatem sed in vetustatem litterae simplicis sunt recumbentes . . . ." On this opposition between the Priest of Shadows and the Priest of Truth and on the resistance offered by obsolete "types and shadows" to the "Advent of Truth," see above, chapter 1 at nn. 21 and 22.

126. *Commentariorum Series* 101, 221: ". . . [as above, n. 124] . . . sacerdotum Caiphas. Videtur autem mihi, quoniam qui ex gentibus crediderunt omnes, unus populus constituti in Christo, per hoc ipsum quod crediderunt in Christum facti sunt causa, ut praecideretur Iudaeorum auditio dextra, secundum quod fuerat prophetatum de eis: 'grava aures populi huius et oculos eorum deprime, ut ne videntes videant et audientes intellegant et convertantur et sanem eos' [Isaiah 6:10]." The whole passage is obviously inspired from Paul's discussion in Romans 9–11.

127. Above at n. 14.

poverty of their faith in Christ.[128] He tends to identify "we who have been called from the Gentiles" with "the Christian people," the "Faithful People of God," and to contrast this Gentile Church, the true Church of God, with the Jewish followers of Christ.[129] Is this perhaps why Origen—at least here in the obvious context—simply ignores Christ's miraculous restoration of the ear of Malchus? That miracle, it is true, is found only in Luke and not in the Matthean material, which Origen is presumably discussing. But so is the fact that it was Malchus' right ear that had been amputated by Peter. That too does not occur in Matthew; yet Origen in his allegorical exegesis has done a particularly splendid job with that little detail. Later commentators will come to the rescue and draw the obvious eschatological conclusion: the miracle is an anagogy that prefigures the ultimate reconciliation of the Jews, when in the words of Saint Paul "all Israel shall be saved."[130] In his Com-

128. *Com. Mat.* 16.12, 512 f. See above, n. 113, and Chadwick, 66, n. 3. The already complex problem of the Ebionites has been unnecessarily complicated by a problem of nomenclature: while Origen and others distinguish between two groups of Ebionites, the first believing in the divinity of Christ, and the second not (both of which, however, rejecting the epistles of Paul, and both of which subject to criticism for their preference for the letter), other Fathers reserve the term Ebionites for the fully heretical group, and call by the name "Nazarenes" the one that is more or less orthodox. Modern authors add to the confusion by also differing in their nomenclature; see Daniélou, *The Theology of Jewish Christianity* (London, 1964), 54–64.

129. *Hom. Num.* 16.9, 151; see above, n. 17: ". . . etiam *nos, qui ex gentibus vocati sumus,* necessario iubeamur 'abstinere nos' sicut 'ab his quae idolis immolantur' ita et 'a sanguine'. . . . *Qui ex Iudaeis Dominum sequebantur* scandalizati sunt et dixerunt: quis potest 'manducare carnes et sanguinem bibere'? *Sed populus Christianus, populus fidelis,* audit haec et amplectitur . . . ." The contrast between *ii qui ex Iudaeis Dominum sequebantur* (on one level, of course, simply the Jewish crowd that followed Christ, but at another surely Jewish Christians) and *nos qui ex gentibus vocati sumus* seems clear enough; it is the second group alone that is identified with *populus Christianus* and *populus fidelis.*

130. The idea will be fully expressed by Rupert of Deutz, *Commentaria in Evangelium Sancti Johannis* 13 (18.10), *CCCM* 9.717: "Quod vero eandem auriculam tactu Dominus apud Lucam sanasse legitur, illud significat, quia quandoque futurum est, ut iterum populo illi dexter et verus Scripturae auditus aperiatur, scilicet cum plenitudo gentium introierit, tunc enim reliquiae Israel salvabuntur." If one can trust the edition of Migne, see also more or less contemporarily with Rupert, *Glossa Ordinaria ad Johannem* 18.11, *PL* 114.418: "Postquam plenitudo [i.e., gentium] subintraverit, dicit Petro per quem totus ordo praedicatorum designatur 'Mitte verbum praedicationis ad Israel.' " Jerome, *Commentariorum in Mattheum Libri* IV (26.51), *CC* 77.257, had prepared the way by interpreting the restoration of Malchus' ear as the conversion of those *qui ex Iudaeis credere voluerunt.* Bede, *In Lucae Evangelio Expositio, CC* 120.388 f., and Paschasius Radbertus, *Expositio in Mattheum, PL* 120.917, follow Jerome. See also on the restitution of the ear and the conversion of Israel, Ambrose, *Expositio Evangelii secundum Lucam* 10.66, *CC* 14.365: ". . . docuit quod aurem habere in specie non deberent [i.e., Iudaei] quam in mysterio non haberent. Sed bonus dominus et ipsi refundit auditum secundum prophetica dicta demonstrans et ipsos si convertantur posse sanari. . . ."

mentary on Romans, Origen has a perfectly Pauline and indeed rather touching exegesis of these very words. Here, however, in the *Commentariorum Series*, the eschatological salvation of the Jews does not enter into the picture; and when Origen, as a sort of afterthought, finally alludes to the healing of Malchus' ear at the end of his commentary on the pericope as a whole, his treatment will be pedestrian and at a strictly literal level.[131]

This pedestrian note is already apparent in Origen's treatment of the Lord's rebuke of Peter. Though the exegesis of this fifth moment does not exactly show Origen at his most exciting, it will be of enormous influence on the later history of the sword pericope. Christ, Origen begins rather platitudinously, did not say "draw" or "unsheath thy sword"; on the contrary, what the Lord said was: "put up again thy sword into his place."[132]

Est ergo gladii aliquis locus, ex quo non licet accipere eum qui non vult perire, maxime in gladio. Pacificos enim vult esse Iesus discipulos suos ut bellicum hunc 'gladium' deponentes, alterum pacificum accipiant 'gladium,' quem dicit scriptura 'gladium spiritus.' Simile autem mihi videtur quod dicit 'omnes qui accipiunt gladium, gladio et peribunt,' id est, omnes qui non sunt pacifici sed belli concitatores, in eo bello peribunt quod concitant, ut sit in eis gladius mysterium belli et litis. Et puto quod omnes tumultuosi et concitatores bellorum et conturbantes animas hominum, maxime ecclesiarum, accipiunt gladium in quo et ipsi peribunt; quoniam 'qui fodit foveam, ipse incidet in eam' . . . .[133]

There is therefore a particular "place" from which one may not take up the sword, if one does not wish to perish, particularly by means of the sword. For Jesus wanted His disciples to be peace-loving, so that they would put down the sword of war and take up in its stead another sword, the sword of peace, which Holy Writ calls "the sword of the Spirit." Indeed the first half of Matthew 26:52, "Put up again thy sword into his place," seems to Origen pretty much the equivalent of the *logion*'s second half: "all they that take the sword shall perish with the sword." In other words, all those who are not peace-loving but incite to war will perish in the very war which they

131. *Com. Rom.* 8.12, 1195/1198. Below, n. 146, for Origen's "afterthought."

132. *Commentariorum Series* 102, 221: " 'Tunc ait ei Jesus: Converte gladium tuum in locum suum.' Mox Iesus ad eum, qui fuerat gladio usus et abstulerat 'auriculam' servi illius dextram, non dicit 'exime gladium' sed 'converte gladium in locum suum.' "

133. Ibid., 221 f.: ". . . [above, preceding note] . . . locum suum. Est ergo . . . [as in text] . . . 'ipse incidet in eam' [Psalm 7:16], quoniam 'convertetur dolor' eorum in caput ipsorum et 'iniquitas' eorum 'in cerebrum' eorum 'descendet' [Psalm 7:17]." For the mysterious *locus* see below, p. 90, and at nn. 148–49.

will have incited, so that for such people "the sword" becomes a sacrament of war and of strife. Origen believes, moreover, that all those who create an uproar, incite to war, and stir up the souls of men (though especially those who stir up the churches of Christ) may be said to have "taken the sword with which they shall perish." In the words of Psalm 7:16: "He who has dug a pit, shall himself fall into that hole."

What in other passages was called "the corporeal sword," "the perceptible sword," "the sword of homicide," or simply "*this* kind of sword" is here called "the sword of war." This is the sword which the disciples took up, because they did "not yet understand the gospel patience taught by the Lord," and were still attached to an Old Dispensation that was passing away; whence the rebuke addressed to Peter. Yet this allegorical structure is little more than a memory: it is in no sense deepened or even exploited by this section of the exegesis. In the first sentence one has the feeling that Origen is going to suggest some sort of additional allegory for the mysterious *topos* or *locus,* "the place" from which the sword is not to be taken. But he quickly veers away and is content with pointing out that "put up again thy sword into his place" is more or less the equivalent of "all they that take the sword shall perish by the sword"; and when at the very end of his exegesis of the pericope Origen has occasion to come back to the problem, "the place" from which one must not take the sword has simply been equated with "the sheath of patience." This is no longer genuine tropology but little more than a moralistic platitude. The same pedestrian tendency is at work in the following sentences: and there is in addition a certain lack of focus. Origen's exegesis seems to hover between the literal and the allegorical or tropological. The sword which the disciples are forbidden to use is indeed "the sword of war"; but it functions at the same time as a "sacrament of war" (*mysterium belli*) and even a "sacrament of strife" in the souls of men and more particularly of strife within the churches. In the end of the Lord's *logion* fades into a commonplace: "he who has dug a pit shall fall into that hole"!

What follows is at least more sharply focused. To an extent, he corrects the uncertainties of his exegesis and emphasizes that Matthew 26:52 has at the very least a simple literal meaning, which is binding on every Christian without exception:

sed et simpliciter audientes, quod dicit 'qui accipiunt gladium, gladio peribunt' cavere nos convenit, ut ne occasione militiae aut vindictae propriarum iniuriarum eximamus 'gladium,' aut ob aliquam occasionem, quam omnem abominatur evangelica haec Christi doctrina, praecipiens ut inpleamus, quod scriptum est: 'cum his qui oderunt pacem, eram pacificus.' Si ergo cum odientibus pacem debemus esse pacifici, adversus neminem gladio uti debemus.[134]

But even for those who listen for the plainer meaning, "all they that take the sword shall perish by the sword" has a significance: for one must beware lest by reason of being in the army, or in order to avenge one's own private wrongs, or indeed for any reason whatsoever, one should unsheath the sword. For the gospel teaching of Christ holds all these uses of the sword to be abominations, since it commands Christians to fulfill what is written in Psalm 119:7: "With them that hated peace, I was peaceable." But if Christians must be peaceable even with those who hate peace, they may use the sword against no one whatever.

Nothing could be clearer. Whatever may be its more "spiritual" significance, Matthew 26:52 has first a plain and literal meaning. Christians are absolutely forbidden to make use of the sword under any pretext whatsoever (*ob aliquam occasionem*): for the teaching of Christ considers all such uses to be abominations (*quam omnem abominatur Christi doctrina*). Throughout his works, Origen insists again and again that "even we who are called from the Gentiles are strictly enjoined to abstain from blood." Despite his allegorism, he believes, with the remainder of the pre-Constantinian Church, that the decree of the Apostolic Council is literally binding. For Origen, as for all his contemporaries, to shed blood is for Christians "a sacrilege and an abomination." This prohibition, moreover, includes both killings undertaken "by reason of self-defense" (*occasio vindictae propriarum iniuriarum*) and killings undertaken "by reason of being in the army" (*occasio militiae*). Like Tertullian in *De Corona* and Hippolytus in *Traditio Apostolica*, Origen obviously believes that Matthew 26:52 forbids Christians to kill even when they are soldiers and are ordered to do so by their commanding officer.[135]

134. *Commentariorum Series* 102, 222: ". . . [above, preceding note] . . . eorum 'descendet.' Sed et simpliciter audientes . . . [as in text] . . . gladio uti debemus."

135. For Tertullian, see *De Idolatria* 19.1–3 (*CC* 2), 1120, cited above, n. 100, and chapter 1, n. 86, as well as the more moderate position in *De Corona* 11.1–4 (*CC* 2), 1056 f., and the article by Rordorf, cited in these notes. For Hippolytus of Rome, see the Latin translation of the Greek original of the *Traditio Apostolica* as reconstructed by Dom Bernard Botte from the extant Coptic, Arabic, and Ethiopian versions (the Latin version of this particular passage being unfortunately lost), as well as from the

A brief *catena*-fragment on Matthew 26:52 seems on superficial reading to contradict this exegesis. "All they that take the sword shall perish with the sword"; but "from this *logion*," Origen asserts in the fragment, "one must except those who lead the soldiers' life."[136] This brief remark clarifies but in no way modifies the longer exegesis in the *Commentariorum Series*. In the longer passage, Origen had asserted that serving in the army (*militare*) is no excuse for "unsheathing" or "brandishing" (*eximere*) the sword in order to kill; in the fragment he points out that the Lord's curse on those who take (*accipere*) the sword must not be misconstrued as extending to those who in peacetime serve in the army and lead the soldier's life. The purpose of the fragment is simply to prevent the sort of rigorist exegesis exemplified in *De Idolatria*: there, it will be recalled, Tertullian had argued in so many words that Matthew 26:52 puts a curse even on the military costume. For Origen, those "surprised by faith" while serving in the ranks need choose between martyrdom and desertion only when faced by a command to kill. To be a soldier is for a Christian a highly dangerous but not an absolutely illicit profession. The anti-literalism of Origen operates therefore on two fronts at once. In the first moment of the sword pericope he faces literalists who would misconstrue the Lord's injunction about buying a sword in order to justify killing in wartime or armed resistance of the Zealot type. In the fifth moment he opposes literalists who would misconstrue the Lord's rebuke of Peter in order to condemn the very profession of the soldier. Origen, to be sure, is no Tertullian and no Hippolytus: he is an exegete and a theologian more than a polemicist and a moralist. In the end, his political morals cannot be separated from his anti-literal exegesis. Nevertheless, his position is, in practice, no different from that of Tertullian in *De Corona* or Hippolytus in *Traditio*

---

parallel versions in the *Apostolic Constitutions*, the *Epitome*, the *Testamentum Domini*, and the *Canons of Hippolytus* (all of which are ultimately derived from the *Traditio Apostolica*). Dom Bernard Botte, *La Tradition Apostolique de Saint Hippolyte. Essai de Reconstitution* (*Liturgiewissenschaftliche Quellen und Forschungen* 39, Münster, 1963), 16, 36: "Miles qui est in potestate non occidet hominem. Si iubetur, non exequetur rem, neque faciet iuramentum. Si autem non vult, reiciatur. Qui habet potestatem gladii, vel magistratus civitatis qui induitur purpura, vel cesset vel reiciatur. Catechumenus vel fidelis qui volunt fieri milites reiciantur, quia contempserunt deum." See below, n. 137, and chapter 4, n. 6, for a more general bibliography on Early Christian pacifism.

136. *Frag. Mat.* 537, 219: "*Hypexaireisthai chrē tou logou toutou tous en strateia[i] zōntas.*"

Apostolica: it is simply the common opinion of the pre-Constantinian Church.[137] There is therefore no contradiction between the fragment and the lengthier exegesis.

The fragment, however, clarifies some puzzling features in that exegesis. Strange as it may seem, Origen treats Matthew 26:52 as a sort of metaphor; and, moreover, as the type of metaphor in which one can not only distinguish the letter from the intended or metaphorical meaning but in which the latter can in turn be distinguished from the allegorical or tropological meaning. A superficial reading of the "letter" would indicate that all those who "take" the sword (including therefore those who have taken on the soldier's belt) fall under the Lord's curse. Yet that is not the "intention of the words": it is not soldiers in general but only those who make use of the sword in order to kill the enemy who come under the curse. Origen nowhere lists Matthew 26:52 among the gospel sayings whose letter is a

137. For Hippolytus, see above, n. 135. For *De Corona* 11.1–4, the key passage is in *De Corona* 11.4, *CC* 2.1057: "Plane si quos militia praeventos fides posterior invenit, alia condicio est, ut illorum, quos Johannes admittebat ad lavacrum, ut centurionum fidelissimorum quem Christus probat et Petrus catechizat, dum tamen suscepta fide atque signata aut deserendum sit, ut a multis actum, aut omnibus modis cavillandum, ne quid adversus deum committatur, quae nec extra militiam permittuntur . . . ." This is, of course, in sharp contrast to Tertullian's more "radical" position in *De Idolatria* 19.1–3, cited above, n. 100, and chapter 1, n. 86. Yet even in *De Idolatria,* Tertullian distinguishes between waging war (*bellare*) and "serving in the army in peacetime" (*militare*). In *De Idolatria,* Tertullian condemns both: but his adversaries who appeal to various articles of military costume, mostly in the Old Testament, and to the bellicose activities of the People of God in order to justify the "waging of war" (*bellare*) are simply dismissed out of hand—they are pleased to play games (*placet ludere*) and not worthy of serious refutation. On the other hand, those who appeal to certain passages of the Gospels (passages which Tertullian himself accepts in *De Corona*) in order to argue that soldiers "of the simple or booted sort" can remain in the army in peacetime, even after baptism, are taken more seriously and refuted by an appeal to Matthew 26:52 (see above, chapter 1, n. 86). The distinction between *bellare* and *militare* was first noted by Henri F. Secrétan, "Le Christianisme et Le Service Militaire," *Revue de Théologie et de Philosophie* 2 (1914) 345–65. For Secrétan, however, who was strongly biased in favor of radical pacifism (the date of his essay is significant), the position of *De Corona* and *Traditio Apostolica* (as well, therefore, as that of Origen, who is not mentioned) is not the common Christian position (for him that is the unique privilege of *De Idolatria*), but only that of "opportunists." Jean-Michel Hornus, *Evangile et Labarum. Etude sur l'attitude du christianisme primitif devant les problèmes de l'état de la guerre et de la violence* (Geneva, 1969), 121 ff. and 128 f., follows in Secrétan's footsteps but far more discreetly. Adolf von Harnack, *Militia Christi. Die Christliche Religion und der Soldatenstand in den ersten drei Jahrhunderten* (Tübingen, 1905), 67 f., is strongly biased in an anti-pacifist direction, and mentions the distinction between *bellare* and *militare* only because he feels that "it clearly demonstrates" Tertullian's "embarrassment" at introducing the quite unheard of doctrine (*bisher Unerhörtes*) of Christian pacifism. Most other writers ignore the distinction; but see Rordorf, "Tertullians Beurteilung," 121, n. 44. See below, chapter 4, n. 6, for a fuller bibliography.

"letter that killeth." Yet he surely believed that Christians owed absolute obedience to the powers that be insofar as that obedience did not force them into conflict with the laws of God.[138] Since he held moreover that to be a soldier was not for Christians an absolutely illicit profession, it follows that those who misuse the letter of the fifth moment to urge Christian soldiers to desert in peacetime are very much like those who urge armed resistance in the first moment. In both cases they will, out of an excess of literal zeal—an "immoderate lust" for the Kingdom of God—have in fact contravened the actual will of Christ. In both cases the death which they will achieve will not be the glorious death of the martyr, but the fruitless "death of the letter." The slight discrepancy between the letter of Matthew 26:52 and its intended or metaphorical meaning serves moreover as a signal for the true pneumatic: beyond the plain intent (which should be obvious even to "those who listen for the plainer meaning") there lurks something "deeper" and more "subtle." The Lord wished to forbid not only warfare and armed resistance but also strife "in the souls of men"; this is the tropological meaning. More specially, he wished to condemn "those who stir up the churches of Christ"; this is the ecclesiological or allegorical meaning. In this case, to be sure, these distinctions are rather mechanical. In fact, the exegesis is unfocused and hovers between the literal and the tropological or allegorical. The mechanistic application of Origenist "spirituality" has all sorts of pitfalls. Mythographic esotericism and overweening complexity are possible dangers. When, as here, "letter" and "spirit" are so close that there is not enough tension for dialectical exegesis, "spirituality," on the contrary, tends to fade into the pedestrian and the commonplace. "He who has dug a pit shall himself fall into that hole": this is the "subtler" meaning of which simpler folk remain unaware![139]

Origen's exegesis of Matthew 26:53 is equally pedestrian, but is at least clearly focused on the literal level. His interpretation, moreover, is essentially the same as in *Contra Celsum*. Christ, Origen asserts, wished to emphasize that He "hath given himself for us all" willingly (Ephesians 5:2). To His rebuke of Peter, He therefore added the following: "or thinkest thou that I cannot now pray my Father and he shall presently give me more than twelve legions of angels" (Matthew 26:53). This is, Origen

138. See below, chapter 4 at nn. 48–56.
139. Above at n. 133.

comments, as if He had said: "you, Peter, only drew your sword and struck the servant of the High Priest, as if in order to offer me your help; but I, if I wished, could ask my Father for a help that is more than human and far better than yours, that is for the help of the angels and not only for the help of one angel but for that of more than twelve legions of angels."[140] Origen then concludes his exegesis of the fifth moment with a long excursus that is of relatively little interest in this context. Christ, he notes, speaks of "legions of angels" by analogy with the legions of soldiers of this world. Nor should the military metaphor cause any surprise: for Luke speaks of "the multitude of the heavenly host," and in Genesis Jacob speaks of "the encampments of the Lord" when he clearly wishes to refer to angels.[141] The fact that Christ speaks of help from legions of angels, Origen continues, does not mean that He is in any way inferior to angels and really needs their help. Perhaps, Origen suggests, even that saying of the Lord's was adapted to Peter's still imperfect understanding: after all, Peter had wished to help the Lord by actually taking up his sword and slicing off the ear of Malchus. In any case, the conclusion is clear: though Christ could have "taken up" not only the sword but many legions of angels, He did not wish to do so, so that through His patience, Scripture might be fulfilled which had prophesied that He would undergo His Passion in this fashion.[142]

140. *Commentariorum Series* 102, 222: ". . . Si ergo cum odientibus pacem debemus esse pacifici, adversus neminem gladio uti debemus [above, n. 134]. Ita volens (ad eum qui non didicerat loquens) docere nos omnes quoniam volens 'tradidit semetipsum pro nobis omnibus' [Ephesians 5:2], addit et dicit: 'aut putas quoniam non possum modo rogare patrem meum, et exhibebit mihi plus duodecim legiones angelorum? [Matthew 26:53].' Tamquam si dicat: 'tu quidem sic gladium exemisti et percussisti principis servum quasi mihi auxilium praestans, ego autem si voluissem poteram rogans patrem non humanum auxilium impetrare sed meliorum, id est 'angelorum' nec unius sed 'plus duodecim legionum.' "

141. Ibid., 222 f.: ". . . [above, preceding note] . . . 'duodecim legionum.' Ex hoc demonstratur quoniam secundum similitudinem legionum militiae mundialis sunt et 'angelorum legiones' militiae caelestis, militantium contra legiones daemonum habitantium in sepulcris. Nam et apud Lucam, 'multitudo militiae caelestis' audita est 'laudantium deum' [Luke 2:13] propter Christi nativitatem. . . . Sed etiam Iacob locum aliquem vocavit 'castra' domini [Genesis 32:2] quoniam militiam illic aspexit angelorum. . . ."

142. Ibid., 223: 'Et adtende: putas quasi inferior angelis salvator aut indigens auxilio angelorum dicebat: 'aut putas quia non possum rogare patrem meum et exhibebit mihi plus duodecim legiones angelorum'?—aut forte secundum aestimationem Petri volentis ei auxilium ferre et gladium proferentis et amputantis auriculam servi talia est locutus? Magis enim angeli opus habent auxilium unigeniti filii dei, quam ipse illorum. Propter hoc et quod scribitur . . . non de filio dei unigenito intelligitur dictum, sed aut in persona Christi de omni viro iusto, quem Christus portabat in corpore suo,

Origen's exegesis here is literal and perfectly straightforward. Only a few points need perhaps be noted. First, Origen apparently felt that some Christians at least might be scandalized by the application of the word "legion" to the angels of the Lord. The anti-militaristic and perhaps anti-Roman feelings in some sections of the community are such that the use of this demonic term needs some explanation. Second, as in *Contra Celsum*, the purpose of the *logion* is seen as primarily apologetic. Christ wished to emphasize that it was willingly that He went unto His death. His arrest and crucifixion are not arguments against His divinity. Third, Matthew 26:53 nevertheless poses certain christological difficulties: if Christ is God, what need does He have for the help of angels? Origen offers his solution with a certain amount of hesitation; but it should be noted that it makes use of the so-called principle of "accommodation." The Logos accommodates His teachings to the spiritual understanding of particular men at a particular time; indeed, this is one reason why the pneumatic must look for a "subtler" meaning even in the very words of Christ.[143] Finally, it is worth stressing how Peter's use of the corporeal sword is equated or at least connected by Origen with Peter's still imperfect and presumably overly "carnal" christology. The Lord whom Peter loved was still the Christ after the flesh. This is why he sought to help Him with the corporeal sword. This is why the Lord, even in His rebuke, sought to adjust His answer to Peter's still imperfect understanding and thus spoke of "help" from legions of angels. It should therefore be clear that the moralistic and pedestrian treatment of the rebuke of Peter does not mean that the christological and allegorical dimension has been in any way forgotten: for by practicing peaceableness and willing nonresistance Christians imitate the willing Passion of their Lord.

Finally, Origen considers Matthew 26:55: "In that same hour said Jesus to the multitudes, 'Are ye come out as against a thief with swords and staves for to take me? I sat daily with you teaching in the temple and ye laid no hold on me.'" This verse

---

aut de Christo secundum humanam eius naturam. . . . Cum ergo posset accipere legiones, nolebat accipere, ut per patientiam eius inplerentur scripturae prophetantes de ipso, quoniam ita eum pati conveniebat."

143. On this principle of accommodation and Origen, see, for instance, Hanson, "Biblical Exegesis in the Early Church," *Cambridge History of the Bible* 1.451, and Wiles, "Origen as Biblical Scholar," 464.

forms a part of the sword pericope really only in Mark and in Luke. John ignores it and Matthew transforms it into a more or less independent, or at least transitional, unit.[144] Origen, however, treats it as still a part of the pericope, presumably under the influence of Mark or of Luke. His exegesis is literal and except for the last few lines is of relatively little interest. The comparison with the thief or robber, Origen begins, is simply meant to indicate that it might be fitting to seize criminals with swords and with staves, since a robber would himself be willing to use such weapons. From both His words and His deeds, however, the Jews must have known that Christ was no robber; they had "daily" associated with Him "in the Temple" and knew how peaceful He was and how much He praised peace. Through both His life and His words, Origen pursues, Christ had attempted to impart to those who would listen what would be of profit to them and would help their salvation; the Jews had no reason to treat Him like a criminal. Nevertheless, Origen concludes, even when He was arrested, Christ did not wish to alter what He had promised. In both words and deeds, He still wished to be of profit to those who were willing:[145]

Et vide postquam dixit ad Petrum: 'Reconde gladium tuum in thecam suam'—quod est patientiae—postquam auriculam restituit amputatam, sicut alter dicit evangelista (quod et summae benignitatis indicium fuerat pariter et divinae virtutis), tunc ista verba locutus est, ut fidelia viderentur ex praecedentibus verbis et factis, ut etsi praeterita benefacta non recordantur, vel praesentia recognoscant.[146]

Therefore, after He had said to Peter "Put up thy sword into the sheath" (John 18:11)—that is to say into the sheath of patience—and after He had replaced the cut-off ear, as is recorded by another evangelist (a sign of both the greatest mildness as

144. *Commentariorum Series* 103, 223 f. See above, Introduction, pp. 4f.

145. Ibid., 223 f.: ". . . si quis 'latronem' vult tenere, non est incongruum 'cum gladiis et fustibus' venire ad eum, quia talis est et latro . . . et . . . paratus est et gladio uti. . . . Ego autem quoniam non sum talis, omnes qui sunt in Iudaea sciunt, alii quidem videntes doctrinam meam et opera mea, alii autem auditum habentes de me . . . quoniam 'cottidie' sedens in loco sancto templi . . . manifestabam quae pertinentia erant ad pietatem et vitam sanam secundum legem dei et per hoc commendabam pacificum me esse. . . . Nunc autem quasi mutatum me aestimatis, ut quasi 'latronem' debere conprehendi putetis? Sed nec in hoc occasionem aliquam invenitis quasi ad verbum mutatum ab eis, quae in primis proposueram, prodesse volentibus verbis et factis."

146. Ibid., 224: ". . . [above, preceding note] . . . verbis et factis. Et vide . . . [as in text] . . . praesentia recognoscant."

well as of godly power), He uttered the words in Matthew 26:55, so that they might appear faithful to what He had previously taught in both words and deeds: for even if the Jews did not remember His previous kindness towards them, they might at least understand what He was offering them now.

Here too the exegesis appears literal and straightforward, at least on the surface. A few points, however, should be stressed, First, the healing of the ear of Malchus is interpreted as both a "sign of the greatest mildness" and as a sign "of godly power." On the one hand, the miracle demonstrates that even at the moment of His arrest, Jesus was filled with divine power. The passivity of His Passion is not therefore an argument against His Divinity. This brief and apologetic remark on the part of Origen will have a remarkable future in exegetical history.[147] On the other, the same act of miraculous healing is also a sign "of the greatest mildness." Here the underlying christological dimension comes close to the surface: the healing of Malchus' ear is both a demonstration of the power of Christ's Divinity and a witness to the peaceableness, the loving kindness, and the lowly humility of His Humanity. Second, the mysterious "place from which one may not"—Origen had insisted in his exegesis of Matthew 26:52—even "take up the sword" is here identified with the "sheath" of John 18:11; and that sheath by what in appearance is a rather pedestrian tropology is then simply reduced to "the sheath of patience." In the context of the christological interpretation given to the healing of Malchus' ear, "the sheath of patience" in which the sword is to remain hidden becomes, however, more than a simple morality: it can be seen as the humble and patient sheath of Christ's Humanity within which the power of His Divinity must remain hidden (yet through which it shines forth) until the Second Coming, when He shall appear again "in power and glory." This at least is the interpretation—which may perhaps be supported by an even more obscure passage in the Homilies on Ezechiel[148]—

147. See Ambrosiaster, *Quaestio 104 de Evangelio Lucae*, *CSEL* 50. 229, see above, n. 117: ". . . [as in n. 117] . . . ambigerentur; inimici vero pro certo haberent datam sibi ab eo potestatem ut haec facerent. Non enim victus apparebat sed tradens se voluntati eorum." Also, Bede, *Commentarium in Lucam*, *CC* 120.384: "Duo gladii sufficiunt . . . [as above, n. 117] . . . audaciam pro Domino certandi et evulsa ictu eius auricula, Domino etiam morituro, pietatem virtutemque doceret inesse medicandi alter . . . [as in n. 117] . . . facere permissos."

148. Origen, *Hom. Ez.* 5.1, 372: ". . . Defert utrumque Salvator 'gladium' et 'ignem' et baptizat te 'gladio' et 'igne.' Eos enim qui non sunt curati baptismo spiritus sancti 'igne' baptizat, quia non potuerunt Spiritus Sancti purificatione purgari." The context

that the subsequent tradition will at least on occasion impart to these few words of Origen's.[149] Third, the literal intent of Origen's exegesis is here simply to contrast the hardness of the Jews with the peaceableness of Jesus. Indeed, this is why Matthew 26:55 is for Origen still part of the sword pericope. All along, the Lord had tried to teach peace to those who would listen: in the Temple through the means of words, in His

---

consists of the four scourges of Ezechiel 14:12–21, famine, wild beasts, sword and pestilence (cf. Revelation 6:8). In practically the whole of Homilies 4 and 5 these four are, of course, spiritualized but still treated as scourges. In Homily 5.1, the sword is first treated in the same fashion, but by juxtaposition with the "fiery sword" and the Cherubim that guard the entrance to Paradise in Genesis 3:24, the scourge of the sword is duplicated: the eschatological sword can both cut and burn (ibid., 371). Origen then, however, is reminded that God's punishments are always medicinal and he cites Matthew 10:34, "I have not come to bring peace but a sword," with its parallel in Luke 12:49 ff.: "I came to cast fire upon the earth," to demonstrate that the Lord sends both fire and sword (ibid., 371 f.). The passage that has just been cited follows, and Origen then returns to the theme that the scourges of God are medicinal and paideutic (ibid., 372, to the end of 5.1). The passage cited seems to identify the sword with ordinary baptism by water, and fire with a still essentially purgative punishment in the afterlife. At the same time, the sword is clearly identified with the Holy Spirit which the Lord in Matthew 10:34 is understood to have promised to send. Yet that Spirit *may*, for Origen, be identified at least in part with the Divinity of Christ: see Origen, *Com. Rom.* 3.8, 948 BD, where the Cherubim that surround the mercy seat in the Ark of the Covenant represent the soul of Jesus and the ark of the covenant His flesh. (See Crouzel, *Théologie de l'Image*, 134, where the passage is discussed.) Normally, of course, Spirit and Word are clearly distinguished by Origen: see, for instance, *De Principiis* 1.3, 5, 54–56 (Butterworth, 33 f.) particularly the fragment preserved in Greek only; also the passage in *Hom. Jos.* 3.2, 303 f., where Origen seems to distinguish three "economies" almost in the sense of Joachim of Fiora (discussed by Daniélou, *Origen*, 124 ff.); and finally, the passage in *Hom. Is.* 1.2, 244 f., where the two Seraphim of Isaiah 6:2 are related to the Trinity and identified, one with the Holy Spirit and the other with "my Lord Jesus." A rather similar connection between Matthew 10:34, Luke 12:49, and a sword appearing in the waters of baptism is made by St. Ephrem the Syrian in *Hymns on the Epiphany* 8.16 (see the discussion by Murray, "The Exhortation to Candidates for Ascetical Vows at Baptism in the Ancient Syriac Church," 64, and *Symbols of Church and Kingdom*, 16). It may be further significant that in the Syriac Church these themes are also often connected with the "fiery sword" of Genesis 3:24; see Murray, "The Lance that Re-opened Paradise," 224–33; see also above, chapter 1, n. 82. For Origen, note also *Com. Mat.* 15.2, 352: "de quo autem gladio non est loci huius exponere" (cited above at n. 48), which suggests that there is a "mystery" of the sword which it is not always the proper time (the Greek text has *kairos* instead of *locus*) to expound.

149. The rebuke of Peter and Christ's refusal to make use of His power (cf. above, n. 117) is given a christological twist by Leo the Great, *Tractatus* LII.4, *CC* 138A, 310. (The paragraph should be read in the context of the whole sermon, ibid., 307–12—note in particular the contrast between *maiestas* and *humilitas*, p. 310, ll. 1–2.) The imagery of the sheath as the flesh of Christ is then developed by Rupert of Deutz, *De Victoria Verbi Dei* 12.17 (ed. R. Haacke, *MGH—Quellen zur Geistesgeschichte des Mittelalters* 5), 391: "Ut quid o tam potens tam fortis divinitas verbi me carnem tuam dereliquisti intus te continens tamquam gladius qui de vagina sua nolit egredi?" The passage occurs only a few lines before Rupert, ibid. 12.19, 391 f., discusses the whole of the sword pericope. Cf. also ibid. 11.27, 367.

life through the example of His deeds. Now Jesus one last time attempts to overcome the hardness of the Jews: in deeds through the restoration of the ear of one of those who had attacked Him, in words by reminding the Jews of His peaceful teachings in the Temple and by rebuking them for coming after Him "with staves and with swords."

Although Origen's exegesis remains literal and fairly pedestrian, the attentive reader is nevertheless reminded of the underlying allegorical structure. The Jews' use of "staves and swords" is in fact an exact parallel to Peter's abscission of the ear of Malchus and his consequent indulgence in armed resistance of the Zealot type. Having rebuked Peter for "not yet clearly entertaining within himself the gospel patience handed unto him" and for still "acting in accordance with the power of defense against enemies given unto the Jews by the Law," the Lord in Matthew 26:55 turns to the Jews and rebukes them for their hardness. Both Peter's use of the sword in defense of the Lord and the Jews' use of "swords and of staves" in attacking Him are each in their own way witnesses of the obsolete and obstinate survival of the Old Dispensation in the face of the advent of Truth. Jesus' own peaceableness and nonresistance, on the other hand, form the foundation stones of the New Dispensation, when "they shall beat their swords into plowshares and their spears into pruninghooks: nation shall not lift sword against nation, neither shall they learn war any more." It is the Jews who are "cruel and thirst for blood," who believe that those who "keep back their sword from blood" are under the curse of Jeremiah 48:10. Christians, however, must shun the bloodthirsty literalism of the Zealots.[150] They are forbidden to use the corporeal sword under any pretext whatsoever: for the teaching of Christ considers all such uses to be a sacrilege and an abomination.[151] On the contrary, Christians must imitate

150. Above, chapter 1 at nn. 71 and 72.

151. For Athenagoras in the second century even attendance at a public execution "no matter how just" was for the Christian *agos kai miasma*, a sacrilege and an abomination, *Libellus pro Christianis* 35, *TU* 4:2, 45; see the discussion by Bernhard Schöpf, *Das Tötungsrecht bei den frühchristlichen Schriftstellern* (*Studien zur Geschichte der katholischen Moraltheologie* 5; Regensburg, 1958), 130 ff. For Minucius Felix, to watch or listen to a homicide even in a theatrical representation is for the Christian a sort of blasphemy: "nobis homicidium nec videre fas nec audire," *Octavius* 30.7, *Loeb Classics* 250, 408. On this whole problem of blood-avoidance and the observance by Christians of the Apostolic Decree, see Ehrhardt, "Der Sonntagsbraten der christlichen Hausfrau," cited above, n. 17. On the relation of blood-avoidance to Christian pacifism, and to Origen's own position, see below, chapter 4 at nn. 5 to 7.

Christ and practice the long-suffering and nonresistance of the Lord's own Passion. The only sword which they may use is "the sword of the spirit."

Origen's exegesis of the sword pericope was destined to live through the ages. To an almost unbelievable extent, later commentators will be influenced by the general exegetical shape which he imprinted on the pericope as a whole—a general structure, which was obviously felt to be highly attractive. Even the details of his exegesis, though sometimes far less felicitous, will condition the subsequent history of the pericope. Insofar as they are successful, these smaller features may simply be copied; or in some cases the congruence between the broader structure and a particular exegetical detail will help later commentators to deepen the meaning or impact of their model, in a way both original and yet according to tradition. Insofar as they are unsuccessful, Origen's exegetical details may, on the contrary, invite later correction; or else they may sharply limit or at least delay the possibilities for further interpretation. For the moment, two tasks remain to be done. First, it will be necessary to develop and generalize the sort of exegetical aesthetics that has been adumbrated in the last few pages. This sort of hermeneutical analysis will be useful precisely because so much of the later history of the pericope is dependent on the shape and structure of Origen's exegesis.[152] Aesthetic criticism is here a necessary part of historical understanding. Aesthetical analysis, moreover, will allow the reader to develop criteria by which exegetical attempts can be judged and therefore understood. Aesthetics will thus insensibly merge into a sort of exegetical philosophy. This aesthetical and indeed at times hermeneutical excursus will be the subject of the next chapter of this study. Second, it will be necessary to place Origen's exegesis of the sword pericope—and indeed his exegetical method as a whole—within the general framework of his theology of politics. This will be the task of the fourth and final chapter.

152. See above, Introduction, pp. 7 and 9f.

CHAPTER III

HERMENEUTICAL INTERLUDE

The aesthetic and philosophical interlude which is the subject of this chapter must begin with a few additional remarks, first on the relative weaknesses and then on the relative strengths of Origen's exegesis. Some of the weaknesses are, no doubt, the result of the rather loose structure of the sword pericope itself, which, as has been seen in the Introduction, is after all a conglomeration of rather disparate material. Thus, even though Origen and the tradition that follows attempt to integrate the first three (and purely Lucan) moments with the remainder, the actual shape of the pericope tends to rebel against this exegetical unity imposed from the outside, and to force the commentator to deal with these first moments in a different way than he does with the latter. Again, the concluding *logia* offer in effect alternate interpretations of the pericope, which it is not all that easy to integrate into a whole. The exegesis of such loosely connected material presents an obvious hermeneutical problem: how does one preserve the autonomy of each section and subsection (an autonomy stressed by the construction of the pericope) and yet deal satisfactorily with the underlying unity? These, so to speak, natural difficulties are, moreover, compounded by the shape and indeed by the very strengths of Origen's own exegetical structure. The pericope is for him essentially an allegory about letter and spirit, an allegory about allegory itself. The general structure of his exegesis depends on the tension between the spiritual or allegorical sword, which the disciples are enjoined to buy in the first, and the corporeal or literal sword, for the use of which they are rebuked in the last moments of the pericope. Like almost any work of art, successful exegesis requires, however, that the whole should be reflected in the parts. At the same time, each moment must remain true to the role which has been assigned to it in the general structure. In this particular case, the two requirements may clash. As a logical structure, Origen's exegetical scheme demands that some moments be interpreted at a purely spiritual, others at a purely literal level; as a symbolic structure, it requires, paradoxically, that each moment should equally express the underlying tension between letter and spirit.

Origen meets with varying degrees of success in attempting to cope with this particular problem. In his treatment of the first four moments the difficulty is more or less successfully evaded. The first moment is, it will be recalled, handled only briefly, and, as it were, *ex parte* in the margin of Origen's discussion of eunuchs or Jewish food restrictions.[1] Essentially it provides Origen with an occasion for presenting his exegesis of the pericope as a whole: obviously there will be no discrepancy between the general structure and the exegesis of the individual moment. In general this will remain true for the subsequent tradition: the problem is solved by using the first moment as an introduction to the whole pericope. The second moment is treated even more briefly in an incomplete *catena*-fragment; but if my interpretation is correct it illustrates how Origen is able to reconcile the requirements of logic with those of symbolism. The general structure assigns to the two swords of Luke a strictly literal meaning: the Lord's command to the disciples to buy themselves a sword is misunderstood by them because of their still Jewish fondness for the letter, and this is why they come up with two swords. The *catena*-fragment suggests, however, that this gemination of swords is interpreted by Origen in Platonic fashion as a reference to the materiality of the number "two" and is opposed by him to the "one" sword of the spirit. While the second moment is thus interpreted at a strictly literal—and indeed material—level, the necessary ten-

1. Above, chapter 2 at nn. 5–13 and at 46–53.

sion between letter and spirit has been nevertheless preserved. The third moment of the pericope would undoubtedly have presented a problem. The general structure would have required Origen to interpret the Lord's "It is enough" at a literal level and it is hard to see how the tension between letter and spirit could have been preserved for that particular moment; but Origen manages to avoid discussing the third moment. The fourth moment is once again a good example of Origen's ability to reconcile the requirements of the general structure, and the role assigned by that structure to a particular moment, with the necessity of expressing in each and every moment the underlying tension between letter and spirit. The general structure once more requires that the abscission of Malchus' ear be treated on a strictly literal level: like the second and third moments, this fourth moment is a result of the disciples' literalist misunderstanding, of their still being mired in the letter of the Law. Nevertheless, as Origen emphasizes, the abscission of Malchus' ear, though blameworthy and condemned by the Lord on the literal level, is nevertheless filled with "sacramental" meaning: for it is an allegory of the spiritual deafness of the Jewish People who from now on will only be able to listen with the left and sinister ear of literal hearing. This sort of *allegoria per antithesim* was much to the taste of the subsequent tradition. The most famous example is perhaps the allegorical treatment of the story of David and Bathsheba. At the literal level, the adultery and the murder on the part of David of Bathsheba's husband, Uriah the Hittite, is, of course, bitterly condemned; but spiritually the marriage of David and Bathsheba becomes a figure of the union of Christ with the True Israel of God; the murder of Uriah, the alien husband, a figure of the overcoming of the Devil to whom the Bride of Christ had formerly been in thrall. Origen's exegesis of the abscission of the ear of Malchus is built on essentially the same lines: a particularly refined example of the allegorist's subtle art.[2]

With Origen's treatment of the last moments of the pericope the conflict between logical structure and symbolic expressiveness becomes apparent. With some exceptions, his tendency here is to emphasize the literal meaning, as is demanded by the general shape and the logical requirements of his exegesis; and this even though that literalism may rob the exegesis of much of its symbolic power. This is true already of his treat-

2. Above, chapter 2 at nn. 118, 122, 123.

ment of the healing of the ear of Malchus: it is given no allegorical meaning and is seen merely as a manifestation of both the mercy and the power of the Lord. Here later commentators will correct the situation and give to the episode the sort of double exegesis that Origen had already given to the preceding moment: the healing of the ear is a manifestation of mercy and power (and thus at the literal level a proper response to both the misunderstanding of the disciples and the misunderstanding of the Jews), but it is also an allegory of the ultimate reconciliation of the people of Israel.[3]

With the Lord's rebuke, the problem becomes particularly acute. Here, Origen attempts a two-level or even three-level exegesis of a sort. At a literal level, the Lord's rebuke of Peter forbids Christians to kill for any reason whatsoever, even in self-defense or by reason of being in the army; at a tropological level, it forbids strife in general; at an allegorical level, it forbids strife more particularly within the churches of Christ. The attempt fails, however: the distance between the three levels of meaning is so minimal that the cause of symbolic expressiveness has not in fact been served. Letter and spirit are here far too close: and the distinction between the two (which forms the basis of Origen's exegesis of the pericope as a whole) is blurred rather than given symbolic expression. The ethics of absolute nonresistance involves an eschatological tension, for by living in the world as if they were already in the next, Christians become witnesses to the eschatological kingdom. In genuine tropology that tension is reflected by a minimum distance between letter and spirit. In this case, however, eschatological expectation and the witness to the Kingdom tend to fade into what has been called "the bourgeois Christianity" of a self-consciously Gentile (and to an extent at least self-consciously respectable) Church.[4] To be sure, insofar as Origen has preserved the literal meaning, he has preserved the ethics

3. For Origen, see above, chapter 2 at nn. 127–131. For later commentators, see Ambrose, *Expositio Evangelii secundum Lucam* 10.66, *CC* 14.365, above, chapter 2, n. 130; Jerome, *Commentariorum in Mattheum Libri* IV (26.51), *CC* 77.257, cited above, chapter 2, n. 106; Bede, *In Lucae Evangelium Expositio*, *CC* 120, 388 f., and Paschasius Radbertus, *Expositio in Mattheum*, *PL* 120.917, who follow Jerome, above, chapter 2, n. 106; most clearly, *Glossa Ordinaria ad Johannem* 18.11, *PL* 114.418, and Rupert of Deutz, *Commentaria in Evangelium Sancti Johannis* 13 (18:10), *CCCM* 9.717, cited above, chapter 2, n. 130.

4. The phrase "bourgeois Christianity" (*bürgerliches Christentum*) as applied specifically to the Gentile Christianity of the Pastoral Epistles goes back to Dibelius; Bultmann calls this sort of *eusebeia* ("piety") a "somewhat faded Paulinism." See W. Kümmel, *Introduction to the New Testament* (London, 1970), 270.

of absolute nonresistance. But his tropology here degenerates into folk-wisdom and the Lord's *logion* into a moralistic aphorism. Post-Constantinian commentators, embarrassed by the radical pacifism of Matthew 26:52, will find it all too easy to retain the "spiritual" aphorism and deny the literal meaning. In a sense they will have brought Origen's rather blurred exegesis into sharper focus.

As for the last two *logia,* Origen opts to treat them on a literal level. Here, to be sure, he is greatly limited by the shape of his material. Both of these concluding sayings are essentially theological and historical comments by the Lord Himself on His mission and His relationship to the Jewish People. In the nature of the case there is very little that can be done by way of allegorization. Nevertheless, Origen does the best he can: for implicitly at least he suggests that the literal meaning of these concluding moments is intimately related to the allegorical shape of the pericope as a whole. In addition, these final comments allow him to point up a christological dimension that had not yet been touched upon. Neither the Jews nor the disciples had understood either the absolute mildness of Christ's humanity or the absolute power of His Divinity. Yet the dialectical relationship between humility and power is in the end the main lesson to be drawn from the pericope as a whole. This is also the sacramental meaning of the ethics of absolute nonresistance. In Origen, to be sure, these christological implications are not fully drawn: and it will remain the task of much later commentators (particularly twelfth-century "conservatives," such as Rupert of Deutz) to unveil what in Origen had only been suggested.[5] In the more immediate future, Origen's lack of explicitness and apparent literalism will allow some of the Fathers of the Constantinian Era to reduce the rebuke of Peter to the merely historical: the Lord told Peter to put his sword back into its sheath not because of any general doctrine of nonresistance but because He wanted to accomplish His Father's will and did not wish Peter to interfere in this particular case.

Origen's exegesis has thus certain weaknesses which to an extent at least will condition the subsequent history of the pericope. Yet the imperfections of his exegesis of some individual

5. Rupert of Deutz, *De Victoria Verbi Dei* 12.17 (ed. R. Haacke), 391, cited above, chapter 2, n. 149. See, in the same note, the citation from Leo the Great, *Tractatus* LII.4, *CC* 138A, 310; also Augustine, *De Ordine* 2.9.27, *CC* 29, 122, cited below, n. 23.

moments do not detract from the immense attractiveness of his exegetical scheme as a whole. This attractiveness will determine the exegetical future even more than the imperfections; it too, moreover, can be analyzed. As has already been noted in passing, the allegory here is primary and self-regarding, for it is in effect an allegory about allegory itself: the opposition between the sword of the spirit which the disciples are enjoined to buy and the corporeal sword, with which Peter presumes to defend his Lord, is treated by Origen as an allegory of the opposition between letter and spirit, and therefore as an allegory of allegory itself. But in an exegetical structure that is primary and self-regarding, the form will necessarily express the content. This is an immense aesthetic advantage and undoubtedly one of the main reasons for the popularity of Origen's scheme for centuries to come.

Aesthetics cannot in this context properly be separated from either hermeneutics or theology: for the primary exegesis gives entry to an underlying exegetical structure, which is both traditional (and indeed absolutely fundamental to the whole of Christian thought) and yet also capable of almost perpetual self-renewal. This is the circular and dialectic structure, which has been briefly described in the context of Origen's exegesis of the two tunics of Matthew 10:10: underlying his primary exegesis of these two tunics there was, it will be recalled, a deeper circular structure in which letter is to spirit as the Old is to the New Man, as superfluities are to Christian simplicity, as externals are to the inner life, as flesh is to the spirit, as the Old is to the New Dispensation, and again (closing the circle) as letter is to spirit.[6] Here in the context of the sword pericope, the circle is more limited and consists of slightly different dialectical pairs. By confusing the sword of the spirit with the corporeal sword, the disciples mistook spirit for letter, since they had not yet grasped the gospel patience handed unto them by the Lord and were still laboring under the power of self-defense against enemies given unto them by the Law. Here corporeal warfare is to spiritual war as letter is to spirit, as the Law is to the Gospel, as self-defense is to patience, and again (closing the circle) as corporeal warfare is to spiritual warfare. Basically, however, the deep underlying dialectical and circular structure remains the same. It can, moreover, be found in a wide variety

6. Above, chapter 2 at nn. 79–83.

of exegetical contexts, is capable of almost perpetual self-renewal because of the wide possibilities of exchange between dialectical pairs, and yet, because of its structural pattern, is expressive of much that is fundamental to Christianity.

The classical example is undoubtedly Paul's own treatment of the Hagar-Sarah pair in Galatians 4:21 ff. There the two wives of Abraham are first of all identified with the Old and the New Covenant, then with the Jerusalem-that-is-today versus the Jerusalem-that-is-to-come, and finally with slavery and freedom. Assimilation with other great Pauline pairs, such as Law and Grace, letter and spirit, death and life, the Old and the New Man, is not explicitly carried out; but when the subsequent tradition makes these identifications it is surely loyal to the spirit of the Pauline structure. When Augustine deliberately assimilates the pairs of Galatians to his Two Cities, he is no doubt profoundly original, yet at the same time perfectly in line with the underlying structure of the Pauline passage.[7] Again in Romans 9:13, Paul connects Esau and Jacob with the Old and the New Dispensation, as well as with the Jews and Christians of his own day: here, too, though the circle is less well worked out than in Galatians, the same basic structure is at least suggested. Similarly, when Tertullian identifies the two edges of the sword of the Apocalypse with the Old and the New Dispensation, it is the same basic structure that underlies his exegesis. Exactly the same is the case in the subsequent tradition of the exegesis of the two cherubim on each side of the propitiatory within the ark of the alliance, or of the exegesis of the two pennies found in the mouth of the fish in the pericope of the Temple Tax. Origen himself uses the structure not only in his exegesis of the two tunics and of the sword pericope, but also, as will be seen, in his own interpretation of the two pennies found in the mouth of the fish as well as in his exegesis of the saying about God and Caesar.[8] In every

7. Augustine, *De Civitate Dei* 15.2, *CC* 48.454 ff.

8. For Tertullian, see *Adversus Marcionem* III.14.3, *CC* 1.526 (cf. also *Adversus Iudaeos* IX.18, *CC* 2.1369). The two cherubim of Exodus 25 and 37, in a tradition that goes back to Philo, represent justice and mercy; see Rupert of Deutz, *De Sancta Trinitate et operibus eius* XIII (*in Exodum* IV.14), *CCCM* 22.767; in John of Salisbury, *Epistola* 145 (*Ad Bartholomaeum Episcopum Exoniensem*), *PL* 199.135C, the same two cherubim have become the temporal and spiritual powers (I owe this last reference to my student, Ms. Janet Gardiner). For the two pennies, see Hilary of Poitiers, *Commentarius in Matthaeum* 17.10–13, *PL* 9.1017 f.: in this elegantly compressed exegesis, the *didrachma* (two pence) and the *statēra* (double *didrachma*) of the pericope are interpreted in a subtly complex way: there are references to body and soul, shadow and

case, the general procedure is essentially the same. Hagar and Sarah are first assimilated to the Old and the New Covenant, then as it were by reverberation to the Jerusalem-that-now-is and the Jerusalem-that-is-to-come and then to slavery and freedom, which brings one back to Hagar and Sarah. Later exegetes will pursue this process of reverberation and insert on the circle either genuinely Pauline pairs such as letter and spirit, or a new pair such as the Two Cities of Augustine, which by exegetical assimilation can be equated with one of the Pauline pairs. Again in the case of the two tunics, Origen first identifies the pair with the Old and the New Man in the Homilies on Luke, with Law and Grace in the Homilies on Leviticus. By reverberation these dualities then suggest to Origen the perhaps non-Pauline but in any case analogous contrasts between the superfluous and ascetic and between the outer and the inner.[9] In the case of the two swords, Origen has first recourse to the only partly Pauline contrast between material resistance and spiritual warfare: by reverberation this then suggests to him the perfectly Pauline opposition between Law and Grace and letter and spirit. Later commentators will feel free to insert new pairs while fully respecting the original structure: for instance, body and soul, works and faith, death and life, material and spiritual power, laity and clergy, and ultimately, of course, even state and church.[10]

In every case the pair in the particular biblical passage is identified either with one of the Pauline dualities on the exegetical circle or with a dialectical pair that is somehow assimilated to them. Second, in most cases (though not in all), this first identification sets up a series of reverberations in the mind

---

reality, Law and Gospel, as well as to the unity of the Four Gospels (cf. below, chapter 4, n. 88). For the two pennies and Origen's own exegesis, see below, chapter 4 at nn. 87–100. For his interpretation of "Render unto Caesar," see below, chapter 4 at nn. 61–83. For these pairs and others standing for the Two Dispensations, see de Lubac, *Exégèse Médiévale* 1.1, 346–51.

9. Above, chapter 2 at nn 75–83. Implicit in Origen's exegesis of the two tunics there is, I think, a contrast between psychic and pneumatic; see above, chapter 2, pp. 67ff. and pp. 79f.

10. For Origen, see above, chapter 2, nn. 118–126 (cf. also chapter 1, n. 80). For the two swords as body and soul, see Alcuin, *Epistola* 136, *MGH—Epistolae* 4, 206; for the same as works and faith, ibid., 207. For the opposition between a sword of life and a sword of death, Paschasius Radbertus, *Expositio in Matthaeum* 12.26, *PL* 120.918. For the beginnings of the application of the two-sword pericope to the traditional doctrine of the two powers, see Henry IV, *Epistola* 13 in *Die Briefe Heinrich IV* (ed. Carl Erdmann, *MGH—Deutsches Mittelalter. Kritische Studientexte des Reichsinstituts für ältere deutsche Geschichtskunde*, vol. 1 [Leipzig, 1937]), 19. (Cf. also ibid., *Epistola* 17, p. 25).

of the exegete so that a number of similar identifications follow. Third, and finally, the subsequent tradition will pick up this reverberating process and come up with still other Pauline or assimilated pairs. As a result of this process of reverberation, generation of new pairs, and assimilation of non-Pauline to genuinely Pauline pairs, the subsequent exegesis will be capable both of absolute faithfulness to tradition and yet also of adaptation to new historical conditions. Faithfulness to tradition will mean faithfulness to the general structure; and the capacity for adaptation, the capacity for the generation of new pairs.

The new pairs, moreover, usually offer original but perfectly genuine insights into the nature of Christianity. The relationship between, say, clergy and laity or between Church and state is something that Saint Paul would presumably never even have thought about; but because these relations are patterned on the duality between Church and world and therefore on that between New and Old Dispensation, a full understanding of their complexity will, in fact, provide both a miniaturized version of, and genuine new insights into, some of the main mysteries of the Christian religion. This capacity for the generation of new yet meaningful dualities is made possible by the structural peculiarities of the original Pauline pairs.

In a sense, of course, all dialectical pairs are capable of being related to each other simply as dialectical pairs, in the sense that the two poles are both opposed to each other and yet united by their complementarity. When new dualities are encountered, they can therefore be fitted into the pre-existing system. Suppose, for instance, that a given tribe has always related the Raw to the Cooked, as Male is to Female, Hunting to Gathering, Animal to Plant, and Dry to Wet.[11] Under the impact of the neolithic revolution, such a tribe will undoubtedly encounter both new items (such as, for instance, wool and linen) which can easily be integrated into the old dualities and new oppositions such as that between Wild Beasts and Domesticated Animals. Out of sheer structural joy,

11. These categories are, of course, only a few among the many such congruences which could be drawn from the works of Claude Lévi-Strauss. See in particular, *La Pensée Sauvage* (Paris, 1962) (English translation, *The Savage Mind* [New York, 1966]); *Mythologiques*, vol. 1, *Le Cru et le Cuit* (Paris, 1964) (English translation, *The Raw and the Cooked* [New York, 1969]); vol. 2, *Du Miel aux Cendres* (Paris, 1966) (English translation, *From Honey to Ashes* [New York, 1973]); vol. 3, *L'Origine des Manières de Table* (Paris, 1968); and vol. 4, *L'Homme Nu* (Paris, 1971).

the nameless tribe may indeed proceed further, and by a process of simple subdivision create a whole series of further dualities. Thus, Domesticated Animals can be subdivided into Hooved and Non-Hooved; while the category of the Hooved may in turn give rise to a distinction between animals with cloven and animals with non-cloven hooves, as well perhaps as to that between animals that chew and animals that do not chew the cud. The new pairs will then be integrated into the older pre-neolithic system. From a purely structural point of view, there is, however, no way of telling whether a new category (Cud-Chewing, for instance) will be assimilated with the Raw-Male-Hunting-Animal grouping or with the Cooked-Female-Gathering-Plant system. To be sure, there may be nonstructural clues: if the Non-Hooved is taboo, it cannot be cooked, and should therefore be classified with the first rather than the second set. On the other hand, people may be reluctant to associate the only meat that can be eaten with the category of Plant rather than with that of Animal: in that case Hooved will be associated with the first set. The Hooved and Non-Hooved, the Raw and the Cooked, the Wet and the Dry, Animal and Plant, are related to each other *merely* as dialectical pairs: the poles are opposed and yet also united because of their complementary functions within each particular system. In such complementary pairs, however, the polarity is nondirectional in the sense that neither pole is necessarily thought of as better than or superior to the other. Neither pole is always marked with either a plus or a minus sign. In such a complementary system, new pairs can be generated, but from a structural point of view the assimilation of new to old poles is purely arbitrary.

Once the nameless tribe has entered history, some of these pairs may, to be sure, become assimilated with others whose poles have positive or negative charges. Thus, some of the categories discussed in the previous paragraph may be grouped together as "pure," others as "impure" food. In addition, impurity may be particularly marked not only at one pole but in cases that are considered anomalous (e.g., in the case of an animal that chews the cud but does not have cloven hooves or in the case of "things that breed in the water" but do not have fins or scales) or again if categories that are considered as sharply distinct are incongruously forced to meet (e.g., animal textiles such as wool and vegetal textiles such as linen). These incongruities or anomalies seem, however, generated in a somewhat arbitrary fashion. Milk and meat products may for some reason not be mixed but fish may be eaten with either; the pig is considered anomalous and impure but birds that are made to fly yet swim in the water remain perfectly kosher. "Pure" and "impure" may in turn be assimilated with "sacred" and "profane," the "inner" and "outer" (the People versus the nations, for instance, or the Levites in the inner, versus the Israelites in the outer, parts of the Temple) and thus once more with males, who can enter the Temple proper, and with females, who, as quasi-gentiles, are restricted to a courtyard, though to be sure an inner one.[12]

These Jewish categories (unlike the hypothetical pre-neolithic and neolithic systems just discussed) are non-arbitrary and directional, largely through the presence of positive and negative poles, and are further structured through the sharply negative emphasis given to anomalies. As has been seen, however, the generation of anomalies remains itself rather arbitrary. Within Christianity, on the other hand, the negative stress on anomalies tends to disappear together with the emphasis on ritual purity and the sharp opposition of Jew and Gentile: after all, what could be more incongruous than a God that becomes man and dies the ignominious death of the Cross or a Jew whose message ultimately is accepted by Gentiles? In Christian grammar, therefore, there is nothing arbitrary about the generation of new structures. Indeed, in the special case of the dialectical pairs on the Pauline circle, there are four distinct parameters which insure directionality and at the same time

12. Though the interpretive shape and many of the details are my own, the attempt to explain the food legislation of Leviticus 11 in Lévi-Straussian terms is not new. See in particular, Mary Douglas, "Deciphering a Meal" in her collection, *Implicit Meanings: Essays in Anthropology* (London, 1975), 249–75 (first published in *Daedalus,* Winter 1972), a thorough reworking of her earlier but still indispensable attempt in *Purity and Danger: An Analysis of Concepts of Pollution and Taboo* (London, 1966), 41–57; see also the brief remarks by Edmund Leach in "Lévi-Strauss in the Garden of Eden: An Examination of Some Recent Developments in the Analysis of a Myth," in E. Nelson Hayes and Tanya Hayes, *Claude Lévi-Strauss: The Anthropologist as Hero* (Cambridge, Mass., 1970), 53 f. The Raw-Male-Hunting-Animal grouping versus the Cooked-Female-Gathering-Plant system and the relations between Hooved and Non-Hooved, Raw and Cooked, Wet and Dry or Animal and Plant (see Wool versus Linen) are derived rather loosely though directly from Lévi-Strauss. The emphasis on incongruities, on "pure" versus "impure" and some of the subdivisions among Jews owe a lot to Mary Douglas. For the overall system and the application to Christianity that follows I must take full responsibility.

protect the dialectical pair against the twin dangers to which all such pairs are exposed: overemphasis on unity to the point that the sense of opposition is lost or overemphasis on opposition to the point that unity disappears. The first of these parameters may be called that of ethical polarization: spirit and flesh, New and Old Dispensation are opposed to each other as good is to bad. The danger here is a manichean exaggeration of the polarity to the point that the necessary unity is no longer felt. The parameter of ethical polarization is balanced, however, by a second parameter, the parameter of hierarchical subordination: the letter is subordinated to the spirit, the Old to the New Dispensation, as the means is to the end or the inferior to the superior. Here the danger is that the element of subordination may be pushed to the point that the inferior may lose its autonomy and in quasi-monophysitic fashion be absorbed by the hierarchical superior. The parameter of hierarchical subordination thus balances the parameter of ethical polarization. By marking the poles of dialectical pairs, both parameters, moreover, provide a simple principle for the nonarbitrary generation of new pairs.

A third, less obvious, and somewhat more complex parameter is provided by the distinction between inner and outer. Flesh and spirit, Old and New Dispensation are related to each other not only as bad is to good or as inferior to superior, but also as the sign is to the thing signified, the shadow to the reality, the envelope to the inner life. As Lévi-Strauss has shown, such concentric structures, unlike the more linear structures, which he calls "diametric," always have a definite orientation: for by definition the "inner" is closer to the governing point, or center, than the "outer." In Christian terms, this means that the "inner" is closer to the center of the universe—which may be equated with either God or Christ—than the "outer." In a sense this concentric parameter is more basic than, and indeed explains, the two linear parameters. The flesh or the Old Dispensation is evil insofar as it is far from God: it is subordinated to the spirit or the New Dispensation insofar as it is farther from Him. At the same time the three parameters must be kept distinct: for each has its own role in the structure of each dialectical pair.[13] As has been seen, the parameter

13. Lévi-Strauss, "Do Dual Organizations Exist?" *Structural Anthropology* (New York, 1967), esp. 137–50. I have not used Lévi-Strauss's term "diametric" for my two linear parameters because, in Christian thought, these parameters are just as "charged"

of ethical polarization tends to exaggerate the element of opposition at the cost of that of unity; while the parameter of hierarchical subordination works in the opposite direction. The concentric parameter on the other hand (as may be only natural if it is thought of as underlying both linear parameters) provides, or at least is more likely to provide, balance in and of itself. In a concentric structure, one is necessarily aware at least at a subconscious level that besides the polarity between "inner" and "outer" there is a third, hidden element—the geometric center, which is the governing point for both "inner" and "outer" and holds the two in balance. In Christian terms, this means that God created (or became incarnate in) the "outer" as well as the "inner," though, to be sure, He created (or recreated) the latter as closer to Him and therefore as better and superior to the former. Unlike the two linear parameters, the concentric structure, in and of itself, keeps in balance the principles of unity and opposition and thus prevents the dialectic from falling apart. Like the two linear structures, however, it assigns plus or minus signs to the two poles and thus provides a third parameter for the non-arbitrary generation of new pairs.

Finally, a fourth parameter, temporal or at least quasi-temporal, is provided by the distinction between old and new. This temporal element is obvious in the case of such pairs as the Two Dispensations, Law and Grace, the Old and the New Man. In all these cases the first pole has precedence in the order of time, but is subordinated, or inferior, to the second in the hierarchical and ethical orders. In the case of pairs such as letter and spirit, or flesh and spirit, this temporal order has been internalized. Letter, for instance, has temporal precedence over spirit in the order of knowing: for the spiritual meaning can only be reached through the literal, and in the hierarchy of the four senses of scripture the literal meaning is therefore first in time. Similarly, the flesh has temporal precedence over the spirit, but in the order of experience: for the natural man before he comes to Christ experiences only the flesh and even the Christian (as long as he remains in the flesh) can experience the spirit only through that flesh.[14]

or "oriented" as the concentric parameter; the parameter of ethical distantiation, moreover, must be distinguished from the hierarchical (Lévi-Strauss equates "charge" with hierarchy) since they tend to break down the dialectic tension from two different directions.

14. Such temporal parameters exist also in the thought of primitive peoples: but the

This temporal parameter is curiously complex, for it involves in effect two opposite conceptions of time. On the surface, everything is relatively simple: the temporal order simply reverses the order imposed by both the ethical and hierarchical parameters. Yet that "the elder shall serve the younger" (Romans 9:12) was obviously felt as intensely paradoxical. Christians shared with the remainder of the pre-modern world the absolute conviction that historical time, like the processes of life, flows from birth to death and thus from a golden age to decadence and destruction. And, like everyone else, they assumed as a matter of course that at any given time within any society the old are naturally wiser and better than the young. Whence the surprise at the paradoxical news that in supernatural time and sacred history this natural order was completely reversed. The ordinary, normal, flow of natural or profane time is not really suspended: on the contrary, an awareness of this natural flow and of its opposition to the flow of supernatural time is necessary for the paradox to remain a paradox, as it obviously does. In effect, the temporal parameter involves two contrary conceptions of the theology of time. In the order of supernatural time, the Old Dispensation is in every respect inferior to the New; insofar as the Coming of Christ has meant the inauguration of the Kingdom of Heaven, Christians must acknowledge that they are New Men, totally belonging to the New Dispensation, that they are, in fact, no longer members of the Old Creation. Yet insofar as the Kingdom of Heaven will be manifested in power and glory only with the Second Coming, the letter, the flesh, the Old Man have not been completely overcome even among Christians; and from that point of view, the fact that the Old Dispensation came first in the order of time gives even now a certain primacy, a certain "firstness" to that Dispensation and to all its concomitants. Even under the New Dispensation, saints are not born but made: in every case, they must struggle out of the flesh, out of the Old Dispensation from which they come. Even saints, moreover, cannot serve God (as Origen acknowledges, it will be seen below) unless they first provide for the necessities of the flesh (e.g., food and drink) and unless they first give to

---

directionality is biographic (e.g., Young vs. Old) or periodic (e.g., Rainy vs. Dry Season), not normally historical; see Lévi-Strauss, *L'Origine des Manières de Table,* 88 ff., 125–38, 156 ff., 211 f., and 298 f.; also *L'Homme Nu,* 118 f. and 540–46.

the world what is still due to the world (e.g., obedience to Caesar).[15] Even today, therefore, the firstness and primacy of the world in the order of natural time balances the primacy of the New Dispensation in the order of salvation. The temporal parameter is thus in effect twofold: what is given a plus sign in the order of supernatural time is given a minus sign in the order of natural time. Christians, to be sure, must serve God rather than this world: but as Origen will emphasize, they cannot serve God unless they first render to the world what is due to the world. As a result of this doubleness of outlook, the temporal parameter has the same effect as the concentric parameter: it tends to keep the dialectic in balance.

The dialectic of the Pauline pairs is thus of a very special kind, both exceedingly dynamic and exceedingly complex. It is dynamic because, unlike many of the merely complementary pairs in the dialectic of other cultures and creeds, the polarity of the Pauline pairs is always charged and directional. It is complex because the charge in the various parameters is not always in the same direction: for the charge on the scale of natural time reverses the charge on the other scales. It is both dynamic and complex because, while two of the parameters tend to balance the dialectic, the two others tend to make it fly apart but in opposite directions. The dynamism and structural complexity mean, moreover, that new pairs can be generated with a great deal of precision: there will be nothing arbitrary about the assimilation of new poles. Some of these new pairs are subjacent in the New Testament, so that they are merely made explicit by the subsequent tradition rather than being truly generated. This is the case, for instance, of the opposition between Church and world. Paul does not explicitly contrast these two terms, but the opposition between the saints and the world in 1 Corinthians 6:2, or the reference to the New Creation in 2 Corinthians 5:17, clearly implies such a duality. All that remains for the Fathers to do is to point up what is obvious already: the world is to the Church as this world is to the next, as the Old is to the New Dispensation, as the flesh is to the spirit. This is easily done; for Church and world are in every respect analogous to the traditional Pauline pairs. The Church is opposed to the world as good is to evil. Yet it is also the world's hierarchical superior in that the world, though it

15. See below, chapter 4 at nn. 64–66.

may resist the Church, was in the last analysis only created in order to serve God. Church and world, moreover, can be distinguished as "inner" is to "outer": for the Church is the light that shineth within the world and alone gives it meaning. Finally, though the world in all these senses is the Church's inferior, it was nevertheless created before the Church: in fact, it simply is (and remains) the Old Creation. Other pairs, on the contrary, are actually generated anew in the sense that nonbiblical ideas or new social realities are integrated into the underlying structure. Such are, for instance, body and soul, psychic and pneumatic, layman and cleric, non-monk and monk, kingship and priesthood, state and Church. In every case the two poles are not merely complementary, but can be distinguished as good is from bad, superior from inferior, inner from outer, and as later in time is from earlier—at least in the order of knowledge and experience.

At their best, medieval meditations on, for instance, the relation between clergy and laity or on that between the material and the spiritual power may reproduce in miniature much of the basic themes of the Christian religion; and, at their best, such miniatures will have a powerful aesthetic and religious effect.[16] The underlying exegetical circle which makes possible

16. A good example of such "miniaturization" from the point of view of the theology of politics is the famous passage from Gelasius' *Tomus De Anathematis Vinculo*, Eduard Schwartz, ed., *Publizistische Sammlungen zum Acacianischen Schisma* (*Abhandlungen der Bayerischen Akademie der Wissenschaften, Philosophisch-historische Abteilung. Neue Folge* 10, Munich, 1934), 14. (The translation given by Brian Tierney, *The Crisis in Church and State 1050–1300* [Englewood Cliffs, N.J., 1964], 14 f., is easily accessible but not fully satisfactory; the German rendering by Hugo Rahner, *Kirche und Staat im Frühen Christentum* [Munich, 1961], pp. 263 ff., is to be preferred.) In the passage, Gelasius nicely connects BC and AD, Jews and Gentiles (before the Coming of Christ), the Devil and Christ, pride and humility, and finally the two powers. Christian "syntax" allows even people not particularly renowned for their theological acumen to "miniaturize" with considerable elegance. A good example of this from the point of view of the theology of politics would be Isidore of Seville, *Sententiarum Libri* III.49, *PL* 83.720 f.: Isidore here interconnects justice and humility, God and Christ, kings as rulers of the people of God and kings as protectors of the Body of Christ, and at the same time opposes "domination" to "condescension." Gregory VII's famous second letter to Hermann of Metz, *Registrum* VIII.21, 546 ff. (ed. Erich Caspar, *MGH—Epistolae Selectae* 2; Berlin, 1930; see also the partial translation in Tierney, *Crisis*, 66 ff.) is a good example of how kingship and priesthood may start by being opposed according to an antithetical (God vs. Devil) pattern (e.g., p. 552, ll. 5 ff.) and end up in a nicely hierarchical and soteriological pattern (e.g., p. 561, ll. 14 ff.). Even late and extremist writings often follow one of the parameters without, to be sure, sufficiently balancing it with any of the others: for instance, the various tracts of the *Antequam essent clerici* type use only one of the temporal parameters, while *Clericis Laicos* begins so antithetically that it has to go super-hierarchical

this sort of miniaturization in a constantly renewed, fresh, and creative fashion is therefore just as legitimate as the much better known linear structure which proceeds by means of the four meanings of scripture. The circular structure, moreover, is particularly applicable to the exegesis of the New Testament, in which many of the dialectical dualities lie close to the surface, and in which the four meanings can be used only indirectly by a sort of reversal to the Old Testament. To be sure, this sort of circular or dialectical exegesis applies only where the text actually involves a pair or duality of some sort, which through exegesis can be equated with one of the dialectical pairs on the circular structure. Where scripture offers no such convenient juncture, the allegorist will have to revert to the Old Testament or else proceed by a linear, but truncated, exegesis in which tropology or anagogy is the only meaning that fully emerges. The presence of any surface pair will thus exert a powerful attraction.

Both the linear and the circular structures are, in fact, derived from the same basic dialectic: the complex relationship between the Old and the New Dispensations, which in exegetical terms is best expressed by typology in the strict sense of the word.[17] But the peculiarities of the Christian conception of Christ as Messiah (and in particular the delay of the Parousia) meant that the tension inherited from Jewish apocalyptic thought between this world or the present age (*ha-ᶜolom ha-zeh*) and the next world or Messianic Age (*ha-ᶜolom ha-bah*), though still essential, was no longer quite enough. Throughout the Old Dispensation, Christ had been expected as He Who Was To Come; and He did in fact come in the Holy Land, thus inaugurating the New Dispensation and the Messianic Age; yet because this world did not accept Him, the Old Dispensation nevertheless survives until Christ will come again in power and glory. The present age is thus profoundly ambiguous. On the one hand, it is the age in which "the mystery which hath been hid from the ages . . . is now made manifest to the saints" (Colossians 1:26); on the other, Christians must resign themselves to the fact that even "now" they only "see as through a glass darkly," that only "then" will they see "face to face" (1 Corinthians 13:12).

---

in order to redress the balance. (I should discuss at least some of this material in the work I hope to publish later.)

17. Above, chapter 1 at nn. 11–25.

The doubleness of the Advent of Christ and the ambiguity of the present dispensation means first of all that the simple dyadic typology inherited from the past is accompanied by and modulated through a more complex triadic—and since one is dealing with Christianity one should not be afraid to say "trinitarian"—structure. Insofar as the "now" of the present is opposed to the "then" of the past, the present is indeed the New Dispensation, for the Kingdom of God has already been realized; insofar, however, as the "now" of the present is opposed to the "then" of an eternity that is still to come, the Kingdom of God is still in the future. The basic dyadic structure has thus become bifurcated and refracted through a triadic, or trinitarian, organization of history.[18] These two interfering structures, moreover, exist not only in sacred history, but are mirrored in equally linear fashion within the biography of every Christian soul. Insofar as the Kingdom is already at hand, the life of every Christian can be divided into "before" and "after Christ": the New Man can simply be opposed to the Old Man, and the biography of every Christian organized in linear and dyadic fashion into, so to speak, BC and AD. Yet, insofar as the Kingdom is still only in the future, Christians know, alas! that conversion is not irreversible. The historical coming of Christ did not mean that the world would necessarily receive Him; in fact, complete acceptance will occur only after the Last Judgment. In the same way, Christ's "biographical" coming into the soul of the individual Christian and His acceptance by each of these faithful become definite only at the moment of death. Here too, therefore, a triadic or trinitarian structure coexists with the more basic dyadic one. These historical and biographical linear structures can be combined in a variety of ways. The two advents of Christ into the soul (at the moment of conversion and at the moment of death) can, for instance, be inserted between their historical analogues, the First and the Second Coming of Christ: this is the later medieval doctrine of the Four Advents of Christ. Or the Coming of Christ into

18. The generation of triads (e.g., Agriculture/Hunting/War) that mediate between the poles of an antithetical dyad (e.g., Life/Death) is typical of Lévi-Straussian syntax; so is the combination of two dyads to form a single triad. See Lévi-Strauss, "Do Dual Organizations Exist?" 145 ff.; *L'Origine des Manières de Table*, 28 f., 34 ff., 212 f., 238 ff., 327 f., 377–84, 396–406; *L'Homme Nu*, 214 f., 430, 515, 536, 550–54. Needless to say, I don't claim that this sort of generation explains the formation of the Trinity by a "more fundamental" Divinity/Humanity dyad. Yet the triadic structure of the Christ-Event is suggestive.

the life of the Christian can (when seen as one) be inserted between the second and third "points" on the historical and triadic "line": it thus becomes the tropological meaning in the exegetical structure represented by the four senses of scripture.[19]

This linear structure has obviously tremendous advantages. It can be used even if there are no actual pairs such as Esau and Jacob, two tunics, two pennies, or two swords in the letter of the text. It brings out not only the essentially dyadic, or dialectical, but the equally important triadic, or trinitarian, structure of Christianity; it preserves the basic historical dimension; and it points up the parallelism between historical and biographical time, between the life of the People of God and the life of its saints. Yet the linear structure, though the multiplication of its meanings is based on the ambiguity of the present dispensation, cannot really reflect that ambiguity. To be sure, a sort of negative tropology is possible within that linear structure: for instance, insofar as Christians have failed to slay within themselves Sihon, "the puffed-up king," "the barren tree," they have failed to become "cities of Israel," they remain "cities of the Amorites," which is to say cities of the Devil.[20] But within that linear structure it is almost impossible to do justice at one and the same time to the messianic and eschatological as well as the worldly aspects of the time in-between. The Pauline pairs, on the other hand, express that doubleness with perfect accuracy. The circular structure can be used to refract this ambivalence throughout all the important sectors of human experience. The human composite, for

19. See above, chapter 1 at n. 15. For the medieval doctrine of the "four advents," see Innocent III, *Sermo* 4 (Dominica Secunda in Adventu Domini), *PL* 217.329 AB: "Quatuor Redemptoris Adventus Scriptura Sacra distinguit: Primum in nube, secundum in rore, tertium in turbine, quartum in igne. In nube carnis, ut mundum redimeret. In rore gratiae ut spiritum illuminet. In turbine mortis ut corpus incineret. In igne iudicii ut saeculum iudicet . . . [ibid., 329D]. . . . Hos quatuor Redemptoris adventus repraesentat Ecclesia in quatuor Dominicis de Adventu Domini . . . ." At ibid. 330 AD Innocent connects the four advents to the four scriptural meanings of the word "Jerusalem," to each of which the Lord may be said to come in its turn. See also Thomas Aquinas, *Sermo in Prima Dominica Adventus*, ed. Jean Leclercq in *L'Idée de la Royauté du Christ au Moyen Age* (*Unam Sanctam* 32; Paris, 1959), 83 ff.: ". . . scire debetis quod quadruplex legitur Christi adventus. Primus est quo venit in carnem. Secundum . . . est quo venit in mentem. Tertius . . . est quo venit in morte iustorum. Sed quartus Christi adventus est quo venit ad judicandum . . . et tunc gloria sanctorum redundabit usque ad corpus. . . . Et propter istos quatuor Christi adventus celebrat forte ecclesia quatuor dominicas de Christi adventu." See also Guillaume Durand, *Rationale Divinorum Officiorum* VI.2 (Lyons, 1551), fol. 155.1, referred to by de Lubac, *Exégèse Médiévale* 1.2, 624, n. 9.

20. Above, chapter 1 at nn. 49–59.

instance, is seen as subject to the dialectic between flesh and spirit or, later, to that between body and soul. Thought, morals, theology, and ritual are subject to the dialectic between letter and spirit, to that between outer and inner, or to that between works and faith. The perception of the society is determined by the dialectic between Jew and Christian, pagan and Christian, secular and religious, and, ultimately, world and Church. Finally, the perception of the Church and of its relation to the world is subject to the dialectic between psychic and pneumatic, layman and cleric, non-monk and monk, and material and spiritual power. The dialectical pairs inserted in the Pauline circle thus allow the exegete to express the radical ambivalence of the present dispensation far better than the tropological level of the linear structure.

Finally, the exegetical circle and the Pauline pairs afford entry into some of the greatest mysteries of the Christian faith, such as the problem of good and evil or the Incarnation. Thus, as has been seen, genuine Pauline pairs such as spirit and letter or the New and the Old Dispensation can be assimilated to salvation and sin, life and death, and through that intermediary transformed into such antithetical pairs as God and the Devil or simply good and evil. Similarly, flesh and spirit can be assimilated to the outer and the inner, and then transformed into the Humanity and the Divinity of Christ and in a sense therefore even into Man and God. To be sure, this sort of transformation can be a little tricky. Neither antithetical pairs nor pairs patterned on the God/Man relation are exactly Pauline pairs: for one thing it is obvious that the element of reversed temporality is lacking. Antithetical pairs, moreover, emphasize the parameter of ethical distantiation to the point that the element of complementarity or unity may be entirely lost; while in the case of pairs such as the Humanity and Divinity of Christ, the emphasis on hierarchical subordination may be such that it is the element of antithesis that becomes submerged. In transformations of this sort there is therefore the risk that the whole of the Pauline circle degenerates into either antithesis or hierarchical subordination. On the other hand, when carefully done, such transformations help prevent both an exaggerated dualism of a manichean type and the sort of exaggerated linkage between God and Man that could easily degenerate into monophysitic pantheism. Thus the linkage of good and evil to the Pauline circle will help the exegete suggest (even without the metaphysical sophistication of an Augustine) that evil is part of the Old Creation and that even the Devil has a role assigned to him by Divine Providence. Similarly, by linking the Humanity and Divinity of Christ to letter and spirit and the remainder of the Pauline circle, the exegete can show (even without the benefit of Ephesus and Chalcedon) that unity does not necessarily entail confusion.

When applied to Origen's discussion of the sword pericope and the subsequent exegetical tradition, these two types of transformation, if considered together, lead to a fascinating though paradoxical effect. On the one hand, Origen's exegetical structure (together with much of the theology of politics of the Church of the Martyrs) will suggest to some later writers that material power is to spiritual power and that Kingship is to Priesthood not only as the Old is to the New Dispensation, but as death is to life and indeed as the Devil is to God or Christ.[21] On the other hand, Origen's brief reference to "the sheath of patience," and the opposition between Christ's divine power and His human long-suffering and nonresistance, which underlies so much of his discussion of the latter moments of the pericope, will suggest (though admittedly only rarely) that the two powers can be fitted into an incarnational pattern.[22] In the first case, Priesthood is to Kingship as the Church is to the world, as God is to Man, and even (through the intermediary of the sort of antithetical transformation that has just been described) as God is to the Devil. In the second, on the contrary, Priesthood is to Kingship as sacrifice and long-suffering are to royal power, as the Humanity of Christ is to His

21. See, for instance, the eleventh-century *De Ordinando Pontifice, MGH. LdL.*1, 14: "Ubi enim inveniuntur imperatores locum Christi obtinere? Si verius liceat nobis dicere, potius offitio diaboli surguntur in gladio et sanguine, ut dum per penitentiam eruantur vitia spirituali resecatione, ipsi insaniant vel in cede vel in membrorum obtruncatione; quod secundum gratiam apud Deum omnino est abhominabile"; also from the same period, Anselm, *Gesta Episcoporum Leodicensium* 66, *MGH. SS* 7, 230 (it is Bishop Wazo of Liège who is addressing the Emperor Henry III): "Alia . . . est et longe a sacerdotali differens . . . vestra [i.e., regalis vel imperialis] . . . unctio, quia per eam vos ad mortificandum, nos . . . ad vivificandum ornati sumus: unde quantum vita morte praestantior, tantum nostra vestra unctione sine dubio est excellentior." See already Alcuin, *Epistola* 17, *MGH. Epist.* 4, 48: "Divisa est potestas saecularis et potestas spiritalis: illa portat gladium mortis in manu, haec clavem vitae in lingua . . ." and, by implication at least, Pope Nicholas I, *Epistola* 156, *MGH. Epist.* 6, 647 and 677: "Sancta Dei Ecclesia mundanis numquam constringitur legibus; gladium non habet nisi spiritalem atque divinum; non occidit sed vivificat."

22. E.g., Rupert of Deutz, *De Victoria Verbi Dei* 12.17, and already Leo the Great, *Tractatus* LII.4, both cited above, n. 5 and chapter 2, n. 149.

Divinity, and ultimately, therefore, as Man is to God. The relationship between the two terms is thus totally reversed!

The paradox can be allayed by a further transformation from a dyadic to a triadic pattern. The two paradoxical pairs, Kingship-Priesthood and Priesthood-Kingship, can then be fused into a progressive triad of the Power-Humility-Power (or Kingship-Priesthood-Kingship) type. This structure (which is in effect triadic and dyadic at one and the same time) is obviously analogous to the familiar Then-Now-Then pattern, which is itself a perfect expression of the radical ambivalence of the time in-between. It can be connected, moreover, with a christological triad in which the Power and Kingship of the pre-Incarnate Logos are related to the humility and Priesthood of Jesus as well as to the Power and Kingship of the Risen Christ. At the same time this dyadic triad expresses both the radical ambiguity and the fundamental unity of power. Until the Parousia, power is something that can be experienced as coming from either God or the Devil. This is the radical ambivalence of the Old Dispensation, which in that sense can be understood as continuing until the Second Coming. This is precisely why in the Christian experience, power—as Augustine will explain in *De Ordine*—should be mediated through the mediation of humility: in this way the Power of God can in the last analysis be distinguished from the power of the Devil. With the Parousia, however, Christ the King will come again in power and glory to judge the quick and the dead and to bind the Devil for all eternity: only then will the fundamental unity of all power (including the power granted to the powers of this world, and to the Devil, the Prince of this world) stand fully revealed.

In the meantime, power, which is not mediated through the intermediary of humility (and in Augustinian terminology "power" that is so mediated is transmuted into "authority"), remains radically ambiguous: for in the present dispensation it may come from either God or the Devil.[23] The exegetical structures which have been discussed in the last few pages are built

23. On the concept of "auctoritas" in Augustine, see Karl-Heinrich Lütcke, *'Auctoritas' bei Augustin* (*Tübinger Beiträge zur Altertumswissenschaft* 44 [Stuttgart, 1968]). On the mediating position of *auctoritas* between *potestas* and *humilitas* and on the danger of devilish tricks, see in particular Augustine, *De Ordine* 2.9.27, *CC* 29, 122: "Auctoritas autem partim divina est, partim humana, sed vera firma summa ea est, quae divina nominatur. In qua metuenda est aeriorum animalium mira fallacia, quae

into the very texture of Christianity: they allow Christians to deal with this radical ambiguity of power even when they lack the theological sophistication or the "political" interests of an Augustine. Origen's theology of politics, however, is not merely expressed through the exegetical dialectic between the corporeal war of the Old Dispensation and the spiritual warfare of the New Dispensation. As will be seen in the next chapter, such a theology of politics is an express part of his basic theological stance.

---

per rerum ad istos sensus corporis pertinentium quasdam divinationes nonnullasque potentias decipere animas facillime consuerunt . . . aut fragilium cupidas potestatum aut inanium formidulosas miraculorum. Illa ergo auctoritas divina dicenda est, quae non solum in sensibilibus signis transcendit omnem humanam facultatem sed et ipsum hominem agens ostendit ei, quo usque se propter ipsum depresserit, et non teneri sensibus, quibus videntur illa miranda, sed ad intellectum iubet evolare simul demonstrans, et quanta hic possit et cur haec faciat et quam parvi pendat. Doceat enim oportet et factis potestatem suam et humilitate clementiam et praeceptione naturam . . . ." See the discussion by Lütcke, 119 ff. The distinction between *auctoritas* and *potestas* will, of course, become crucial in the language of Gelasius. Much of this will be spelled out in the work I hope to undertake on the origins and early stages of the medieval doctrine of the two swords of Luke (see above, Introduction, p. 7). In the meantime, on the time "in-between," on dyads turning into triads, and on the Then-Now-Then progression, see above, pp. 119 ff., as well as below, chapter 4, pp. 175 ff.

CHAPTER IV

THEOLOGY OF POLITICS

The first chapter of this book dealt with Origen's exegesis of the "letter" of the Old Dispensation; the second with his exegesis of the "spirit" of the New; the third with certain dialectical principles that underlie his hermeneutics. The present chapter will attempt to show how the same dialectic between "letter" and "spirit" illuminates what, for want of a better term, may be called his political ecclesiology. The discussion will begin with an examination of the theology of politics implicit in Origen's *Contra Celsum;* it will continue with an analysis of his exegesis of Romans 13:1 ff. in the Commentary on Romans; and will end with a discussion of the Commentary on Matthew and its exegesis of Matthew 22:21, "render unto Caesar the things that are Caesar's, but unto God the things which are God's."[1]

1. On Origen's political thought remarkably little has been written. See the illuminating remarks by Ehrhardt, *Politische Metaphysik von Solon bis Augustin* (Tübingen, 1959–69), 2.204–22, as well as 2.204, where this scarcity is deplored. See also the brief but cogent lines by W. H. C. Frend, *Martyrdom and Persecution in the Early Church: A Study of a Conflict from the Maccabees to the Donatists* (Garden City, N.Y., 1967), 391–97. But the best on the subject are probably still the few pages by Erik Peterson, "Der Monotheismus als Politisches Problem" (*Theologische Traktate;* Munich, 1951), 79–85. As for Guigliemo Massart, *Società e stato nel cristianesimo primitivo. La concezione di Origene* (Padua, 1932), one can only concur in the judgment of Peterson, "Der Monotheismus," 132, n. 123: "Das Buch ist ohne jeden Wert."

Origen's pacifism is expressed not only in his comments on Matthew 26:52, but also—and indeed much more clearly—in his *Contra Celsum.* The pacifism of Christians as a people, he insists in that work, is indeed their most noticeable characteristic. With that argument, for instance, in Book Three he attempts to refute Celsus' thesis that both Jews and Christians are a rebellious people, whose very origins began in revolution: the Jews in a rebellion against the Egyptians, the Christians in a revolt against the Jews. Whatever may be true of the Jews, the Christians' peaceable beginnings, Origen claims, shine forth even in their present lives: "for if Christians had drawn their origin from a revolt, they would never have submitted to laws, which were so gentle that they made them unable to defend themselves against their persecutors."[2] Later, in Book Five, Origen develops the same point in more eschatological terms. Christians, Celsus maintains, do not know "where they have come from, or who is the 'author' of their traditional laws; in fact, they originated from Judaism . . . [and] rebelled against the Jews." The refutation is simple: "to those who would ask us where we have come from or who is our author, we reply that we came in accordance with the commands of Jesus to beat the spiritual swords that fight and insult us into ploughshares and to transform the spears that formerly fought against us into pruninghooks. No longer do we take the sword against any nation, nor do we learn war any more, since we have become sons of peace, through Jesus, who is our author, and no longer follow our traditional customs, by which we had been 'strangers to the covenants [Ephesians 2:12].' "[3] Christians, for Origen, have thus become the New People of God by abandoning the customs of their Gentile ancestors and replacing the Jews as Sons of the Covenant: as such they fulfill in their persons the eschatological peace prophesied in Isaiah 2:4 and Micah 4:3.

Indeed, it is essentially because of this eschatological role that Christians, Origen insists, are forbidden to fight in the

2. *Contra Celsum* 3.8, 2, 26–29; *GCS* 2, 208 f.; Chadwick, 132. In Koetschau's edition in the *GCS* as well as in Chadwick's translation, the passage is part of 3.7, but Chadwick's suggestion (p. 512) that parts of 3.7 and 3.8 should be inverted has been followed by Borret (*Contre Celse* 1, 47 f. and 3, 27, n. 1) so that in the *Sources Chrétiennes* edition the passage has become part of 3.8 as indicated above. See above, the second note to the Abbreviations p. xiv and chapter 1, note 3, for the fourfold method of citing *Contra Celsum* I have used, as well as for my preference for the *Sources Chrétiennes* edition. In what follows, I have used with only a few changes the excellent translation of Chadwick.

3. Ibid., 5.33, 3, 96–101; *GCS* 3, 34; Chadwick, 289 f.

Emperor's wars. Toward the end of his *True Logos*, Celsus criticized Christians for their lack of patriotism: "if everyone," he argued, "were to do the same as you, there would be nothing to prevent [the Emperor] from being abandoned, alone and deserted, while earthly things would come into the power of lawless and savage barbarians,—and nothing more would be heard either of your form of worship or of the true wisdom!" Yet all men within the Empire, Celsus insisted, should "help the emperor . . . fight for him, and be fellow-soldiers if he presses for this."[4] Origen does not deny that Christians are forbidden to fight even if the Emperor "presses for this." But the arguments of "those who are alien to the faith and demand that Christians fight for the state and kill men" can be easily disproven. After all, Origen points out, even the pagans believe that their priests (or at least some of them) "should keep their hands undefiled, so that they may offer the customary sacrifices with hands unstained by blood." When war comes, such priests are not in fact asked to join in the killing. All Christians, however, form a priestly people who, as worshippers of the One True God, must keep their hands unstained, so that their prayers "for those who fight in a just war and for the emperor who reigns righteously" might be heard in Heaven. Indeed, these priestly Christians, who by their prayers can alone destroy "the demons who stir up war, violate oaths and disturb the peace, are of more help to the emperor than those who *seem* to be doing the fighting," for they achieve far more than the "soldiers, who go out into the lines to kill all the enemy troops that they can." Thus, Christians "do not become 'fellow-soldiers with the Emperor, even if he presses for this,' yet [they] fight for him and compose a special army of piety through their intercession with God."[5]

The ambivalence of Origen's attitude towards warfare is apparent. Celsus' accusation cannot be gainsaid. Christians are indeed a sect of radical pacifists: they do not fight for the Empire, even if "pressed" to do so. In the words of 1 Peter 2:9, they form "a chosen generation, a royal priesthood, an holy nation, a peculiar people": they are the priestly worshippers of the True God, who must keep their hands undefiled and may not therefore "go out into the lines to kill all the

4. Ibid., 8.68 and 73, 4, 330 f. and 344 f.; *GCS* 3, 284 and 290 f.; Chadwick 504, 509.

5. Ibid., 8.73, 4, 346; *GCS* 3, 290; Chadwick, 509. (Emphasis mine.)

enemy troops that they can." Origen's opposition to Christian participation in warfare is, it should be noted, quite openly based on the act of killing. There is not a word about the points so dear to anti-pacifist historians: nothing about the military oath, nothing about the pagan sacrifices soldiers supposedly had to perform.[6] Because they are the priestly worshippers of the Most High, who share the eternal priesthood of Christ, they form the entering wedge of the eschatological kingdom even in this world: as such, they have beaten their swords into ploughshares and their spears into pruninghooks, they no longer use the carnal weapons of the Old Dispensation. On the other hand, as long as this world persists, warfare cannot cease: but for Christians (and only for Christians) it has been transmuted into a far more intense, far more important, and more directly eschatological form of warfare, the warfare of the spirit. In the words of Ephesians 6:12, they no longer "wrestle against flesh and blood, but against principalities and powers, against the rulers of the darkness of this world, against the spiritual hosts of wickedness in the high places." In particular, they wrestle against "the demons who stir up war," "violate pacts," and "disturb the peace." In a "just war" fought by an emperor who "reigns righteously," they fight therefore by praying for the success of the imperial armies: and because they are, all of them without exception, the priests of the Most High, their prayers are far more effective than the puny efforts of merely carnal soldiers, who only "*seem* to fight," and "go out into the lines to kill all the enemies that they can."

As it was for Athenagoras in the second century, so it is with Origen in the third: as long as this world persists, cosmic forces

6. In addition to the bibliography listed above, chapter 1, n. 86, chapter 2, n. 17, and particularly nn. 137 and 151, see on Early Christian pacifism, Henri Leclercq, "Militarisme," *DACL* 11.1108–81 (1933), and Anna Morisi, *La guerra nel pensiero cristiano dalle origini alle crociate* (Florence, 1963), which are strongly biased in an anti-pacifist direction. C. J. Cadoux, *The Early Christian Attitude to War* (London, 1919), is somewhat out of date and slightly biased with a pro-pacifist slant but remains indispensable. R. H. Bainton, "The Early Church and War," *Harvard Theological Review* 39 (1940) 189–212; Hans von Campenhausen, "Der Kriegsdienst der Christen in der Kirche des Altertums," *Festschrift Karl Jaspers* (Munich, 1953), 255–64 (translated under the title "Military Service in the Early Church" in H. v. Campenhausen, *Tradition and Life in the Church, Essays and Lectures in Church History* [Philadelphia, 1968], 160–70); and Jean Daniélou, "La non-violence dans l'Ecriture et la tradition," *Action Chrétienne et non-violence. Compte-Rendu du Congrès National "Pax Christi"* (Paris, 1955), 9–32, are reasonably unbiased. Harnack's *Militia Christi*, and particularly Hornus' *Evangile et Labarum* (both cited above, chapter 2, n. 137) remain indispensable despite their respective biases.

of evil will remain at work. Until the Second Coming, there will be criminals, there will be aggression, there will be trampling on the rights of others. These evils must be resisted, but they must be resisted on two levels. Non-Christians go on fighting with the carnal weapons of the Old Dispensation: it is they who undertake "just" executions, who "reign righteously," who wage "just" wars. Christians, however, because they are conscious and direct participants in the eschatological struggle, must fight with weapons of another kind. No matter how just the war, they may not fight in fleshly fashion; no matter how just an execution, they may not even attend one.[7] The ambivalence of the Early Christian attitude towards war is thus merely a part of the dialectical relation between Old and New Dispensation.

Origen's attitude towards war and violence must, moreover, be understood within the total context of his political ecclesiology, such as it is.[8] In the texture of his theology of history, three more or less simultaneous events stand out as closely interwoven: the spread of the Church, the collapse of the Jewish state, and the success of the Roman Empire. Their interrelationship is made clear in several important passages of *Contra Celsum*. Celsus himself made use of the apparent contradiction between the political nature of Judaism under the Old Dispensation and the radically nonpolitical nature of the Church. Why did God, he asks, give laws by Moses "that the Jews were to become rich and powerful and massacre their enemies, while His Son, the man of Nazareth, gave contradictory laws, saying that a man cannot come to His Father, if he is rich or loves power, and that a man who has been struck once should offer himself to be struck once more? Which is wrong? Moses or Jesus?"[9] The answer, Origen contends, is simple: "neither is wrong, neither Moses nor Jesus."[10] The same God sent both Moses and Jesus; but it was not "possible for the structure of life of the ancient Jews to remain unchanged, if they were to obey the *politeia* enjoined by the Gospel."[11] What has changed

7. For Athenagoras and just executions, see above, chapter 2, n. 151.

8. For the lamentable lack of bibliography, see above, n. 1. For Origen's political ecclesiology, see essentially the remainder of this section.

9. *Contra Celsum* 7.18, 4, 54 f.; *GCS* 3, 169; Chadwick 409.

10. Ibid., 7.25, 4.72 f.; *GCS* 3, 176; Chadwick, 415.

11. Ibid., 7.26, 4,72 f.; *GCS* 3, 177; Chadwick, 415. In the original, *politeia* is used twice, both to render what I—following Chadwick—have translated by "structure of life," and for the *politeia* I have kept in my translation.

between the two Dispensations is not the nature of God, but the very *politeia* or "structure of life." The Law enjoined the ancient Jews to kill their enemies as well as criminals who had been judged to be deserving of death; the Gospel enjoins Christians not to resist evil through physical means. The point, moreover, as Origen emphasizes, is emphatically a political one: the Jews of the Old Dispensation, "who had an autonomous political life [*politeia*] and a country of their own" were badly in need of "the power to go out against their enemies, to fight for their traditional customs, and to punish adulterers and murderers" by making use of the death penalty if necessary. Had they not had such powers, "the inevitable consequence would have been their utter and complete destruction."[12] With the coming of the New Dispensation, however, the same God, Who "long ago had given the Law and has now given the Gospel of Jesus Christ, did not wish the way of life of the Jews to continue and so destroyed both their state and their Temple."[13] The political autonomy, the "structure of life," of the ancient Jews "did not fit in with the gathering in of the Gentiles"; after all, these Gentile Christians could not very well "conduct their society according to the literal interpretation of the law of Moses, since they were subject to the Romans."[14] Providence therefore had the Romans destroy the Jewish state together with the Jewish Temple; while simultaneously the same Providence "increased the success of the Christians," despite the persecution of the Roman Emperors.[15]

While the replacement of the corporeal by the spiritual sword is a product of the passover from the Old to the New Dispensation, that process is, in a sense, completed only with the destruction of the Second Temple and the end of the Jewish People as a political structure. The truly universal, truly catholic, Church is, for Origen, the Gentile Church, the Church that "was called from the *Gentes* or Nations," and such a Church of the Nations could not have "fitted" into the political "structure of life" that had been normal for the separatist Jewish state. Because Jewish life under the Old Dispensation had assumed a political form, it was natural that the Jews should have had the power to go to war against their enemies without, and to inflict the death penalty on those who criminally threatened the

12. Ibid., loc. cit.; *GCS* 3, 177; Chadwick, loc. cit.
13. Ibid., loc. cit.; *GCS* 3, loc. cit.; Chadwick, 416.
14. Ibid., loc. cit.; *GCS* 3, loc. cit.; Chadwick, 415.
15. Ibid., 4, 72–75; *GCS* 3, 176; Chadwick, 416.

structure of society from within. But because God intended Christianity to spread among the Gentiles, it could not remain associated with the Jewish (or indeed with any other) particularist state. God therefore allowed a universal Empire to destroy the Jewish state, and at the same time crowned with success the spread of the Church.

Underlying the argument is the assumption that the People of the New Dispensation could have been deprived of the political independence of God's former people only because the greater part of the Gentiles, among whom the Gospel was to spread, were already subject to a single Empire. As subjects of an Empire that has brought law and order to every corner of the known universe, Christians no longer need "the power to go out against their enemies and to punish adulterers and murderers": such corporeal functions (the absolute necessity of which it does not occur to Origen to question) are now performed by the Roman Empire. Even before the Constantinian Revolution, the Roman Empire thus took its place within providential history. Its providential and indeed eschatological role was, moreover, perceived in more positive fashion than it was in the West. For Origen, the Empire is not merely the fourth and last Empire of Daniel 2:40, as it was for Irenaeus and Hippolytus; nor the power "that holdeth" Antichrist at bay of 2 Thessalonians 2:7, as it was for Tertullian. For Origen the birth and expansion of the Empire is intimately bound up with the spread and the very survival of the Church as a radically nonpolitical (or trans-political) structure, and therefore with the very unfolding of the Christ-event.[16]

That this is indeed Origen's conception of the role of the Empire is confirmed by a famous passage in Book Two of *Contra Celsum.* The prophecy of Psalm 71:7, "in his day shall righteousness flourish and abundance of peace," has been, Origen maintains, fulfilled with the birth of Christ. For at that time "God was preparing the nations for His teaching by submitting them all to one single Roman Emperor, so that the unfriendly attitude of nations to each other, caused by the existence of a large number of kingdoms, might not make it more difficult" for the Apostles to spread the word of God. This explains

16. For Irenaeus, see *Adversus Haereseos* 5.26.1 (*Sources Chrétiennes* 153) 324 ff.; for Hippolytus, see *Eis ton Danila* 4.5 (*GCS* 1) 196; 4.6, 199; and 4.7, 202; also below at nn. 34–38. For Tertullian's gloss on 2 Thessalonians 2:6–8, see *De Resurrectione Mortuorum* 24.18 (*CC* 2.952); also more generally on the same theme, *Apologeticum* 32.1 (*CC* 1.142 f.) and *Ad Scapulam* 2.6 (*CC* 2.1128).

why "Jesus was born under Augustus, the Emperor who reduced, as it were, to the uniformity of a single Empire most of the peoples of this earth. The existence of a plurality of kingdoms would have hindered the spread of the teaching of Jesus throughout the inhabited world, not only for the reason that has just been given, but also because men everywhere would have been forced to do military service and to wage war in defense of their fatherland." Indeed, "how could this teaching, which preaches peace, and does not allow men to take vengeance even on their enemies have had any chance of success, if the state of the world with the advent of Jesus had not been changing everywhere to a more peaceful condition?"[17]

Origen's argument is essentially twofold. First, the overcoming of polyarchy by the monarchy of the Empire meant an opening of external frontiers and a softening of the differences and consequent distrust that used to separate nations from each other. Since the Catholic Church is a Gentile Church, that is, a universal Church, called from all the nations, this blurring of national differences was an essential prerequisite for its spread. Though this is a point Origen does not emphasize in the context, the victory of monarchy over polyarchy can be seen, moreover, as a reflection of the defeat by monotheism of the polytheistic principalities and powers, of Christ's triumph over idols and demons at the time of His Resurrection.[18] Second, the existence of the Empire and of the *Pax Romana,* which it has been able to enforce, has meant that the spread of a sect of such radical pacifists as the Christians becomes a political possibility. Without the Roman Peace, men everywhere would still be "forced to do military service and to wage war in defense of their fatherland" as in the bad old days. With universal conscription, how could a sect of radical pacifists, such as the Church of the Christians, "have had any chance of success"?[19] Elsewhere in the *Commentariorum Series,* that second point is, moreover, given a distinct eschatological twist. In the so-called little apocalypse of Matthew 24, the Lord's prophecy that just before the Second Coming "nation shall rise against nation and kingdom against kingdom" points, according to Origen, to a

17. *Contra Celsum* 2.30, 1, 360 ff.; *GCS* 2, 157; Chadwick, 92. See the brief but excellent discussion by Peterson, "Der Monotheismus," 82 ff. In my translation and paraphrase of this particularly important passage I have been influenced by Borret's translation in *Contre Celse* and by Peterson's as much as by Chadwick's.

18. See Peterson, "Der Monotheismus," 83 f.

19. Above, n. 17.

sort of process of cosmic compensation. The First Advent of Christ "brought peace to many of the nations," and fulfilled the prophecy of Psalm 71:7, for the sake of the increase of the churches of Christ, "the peace of this world was multiplied, so that men should no longer be forced to go to war and fight for their fatherland, as had been the case until then." But with the approach of the Second Coming, it is the prophecy of Matthew 24:12 which will be fulfilled, and battles and warfare will increase once more.[20] The *Pax Romana* is thus a special feature of the interim period between the First and the Second Coming, vouchsafed to the world for the sake of the spread of the churches of Christ.

In the last book of *Contra Celsum,* Origen briefly considers the possibility that with the hypothetical conversion of the whole of the Empire the interim peace given unto the world might be expanded unto a higher stage. Celsus—in one of his more telling strokes—had suggested that if all Romans were to become Christians the same would happen to them as happened to the Jews: "instead of being masters" of the world, the Romans would be "left no land or home of any kind."[21] Origen's answer is lengthy and not always easy to follow—in part because he seems to have been of two minds on the issue. At first he appears rather tempted by the utopian (and Eusebian) vision of the Christian Empire that Celsus cleverly dangles before him. If the whole Empire were to believe, Origen insists, the Romans would in fact be able to subdue their enemies through prayer alone; indeed they would no longer "fight wars at all since they would be protected by divine power."[22] As the argument progresses, however, he begins to have second thoughts. To be sure, the possibility that one day all "the inhabitants of Asia, Europe, and Libya, both Greeks and barbarians even at the furthest limits" of the earth will be united under a single law is immensely attractive: indeed, there is something inevitable about the union of "every rational being"

20. *Commentariorum Series* 37,69: ". . . Sicut adventus Christi in plurimis gentibus divina virtute fecit pacem, secundum quod dicit propheta de illo 'orietur in diebus eius iustitia et abundantia pacis donec extollatur luna' [Psalm 71:7] et sic pax multiplicata est mundi propter incrementa ecclesiarum futura, ut ea pax salutis multorum fiat occasio, dum non coguntur exire ad bella et pugnare pro patriis sicut pridem fiebat—sic consequens est et, cum propter abundantiam iniquitatis refriguerit 'caritas multorum' [Matthew 24:12] et ideo dereliquerit illos deus et Christus eius, iterum fieri proelia. . . ." See Peterson, "Der Monotheismus," 133, n. 125.

21. *Contra Celsum* 8.69, 4,332 f.; *GCS* 3, 285; Chadwick, 505.

22. Ibid., 8.69–70, 4, 332–8; *GCS* 3, 285; Chadwick, 505 f.

under the rule of the Logos.[23] In the end, however, Origen regretfully concludes that such a state of absolute peace "is probably impossible for those who are still in the body; though it is certainly not impossible after they have been delivered from it."[24] The proto-Eusebian vision of a Christian Empire, in which swords have been beaten into plowshares while the world still persists, has occurred to Origen and he is clearly tempted by that vision; but it would seem that ultimately he has overcome that temptation.[25]

Origen's theology of contemporary history is thus reasonably clear. At the same time as the separatism of the Jewish state was replaced by the catholic Christianity of a Church of the Nations, the nations themselves were externally drawn together into a universal Empire. The *Pax Romana*, moreover, meant not only an opening up of frontiers, but also that whatever warlike activities were still needed could be safely left to a small and professional army. It was no longer necessary for all citizens to fight for their country; the spread of a religion of radical pacifists now became possible. This peace of the Roman Empire remains, however, an essentially worldly peace: and even as a peace of this world it prevails neither forever, since it will be terminated by the wars which will announce the Second Coming, nor in all respects, since police operations to keep the barbarians at bay remain a necessity even now. The dream of absolute and universal peace should in all likelihood be relegated until the end of the world. Still, just as the gentleness of the life of the Church is a prefiguration of Heavenly Peace, so in a far more external and imperfect fashion is the *Pax Romana*. From this double perspective, the one "spiritual" and from within the Church, the other more "literal" and from without, it can be said that even now "swords have been beaten into ploughshares and spears into pruninghooks."[26]

To an extent, the Empire of Rome is thus, for Origen, a curious counterpart to the Church of Christ. It destroyed the political structure and the external worship of the Jews according

23. Ibid., 8.72, 4, 340; *GCS* 3, 288; Chadwick, 507.

24. Loc. cit., 4, 344; *GCS* 3, 290; Chadwick, 508.

25. See the analysis in Peterson, "Der Monotheismus," 78–82, with nn. 120 and 133; in my interpretation I have on the whole followed Peterson, though I see Origen as a little closer to the position of Eusebius. Others, e.g., Pierre de Labriolle, *La Réaction Paienne* (Paris, 1942), 150, and Schöpf, *Tötungsrecht*, 224, take the passage as a literal prediction of a Christian Empire.

26. Isaiah 2:4 (Micah 4:3); see above, n. 3.

to the letter, precisely at the time at which "in spirit" Israel according to the flesh was being replaced by the New People of God. The political spread of the Empire, moreover, parallels (and indeed mysteriously echoes and countenances) the spiritual spread of the churches of Christ. Yet, like that of any good Christian, the attitude of Origen towards the world and the political powers that be is necessarily dialectical. By asserting that Christians fight more effectively than soldiers when they pray for those who wage war in a "just" cause, he may, to be sure, have provided a model for later apologists of "the just war." The distinctly eschatological role which he assigns to the Empire may be seen as anticipating Eusebius and the whole political theology of the Byzantine East.[27] Yet his theology of politics has a negative as well as a positive aspect. Not only does Origen insist (in the same last book of *Contra Celsum*) that Roman magistrates who order Christians "to act contrary to the precepts enjoined by Jesus" ought to be resisted; he goes beyond this to point out that in such cases the Empire exhibits distinctly demonic characteristics: resistance to commands of this sort simply means that Christians "refuse to obey the demons who have been allotted the earth."[28]

The very first book, moreover, of *Contra Celsum* begins with the statement that Christians have a God-given right to break the Roman Laws against illicit associations. "For suppose," Origen argues, "that a man were living among the [savage] Scythians with their laws against nature, and that he had no opportunity to go elsewhere and were compelled to live among them: such a man would rightly form associations with like-minded people, even though this were against the laws of the Scythians." Indeed, Origen pursues, "just as it would be right for people to form associations to kill a tyrant, who had seized control of their city, so too—since the Devil and Falsehood reign as tyrants—Christians form associations, against the Devil, in opposition to his laws, in order to save others, whom they might persuade to abandon that law, which is like that of the Scythians or a tyrant."[29] Insofar, therefore, as it attempts to

27. Cadoux, *Early Christian Attitudes*, 134 ff. and 207 f. Morisi, *La Guerra nel pensiero*, 60; Schöpf, *Tötungsrecht*, 222 ff.; Daniélou, "La non-violence," 25. See above, nn. 5 and 17.

28. *Contra Celsum* 8.55, 4, 300; *GCS* 3, 272; Chadwick, 494. See the remarks by Ehrhardt, *Politische Metaphysik* 2.207 f.

29. *Contra Celsum* 1.1, 1, 78 ff.; *GCS* 2, 56; Chadwick, 7. For much of this paragraph, see Ehrhardt, *Politische Metaphysik* 2.204 ff.

force Christians to go against the Law of God, Roman Law becomes something worse than the laws of savages and tyrants. To be sure, such laws are not properly law at all: for Origen has borrowed from Stoicism and Middle Platonism the notion that positive laws which contravene natural law are not laws in any sense of the term.[30] But laws which attempt to force Christians "to act contrary to the precepts enjoined by Jesus" are even worse than the negation of law: they are instruments of "the demons who have been allotted the earth." For Christians to resist such laws is part of the general process of spiritual warfare in which they are, in any case, perpetually engaged. To rebel against the Empire and its illicit legislation means in such circumstances simply to fight the Devil and his Law.[31] If the Empire can be an instrument of Providence, it can under other circumstances become an instrument of the Devil. Like that of his Western contemporaries, Origen's theology of politics is distinctly dialectical.

Yet there is in this respect a certain difference in emphasis and style between East and West. Tertullian recognizes the providential and even eschatological role of the Roman Empire; but the militant opposition of the Empire—the "encampment of darkness" fighting under the "standards of the Devil"—to the Church—the "encampment of light" fighting under the standards of the Cross—remains a major manifestation of the cosmic struggle between the forces of good and evil.[32] For Origen, on the other hand, the theme of the demonic Empire is more in the background. It is subordinated at least to a certain extent to a form of spiritual warfare that has been internalized within the soul of the individual Christian.[33] The providential role of the Empire is, on the contrary, very much in the foreground of his theology of history: for the spread of the Empire echoes and countenances the spread of the Church. In this respect, Origen may be profitably contrasted with his slightly older Western contemporary, Hippolytus of Rome. To be sure, even Hippolytus is by no means one-sided; after all, he too remains

30. William A. Banner, "Origen and Natural Law," *Dumbarton Oaks Papers* 8 (1954) 51–84; Ehrhardt, *Politische Metaphysik* 2.218 f.

31. Above, nn. 28 and 29.

32. Above, chapter 2, n. 100.

33. The contrast is perhaps a little exaggerated by Ehrhardt, *Politische Metaphysik* 2.228 ff.; after all, even Origen believes that the Christian's spiritual warfare has an eschatological and therefore an ecclesiological and historical dimension; see above, chapter 1 at nn. 38–41.

a reasonably orthodox Christian. He believes with everyone else that obedience is due the Empire and all "the powers that be" and he offers a perfectly literal exegesis of Romans 13:1 ff.[34] Yet his more characteristic point of view is that of the Apocalypse. He still follows the ancient tradition which sees in the number of the beast a cryptogram for the word "Latin";[35] and he equates the Roman Empire with *anomia*, pure anarchy, or the simple negation of Law.[36] Indeed, in his most apocalyptic mood, he looks forward to the dissolution of the Empire into ten "democratic" states just before the end of the world: for the ten toes of the statue in the dream of Nebuchadnezzar in Daniel 2:42 represent the democracies which are soon to come.[37]

Unlike Origen, moreover, Hippolytus does not see in the coincidence of dates between the birth of Christ and the reign of Augustus evidence for the positive and indeed providential role of the Roman Empire; on this point his theology of history is in fact the exact counterpart of that of Origen. "While Christ was being born in the twelfth year of Augustus (under whom the Empire had its origin) and while the Lord was calling together all nations and all tongues and thus created the Faithful People, the People of the Christians," at the very same time, Hippolytus emphasizes, "the kingdom of this world, which rules through the power of Satan, aped this action of the Lord's in exact imitation, and—on its side—gathered together the most famous from all the peoples of the earth, gave them the name of 'Romans,' and prepared for war." Indeed, Hippolytus pursues, this is why the first census of the world took place under Augustus, precisely at the time of the birth of Christ, "so that the people of this world, who bear the inscription of

34. Hippolytus of Rome, *Eis ton Danila* 3.23 (*GCS* 1.1), 164 ff.

35. Hippolytus, *De Antichristo* 50 (*GCS* 1.2), 34. The same exegesis occurs already in Irenaeus, *Adversus Haereseos* 5.30.3 (*Sources Chrétiennes* 153), 380 ff. See Ehrhardt, *Politische Metaphysik*, 128 and n. 1. Most of the remainder of the paragraph is based on Ehrhardt's discussion, *Politische Metaphysik*, 125–33.

36. Hippolytus, *Eis ton Danila* 4.6 (*GCS* 1), 198. Ehrhardt, *Politische Metaphysik* 2.125 f.

37. *De Antichristo* 27 (*GCS* 1.2), 19; Ehrhardt, *Politische Metaphysik* 2.127; and Frend, *Martyrdom and Persecution*, 375. Frend, 376, assumes that this involves on the part of Hippolytus a certain sympathy for classical republicanism or for local institutions suppressed by Roman imperialism. Ehrhardt, at 127, n. 5, says that one cannot decide whether there is here any influence of the "democratic" attitudes assumed by much of the philosophical opposition in Rome. Or is it rather that Hippolytus' hatred for Rome is so great that he wishes not only its destruction through division but the utterly shameful decadence of the lowest of all possible forms of government?

the earthly king, should be called 'Romans,' while those who believe in the King of Heaven and bear upon their forehead the sign of victory over death should be called 'Christians.'"[38]

The contrast with Origen is almost too good to be true. For Origen, "Jesus was born under Augustus" because at that time "God was preparing the nations for His teaching by submitting them all" to a universal Empire.[39] The *Pax Romana* was both a foreshadowing and shadow of the spread of the Church. To that extent at least the Empire was both providential and indeed a sacramental imitation (albeit a rather distant and external imitation) of the Church. For Hippolytus, on the other hand, the imitation is not providential; it is sacrilegious aping. The Empire imitates the Church, yes; but precisely in the fashion in which at the beginning the Devil tried to imitate God, and in which at the end Antichrist will attempt once more to simulate Christ. The Empire is not a pale and imperfect echo of, and an unwitting instrument for, the Church. It is the anti-Church. Origen is a self-conscious member of the Church of the Gentiles, and, in his way, a proud participant of the Hellenic world, even perhaps a reasonably contented citizen of the Roman Empire. Hippolytus of Rome, though perhaps not exactly a Jewish Christian, is filled with the apocalyptic expectations of late Judaism and Jewish Christianity, even more than Tertullian. Perhaps, in the East, Christianity left the ghetto at an early enough date so that a Gentile self-consciousness developed in counterpoint to the remnants of Jewish Christianity; while in the West, far removed from the events of Judaea, and where Christians remained, in most regions, a much smaller minority, such a polarization never took place.[40]

Origen and Hippolytus are Christians; they are not Manicheans. This is why Hippolytus can hold that the Empire is essentially a demonic power and yet without schizophrenia remind the faithful that they must obey "the powers that be." Similarly, this is why Origen can assign to the Roman Empire a providential, eschatological, and indeed ecclesiological function and yet believe that when it opposes the Law of God the

38. Hippolytus, *Eis ton Danila* 4.9 (*GCS* 1.1), 206. My rendering is largely based on the German translation by Peterson in "Der Monotheismus," 85 (Peterson himself closely follows Bonwetsch's translation in the *GCS*). It was Peterson who first noted the contrast between this citation of Hippolytus and the passage from Origen in *Contra Celsum* 2.30.

39. Above, n. 17.

40. See the similar ideas in Frend, *Martyrdom and Persecution*, passim.

Empire is a direct representative of the Devil. For Christians, after all, unlike Manicheans, the Devil too is unwittingly a Servant of the Lord. Contemporaneously with Origen, the Pseudo-Clementine Homilies, which, though containing obvious Gnostic strains, can on occasion be taken as witnessing the tradition of the Great Church, make the point in very striking terms. In fairly traditional phraseology, Pseudo-Clement sharply opposes two kingdoms, the Kingdom of Christ and the Kingdom of Satan. Both Kingdoms, however, were established through the ordinance of Heaven; for the Devil "has been chosen by God to rule by means of law over the present and transitory world, his nature being such that he rejoices in the destruction of the wicked." The Kingdom of Satan can therefore be equated with "the kingdom of those who are now kings upon the earth."[41] Like the Devil, the kings of the earth have been appointed to punish the crimes of the wicked by means of worldly law. Like the Devil, pagan kings may not acknowledge the power of the Most High; but like him they are nevertheless God's servants. Thus, even when the powers that be are seen as servants of the Devil, they nevertheless remain the ministers of God. The corollary is that insofar as these ministers of God do not acknowledge their total dependence on the Most High, they remain potentially the servants of the Devil.

So far Origen's political ecclesiology has been examined largely from the vantage point of the theology of history contained in *Contra Celsum.* Theology of history normally tends to be eschatological in outlook. Insofar as that eschatology is "realized" or present-minded, it tends to look at everything from the point of view of the triumph of Christ; insofar as that eschatology is "consequent" or futuristic, it tends, on the contrary, to look at everything from the point of view of a still virulent struggle between Christ and the Devil. As a result, the dialectical relationship between Church and world tends either to be exaggerated and transformed into antithesis or, on the contrary, to be mitigated and transformed in accordance with an incarnational pattern. In the first case, Empire and Church are opposed not only as Old Creation is to New Dispensation but as Devil is to God. In the second, the Empire functions

41. *Pseudo-Clementine Homilies* 20 [K] 2 (*GCS* 42), 268 f.: I have used the translation by Per Beskow, *The Kingship of Christ in the Early Church* (Stockholm, 1963), 245 f. On the general significance and relative orthodoxy of these Homilies, and particularly on their political ideas, see the excellent discussion, ibid., 242–57.

rather as the sacramental penumbra, the image or reflection of the Church; it is assigned the role of outer and fleshly hull to the Church's inner and spiritual core.[42] When Origen in *Contra Celsum* is writing as an anti-pagan polemicist, the stance which he adopts is naturally that of the first, "exaggerated," or antithetical type, an attitude which, as has been seen, is actually less typical of Origen than of his Western contemporaries. On the contrary, when as is more frequent, Origen's tone in *Contra Celsum* is that of the apologist, the emphasis is more on a rapprochement between Empire and Church: the dialectical pattern adopted then tends to be of the "mitigated" or incarnational type.

Origen's theology of politics finds expression, however, not only in *Contra Celsum*, but also in his exegetical works, particularly in his exegesis of the two main political passages of the New Testament: Romans 13:1 ff., "Let every soul be subject to the higher powers," and Matthew 22:21, "Render therefore unto Caesar, the things which are Caesar's." Here the political dialectic is neither exaggerated nor mitigated, but resembles the balanced dialectic of the Pauline circle. In these exegetical passages (which are neither polemical nor apologetic) the state is not seen as demonic nor as a reflection of the Christ-event. The state, to be sure, is still conceived as both helping and hindering the work of the Church and its purpose as ultimately determined by God. Yet its functions remain, so to speak, on a natural—one might even say on a secular—plane. From that perspective, the powers that be are, to use an expression that goes back to the fourth-century Council of Antioch, essentially *exterae potestates*, "external powers," powers that are neither demonic nor closely intertwined with the Christ-event but simply external to the Church;[43] or in the pregnant words of

42. On the contrast between Albert Schweitzer's "consequent" and Dodd's "realized" eschatology and their reconciliation in much of contemporary biblical scholarship, see the excellent historiographical presentation by Norman Perrin, *The Kingdom of God in the Teaching of Jesus* (London, 1963).

43. *Council of Antioch* (341), canon 5, Mansi *Sacrorum Conciliorum Nova et Amplissima Collectio* (Florence, 1759–97), vol. 2, 1131 f. The canon was received at Chalcedon and has thus been edited in modern times; see Eduard Schwartz, *Acta Conciliorum Oecumenicorum* 2.1.2 (Berlin, 1933), Chalcedon *Actio* III, canon 90, 118.90. The crucial Greek phrase is *dia tēs exōthen exousias hōs stasiōdē auton epistrephesthai*. See the late fifth-century Latin translation in the *Collectio Canonum* of Dionysius Exiguus, Mansi *Concilia*, vol. 2, 1322: "Si quis presbyter . . . episcopum proprium contemnens se ab ecclesia sequestravit . . . et commonenti episcopo . . . nec consentire vel obedire voluerit . . . tamquam seditiosus per potestates exteras opprimatur."

Irenaeus in the second century, powers that "have been appointed by God for the utility of the Gentiles."[44] From that "secular" point of view, "the powers that be" are indeed "ministers of God"; yet they remain "gentile" powers, essentially foreign to the People of God. No doubt, good Christians would be murdered in their beds, or at least deprived of all the necessities of life, if such powers had not been appointed to lord it over the kingdoms of the Gentiles—just as Jews in northern climes would freeze to death during the winter sabbath had they not their Gentiles to light their fires for them.[45] From that perspective, both powers, the Christian power of the bishops within the Church and the Gentile power, the power of kings without, are equally necessary; both have been established by God, the one through Christ, the other through the original act of creation of the world. Yet the royal power is not seen as either in the sacramental penumbra of the Church or as a demonic entity in the darkness without; it is seen instead as an essentially pre-Christian, "secular," power appointed primarily for the utility of those who do not yet belong—or at least do not yet fully belong—to the People of God.

That this sort of cool and balanced dialectic should come to the fore in Origen's exegesis of Romans 13:1 ff. and Matthew 22:21 is perhaps not surprising: for it may well be argued that this "secular" view of the state was, in fact, the one intended by Jesus or Matthew and quite possibly also the one intended by Paul in Romans.[46] Origen, in any event, explicitly interprets Romans 13:1 ff. by means of Matthew 22:21, so that for

---

Note the role that the fifth canon of Antioch (in the rendition of Dionysius Exiguus) played in the Investiture Controversy, e.g., Manegold of Lautenbach, *Ad Geberhardum* 33, *MGH. LdL.*1, 369 f. Note that in a letter of the sixth-century Pope Pelagius I (559–63) the "external power" (*exōthen exousia*) of the fifth canon of Antioch or the *exterae potestates* of Dionysius are rendered by *saeculares potestates:* see Henricus Denzinger and Adolfus Schönmetzer, *Enchiridion Symbolorum Definitionum et Declarationum de rebus fidei et morum* (Barcelona, 1963), 157.447.

44. Irenaeus, *Adversus Haereseos* 5.24.2, ed. W. W. Harvey (Cambridge, 1857), vol. 2, 389: "Ad utilitatem ergo gentilium terrenum regnum positum est a Deo: sed non a diabolo, qui numquam omnino quietus est, imo qui nec ipsa quidem gentes vult in tranquillo agere; ut timentes regnum hominum, non se alterutrum homines vice piscium consummant, sed per legum positiones repercutiant multiplicem gentilium injustitiam." Note the distinctly embarrassed attempt by Werner Affeldt, *Die Weltliche Gewalt in der Paulus-Exegese* (Göttingen, 1969), 41, to gloss away the "pagan" nature of the state in the passage: in contrast, see the excellent discussion by Ehrhardt, *Politische Metaphysik* 2.113 f.

45. Cf. above, chapter 2 at nn. 71, 75–79, and also at n. 150.

46. See, for instance, Oscar Cullmann, *The State in the New Testament* (New York, 1956), 55–70.

him the Pauline text becomes an authority for the radical distinction between Church and state. The matter, however, is complicated by the fact that Origen's exegesis of Matthew 22:21 has to be put together from at least four separate and apparently contradictory passages: his brief remarks in margin of his interpretation of Romans 13:1 ff. in the Commentary on Romans; a lengthy exegesis of Matthew 22:21 in its proper place in the Commentary on Matthew (to which may be added a short appendix in which Origen rehearses without endorsing a quite different and apparently traditional interpretation of the same passage); a relatively brief commentary on the Lucan parallel to Matthew 22:21 (: Luke 20:25) in his Homilies on Luke; and finally his exegesis of the pericope of the Temple Tax (i.e., the episode of the coin found in the mouth of a fish in Matthew 17:24 ff.), a pericope which Origen tends to equate with the payment of tribute to Caesar in Matthew 22:21.[47]

Origen's exegesis of Romans 13:1 ff., though it interlocks with his exegesis of Matthew 22:21, is relatively autonomous. In the Commentary on Romans, Origen's first remarks on the beginning of the verse, "Let every soul be subject to the higher powers," concentrate on Paul's use of the word "soul"; the Apostle, he notes, says that it is the "*soul*" that is subject to the powers that be, "for he would never have said, 'let every *spirit* be subject to the higher powers.' "[48] Origen's exegesis here is clearly influenced by the trichotomous anthropology, which he borrowed in part from Paul, and according to which man was divided not simply into body and soul but into body, soul, and spirit. In the social theology of the school of Alexandria, the lower part of man, the body, corresponded to the so-called hylics (from *hylē*, "matter"), men who remained essentially material, that is to say primarily pagans or Jews; the inter-

47. *Com. Rom.* 9.25, 1226C, below at n. 51; *Com. Mat.* 17.25–27, 653–661, below, nn. 61–65; ibid., 17.28, 661–663, below, n. 66; *Hom. Luc.* 39, 219–221, below, nn. 67 and 68; *Com. Mat.* 13.10–13, 206–213, below, nn. 89–94 and 97–100. See also *Hom. Ez.* 13.2, 445, below, n. 95. All these passages are discussed though rather briefly and from a different perspective in the excellent study by Henri Crouzel, *Théologie de L'Image de Dieu chez Origène* (*Etudes publiées sous la direction de la Faculté de Théologie S. J. de Lyon-Fourvière* 34; Paris, 1956), 193–96.

48. Origen, *Com. Rom.* 9.25, 1226B: "Videamus ergo nunc quid etiam in consequentibus adjungat Apostolus 'Omnis potestatibus sublimioribus subjaceat.' Videtur mihi in hoc valde laudabiliter animam nominasse quam subjacere potestatibus jubet. Numquam enim dixisset, 'omnis spiritus subjaceat potestati' sed 'omnis anima.' De qua differentia saepe jam diximus, quod interdum per animam, interdum per carnem, interdum per spiritum, homo nominatur . . . ." For this exegesis of Origen's, see also Affeldt, *Die weltliche Gewalt in der Paulus-Exegese*, 43–53.

mediate part, or soul, corresponded to a second class of men, the "psychics," essentially the average Christians—the simpler folk—who were more or less capable of salvation, but to whom the higher mysteries were closed; finally, the highest part or "spirit" corresponded to the highest class of men, the "pneumatics," that is to say the ascetic intellectual elite, the saints who alone were capable of reaching these mysteries.[49] Thus Paul, according to Origen, would never have said that every "spirit" should be "subject to the higher powers." Indeed, Origen pursues, if we are the sort of "spirituals," the sort of "pneumatics" who are so "joined unto the Lord that we are one spirit with Him" (1 Corinthians 6:17), we are said to be subject to the Lord. But if we are not yet such, but still share the common "soul," that has within itself something of the "world," then the precept of Paul must be followed and we are obliged to subject ourselves to the powers that be.[50]

Origen then briefly notes that this distinction between "soul" and "spirit" is the equivalent of the distinction between "Caesar" and "God" and that Matthew 22:21 thus helps explain Romans 13:1 ff.; for in Matthew the Lord Himself has taught that

> hi qui habent in se superscriptionem Caesaris, reddant Caesari quae sunt Caesaris. Petrus et Johannes nihil habebant quod Caesari redderent; dicit enim Petrus: 'Aurum et argentum non habeo.' Qui hoc non habet, nec Caesari habet quod reddat, nec unde sublimioribus subjaceat potestatibus. Qui vero habet aut pecuniam aut possessiones, aut aliquid in saeculo negotii, audiat: 'Omnis anima potestatibus sublimioribus subjaceat.'[51]

Those who bear in the coinage of their person Caesar's inscription should render unto Caesar the things which are Caesar's. According to the pericope in Acts 3:1 ff., however, Peter and John had nothing which they could render unto Caesar: this is why Peter said in Acts 3:6, "Gold and silver have I none." Indeed, who has no gold or silver has nothing to render unto Caesar and nothing by means of which he might be subject to

49. See Daniélou, "L'Unité des Deux Testaments," 29; also above, chapter 2 at nn. 23–38.

50. Origen, *Com. Rom.* 9.25, 1226C: ". . . Et si quidem tales sumus qui conjuncti Domino unus cum eo spiritus simus Domino dicimur esse subjecti. Si vero nondum tales sumus, sed communis adhuc anima est in nobis quae habeat aliquid hujus mundi, quae sit ei aliquo alligata negotio, huic praecepta Apostolus ponit, et dicit ut subjecta sit potestatibus mundi: quia et Dominus dixit, ut hi . . . [see below in text] . . . subjaceat."

51. Ibid. See Crouzel, *Théologie de l'Image*, 194.

the higher powers. Who, however, has money or possessions (or anything that pertains to the business of this world) should listen to Saint Paul: "Let every soul be subject to the higher powers."

Someone, Origen pursues, might well object: "What? That power, which persecutes the servants of God, makes war upon the faith and subverts all religion, is supposed to come from God?" The answer, however, is simple. Everyone knows that the powers of the body, such as sight, hearing, and indeed all senses, are gifts from God, yet it lies within the province of human freedom to use them for either good or evil; indeed, this is why God justly punishes their misuse. In the same way, the power of earthly rulers is given unto them, in the words of 1 Peter 2:14, "for the punishment of evildoers and for the praise of them that do well." Those who execute the power which they have received, not in accordance with the divine command but in accordance with their own impiety, fall therefore unto the just judgment of God.[52] When Paul forbids resistance, Origen provisionally concludes, this prohibition must not therefore be understood to apply to the powers insofar as they persecute the faith (for in such cases we must, in the words of Acts 5:29, "obey God rather than men") but only to the powers in "the ordinary, common exercise of their functions," or in the words of Romans 13:4, when it is indeed the case that "rulers are not a terror to good works but to the evil."[53]

This restrictive conclusion, however, is merely provisional. What is so striking, Origen continues, every time he rereads the passage, is that Saint Paul should call the worldly power

52. Ibid., 9.26, 1226 f.: " 'Non est enim,' inquit, 'potestas, nisi a Deo.' Dicit fortasse aliquis: 'Quid ergo? Et illa potestas, quae servos Dei persequitur, fidem impugnat, religionem subvertit, a Deo est?' Ad hoc breviter respondebimus. Nemo est qui nesciat quod et visus nobis a Deo donatus est, et auditus, et sensus. Cum ergo a Deo habeamus haec, in potestate tamen nostra est ut visu vel ad bona vel ad mala utamur: similiter et auditu, et motu manuum, et cogitatione sensus: et in hoc est justum judicium Dei quod his quae ille ad usus bonos dedit, nos abutimur ad impia et iniqua ministeria. Ita ergo et potestas omnis a Deo data est 'ad vindictam quidem malorum, laudem vero bonorum,' sicut idem Apostolus in subsequentibus dicit. Erit autem justum judicium Dei erga eos qui acceptam potestatem secundum suas impietates et non secundum divinas temperant leges."

53. Ibid., 9.27, 1227B: "Et ideo dicit: 'Itaque qui resistit potestati, Dei ordinationi resistit; qui autem resistunt, ipsi sibi damnationem acquirunt.' Non hic de illis potestatibus dicit quae persecutiones inferunt fidei; ibi enim dicendum est: 'Deo oportet obtemperare magis quam hominibus,' sed de istis communibus dicit 'quae non sunt timori boni operis, sed mali'; quibus utique qui resistit, ipse sibi damnationem pro gestorum suorum qualitate conquirit."

and the judges of this earth "the ministers of God": and that not just once but two or three times! Yet, once more, how is it possible for the judge of this world to be the minister of God? Origen suggests another solution: the Apostolic Council, he notes, enjoins Gentile Christians (and therefore those whom Origen is addressing) to do no more than to abstain "from meats offered to idols and from blood and from things strangled and from fornication" (Acts 15:29). What then about murder, adultery, theft, sodomy, and other crimes normally punished by all laws whether human or divine? Are Christians given license to commit these abominations?[54]

Sed vide ordinationem Spiritus sancti: quoniam quidem caetera crimina saeculi legibus vindicantur et superfluum videbatur esse ea nunc divina lege prohiberi, quae sufficienter humana lege plectuntur; illa sola de quibus nihil humana lex dixerat et quae religioni videbantur convenire decernit. Ex quo apparet judicem mundi partem maximam Dei legis implere. Omnia enim crimina quae vindicari vult Deus, non per antistites et principes Ecclesiarum sed per mundi judicem voluit vindicari; et hoc sciens Paulus recte eum ministrum Dei nominat et vindicem in eum qui quod malum est agit.[55]

But behold the ordination of the Holy Spirit! Since other crimes are avenged by the laws of this world, it seemed superfluous to forbid them through divine law, when they were already sufficiently punished through the legislation of men. The Apostolic Decree therefore determined only such matters as were not dealt with by human law and which seemed to pertain particularly to affairs of religion. From all this it follows that it is the judge of this world who executes the major part of the law of God. For God did not want all the crimes for which He wished to extract vengeance to be punished by the bishops and princes of the Church, but by the judges of this world. In

54. Ibid., 9.28, 1227 f.: ". . . 'Dei enim minister est' . . . . Movet me in his sermonibus Paulus quod potestatem saeculi et judicem mundi Dei ministrum dicit; et hoc non semel, sed secundo et tertio repetit. Velim ergo requirere quomodo judex mundi Dei minister sit. Invenimus scriptum in Actibus Apostolorum, quia convenientes in unum apostoli statuerunt decreta quae observare deberemus nos qui ex gentibus credidimus Christo. . . . In his . . . praeceptis in quibus dicit nihil amplius imponendum esse oneris his, qui ex gentibus credunt, nisi ut abstineant se ab his quae idolis immolantur, et sanguine, et suffocatis et fornicatione, neque homicidium prohibetur, neque adulterium, neque furtum, neque masculorum concubitus, neque caetera crimina quae divinis et humanis legibus puniuntur. Quod si illa sola quae supra memoravit, observanda dicit esse Christianis, videbitur eis de caeteris dedisse licentiam. Sed vide ordinationem . . . [see below, next note] . . . quod malum est agit."

55. Ibid., 1228B.

knowledge of this, Paul rightly, therefore, calls the latter "the minister of God and a revenger to execute wrath upon him that doeth evil."

Having thus shown that "the judges of this world" are ministers of God, while yet sharply distinguishing their function from that of "the bishops and princes of the Church," Origen can now conclude his whole exegesis by coming back once more to the problem of resistance and by presenting to the Roman authorities what is in effect an affidavit for Christian nonsubversion. Paul, he notes, emphasizes in Romans 13:5 that "ye must needs be subject, not only for wrath, but also for conscience sake." By these words, the Apostle

> ordinat . . . Ecclesiam Dei, ut nihil adversi principibus et potestatibus saeculi gerens per quietem et tranquillitatem vitae opus justitiae et pietatis exerceat. Si enim ponamus, verbi gratia, credentes Christo potestatibus saeculi non esse subjectos, tributa non reddere . . . nulli timorem, nulli honorem deferre, nonne per haec rectorum et principum merito in semetipsos arma converterent et persecutores quidem suos excusabiles semetipsos vero culpabiles facerent?[56]

Paul, therefore, so ordained the Church of God that attempting nothing that was hostile against the princes and powers of the world it might carry out its work of righteousness and godliness through a quiet and peaceable life. For suppose, by way of hypothesis, that those who believe in Christ were not subject to the secular powers, did not pay tribute, offered fear to no one and honor to no one, would they not through such behavior rightly turn upon themselves the weapons of these regents and princes and absolve their persecutors while condemning their own persons?

In both patristic and medieval exegesis, this strictly literal approach is the customary way of dealing with the Epistles of Saint Paul. The Pauline corpus contains little that is either history or parables: it therefore does not lend itself with ease to allegorical interpretation.[57] As a result, Origen's exegesis of Romans 13:1 ff. seems perfectly literal and straightforward, at least on the surface. Nevertheless, several points need explaining even at this preliminary stage.

56. Ibid., 9.29, 1229: "'Ideo necesse est subditos esse non solum propter iram sed et propter conscientiam' . . . . Ordinat . . . [as in text] . . . facerent." At ibid., 9.30, Origen shifts to a tropological exegesis of Romans 13:7 f. that is not relevant in this context.

57. See de Lubac, *Exégèse Médiévale*, vol. 1.2, 668 ff.

First, there is the matter of the last paragraph: at first sight it may seem a little obscure. The key to its understanding is provided, however, by 1 Timothy 2:1 ff.: "I exhort therefore that first of all supplications, prayers, intercessions and giving of thanks be made for all men: for kings and for all that are in authority; that we may lead a peaceable life in all godliness and chastity [*ut quietam et tranquillam vitam agamus in omni pietate et castitate*]."[58] Origen's exegesis of Romans 13:5 ("ye must needs be subject not only for wrath, but also for conscience sake") thus combines Paul's injunction about "tribute," "honor," and "subjection" in Romans 13:6 with the supposedly Pauline decree in 1 Timothy 2:1 ff. As a result, the whole of Romans 13:1 ff. thus becomes an affidavit for nonsubversion. Here in his conclusion Origen seems to combine the two alternatives which he had distinguished elsewhere in his exegesis. The Christian must obey the powers that be—"and that not only for wrath, but also for conscience sake"—"in the ordinary common exercise of their functions" because insofar as "the judges of this world" exercise the power actually given unto them from on high they are indeed the ministers of God. But even if the state authorities "execute the powers which they have received not in accordance with divine law but in accordance with their own impiety" and persecute the faith, active resistance is strictly forbidden; even though in such cases the powers that be do not function as ministers of God, at least in the strict sense of the word "minister." Christians must not return evil for evil; in fact, subversion or active resistance of the Zealot type on the part of the Church would only result in absolving the powers of their guilt and in transferring that guilt unto the heads of the faithful. The ideal of nonresistance is so important that "to attempt nothing that is hostile against the princes and powers of this world" was built into the very order of the Church. When the powers that be act "in the ordinary, common exercise of their function," the Church will praise these powers as "ministers of God"; but even when state authorities subvert the powers which they have received, the Church (which belongs to the Spirit) will not share in that subversion by indulging in material resistance.

Second, at least as a tentative hypothesis, the trichotomous anthropology which opens Origen's exegesis should probably

58. Rufinus in his translation seems to have followed a New Testament text that is at least very close to the Vulgate; see the citations quoted in the preceding notes.

be connected with the comparison between the powers that be and the powers of the body that immediately follows, as well as with the contrast between Church and state, which informs the whole of the remainder of his commentary. Those who still share the "common soul" that has within itself "something of the world" must subject themselves to the powers that be: but if this is true of the common folk of "psychic" Christians who have kept within themselves only "something of the 'world'," all the more must this be the case of the mass of "hylic" unbelievers who are altogether outside the Church. The non-Christian is totally subject to the hylic or material power of the state, which is rightly compared to the powers of the body; the psychic Christian is subject to that power to the extent that his "soul" (which defines him, just as the body defines the pagan and the spirit defines the pneumatic) has kept within itself "something of the world," that is, to the extent that he has been unable to abandon all possessions or is still capable of the sort of crime which is punished by the laws of the state; the pneumatic saint, who at baptism or later has truly become a son of the Church and given up everything that belongs to the world, is totally freed from all such subjection. As will be seen below, from Origen's exegesis of Matthew 17:24 and 22:21, this simple contrast between psychic and pneumatic does not really correspond to the inner reaches of his thought; yet here in the Commentary on Romans the psychic or half-worldling does seem to mediate between the pagan and the true pneumatic.

Third, even in the Commentary on Romans there is an apparent contradiction insofar as the problem of resistance is concerned. In the first half of his exegesis, Origen seems to suggest that resistance is forbidden against the powers that be in "the ordinary, common exercise" of their functions; but that when the powers of the state engage in persecution, Christians should remember that they must "obey God rather than man." Later, on the other hand, he indicates that resistance on the part of Christians—even in the face of persecution—is as serious a crime as persecution on the part of pagans. At one level, of course, the apparent contradiction can be easily resolved. Passive resistance (leading to martyrdom) is a duty, for it is God who must be obeyed rather than man: this sort of resistance to the hylic power of the state frees even the psychic from the shackles of the world and through martyrdom allows him to reach the status of pneumatic. Active resistance, on the other hand, is a sin for all Christians, since it is precisely because the Church would be defiled by the use of force that state power remains necessary even under the New Dispensation. Recourse to material force, as a matter of fact, turns the pneumatic, filled with zeal for the Kingdom of God, into a judaizing Zealot, in somewhat the same way as the persecution of God's People turns the "useful" Gentile—the minister of God—into a pervert who has subverted the power with which he has been entrusted. At the beginning of his exegesis, Origen posits the psychic or half-worlding as mediating between the Gentile and the true pneumatic. Yet at the end of that exegesis, the pneumatic has been transformed into a Zealot and the Gentile power of the state from the minister into the persecutor of God; while somewhat unaccountably the psychic—and not the pneumatic—has been transformed into the orthodox Christian equally opposed to both forms of violence. How this transformation has been accomplished will become clear only from Origen's exegesis of Matthew 17:24 and Matthew 22:21.

The fourth, and by far most important, point has to do with Origen's use of Matthew 22:21 ("Render unto Caesar . . ."). On the surface, his exegesis here is limited to a few very brief remarks. Very early in his commentary, the distinction between the "soul" of Romans 13:1 and the "spirit" of the trichotomous system of anthropology is equated with the distinction between Caesar and God. Through the intermediary of Acts 3:6 ("Gold and silver have I none"), that duality is then transformed into an opposition between possessions and absolute poverty. This transformation too may seem a little puzzling: as will be seen below, it must ultimately be understood in terms of Origen's exegesis of the pericope of the Temple Tax (Matthew 17:24 ff.) and of his equation of that pericope with the pericope of Matthew 22:21.[59] On the surface the point is a rather limited one. Those who have money or possessions must pay taxes; those who have understood Christ's counsel of perfection and practice absolute poverty have nothing "to render unto Caesar." For the remainder of the exegesis, Matthew 22:21 disappears from the foreground of Origen's thought.

Nevertheless, even at this stage one receives the impression that, below the surface, the parallelism which Origen sees between Romans 13:1 ff. and Matthew 22:21 is a thread that colors the whole texture of his exegesis. The Pauline text is for

59. Below at nn. 97–105.

once devoid of dualities of any kind; yet from the moment that Origen introduces the distinction between God and Caesar, his exegesis becomes a commentary on a whole series of disjunctions, all of which are simply a reflection of the distinction between Church and state. Where do these dualities and that distinction come from if not from Matthew 22:21? The point is perhaps least clear in the philosophical excursus which forms the second part of Origen's exegesis. Here he distinguishes not between Church and state but between power as such and the misuse of that power on the part of those who hold it. Nevertheless, already here Origen's purpose obviously is the necessary mediation between God and world. Having, to all appearances, established in the first section that Christians who are already perfected owe nothing to Caesar, Origen in the second and third sections of his exegesis is faced with the problem that many a Christian will oppose world to Church as persecutor is opposed to persecuted: how then can the worldly power be the minister of God? In this section, the problem of ministeriality is solved by the distinction between power and its use and the analogy of the powers of the body. The third section, on the other hand, is directly governed by the distinction between Church and state. Here too, Origen begins with the antithesis between God and world: "but how is it possible for the judge of this world to be the minister of God?" The paradox here is solved through a series of intermediate dualities. Divine Law, to be sure, is radically distinct from human law and the "bishops and princes of the Church" are radically distinct from "the judges of this world": yet the disjunction is the result not so much of demonic resistance on the part of the world as of God's own decision to restrict the jurisdiction of His Church to "matters pertaining particularly to affairs of religion." God Himself distinguished between Church and state. Insofar as the world resists the ordinance of God, it is in opposition to Him and, since the Coming of Christ, in opposition to the Church. Yet both world and Church were created by God through His Word; in Him they are ultimately united. Christ's distinction in Matthew 22:21 thus confirms God's ordinance (while the act of self-denial by the Apostolic Council confirms that distinction on the part of the Church) and mediates between that unity and that opposition. Finally, though in a less obvious way, the disjunction between Church and state remains the organizing theme for the fourth and final section of

Origen's exegesis. Nonresistance to persecution (which is thought of as characteristic of orthodox Christianity) is equally opposed to two parallel forms of violence, which are in effect two parallel forms of usurpation: actual usurpation on the part of the pagan state which prevents the worship of the One True God and thus interferes "in matters which pertain particularly to affairs of religion"; and hypothetical usurpation on the part of a church indulging in Zealot "heresy," since the Church unlike the state is restricted to a life of "peace and quiet" and thus may not engage in active resistance even to persecution.

For Origen, the whole of Romans 13:1 ff. thus becomes an authority for the thoroughgoing, though in no sense antagonistic, distinction between Church and state. There are hints that the ministeriality of the state remains paradoxical because of the eschatological opposition between God and world. This antithetical dimension remains, however, very much in the background and is overshadowed by Origen's emphasis on the ministerial nature of the state. Church and state are here depicted as essentially parallel structures, both equally part of a hierarchy that culminates in God, Who established both as His servants. While the two are sharply distinguished, there is no explicit emphasis on the contrast between their methods or functions. On the surface therefore Church and state do not in this context act as poles of a dialectical dyad. On the contrary, they seem to function rather as a set of twins: what Lévi-Strauss has called a dioscuric pair. At the explicit level at least, in Origen's exegesis of Romans 13:1 ff., both equally mediate between God and the crimes committed in this world. The Church is the minister of God for the punishment of crimes dealing with "affairs of religion"; the state is the divinely appointed avenger for all other crimes. As Lévi-Strauss has pointed out, however, such dioscuric pairs usually conceal a strongly dialectical element:[60] in this case the ambivalence in the relationship between Church and world. In the present context, Origen only hints at this ambivalence: but because of this ambivalence the ministeriality of the worldly power remains a paradox.

Below the surface, moreover, it is clear that Church and state are not in truth parallel structures. For while the state's

60. See, for instance, Lévi-Strauss, *The Raw and the Cooked*, 333, and *L'Homme Nu*, 190 ff., 205 f., and 211 f.

negative role as an avenger of crimes is for Origen, as indeed for all the Fathers, its essential and perhaps indeed only function, the same is not true of the Church. On the contrary, the negative or coercive function of the Church is only a minor and in a sense paradoxical aspect of its redemptive or life-giving role. But in Origen's exegesis of Romans 13:1 ff., only that negative aspect comes to the fore. Both the ambivalent nature of the ministeriality of the state and the essentially redemptive nature of the Church's functions remain therefore very much in the background. This is why on the surface Church and state can take on the appearance of parallel structures. From this deliberately limited point of view, the functions of both Church and state have been determined by the same Providence. This is why the functions of the state (and in an odd way even the functions of the Church) are in this context seen from an essentially "secular" viewpoint: for this is what happens when the redemptive nature of the Church and of the Christ-event, as well as the demonic aspects of both world and state, are not allowed to play a commanding role. The state is therefore seen as "an external power," strictly separate from the Church, with functions that are neither demonic nor redemptive, but "appointed by God for the utility of the Gentiles" or at least for the utility of those "psychic" Christians who have not yet reached the pneumatic perfection of absolute poverty and freedom from sin. Church and state collaborate in fulfilling the commands of Providence; but the ideal relation between the two is, for Origen, patterned not so much on a concordat as on a pact of nonaggression. This sort of Christian "secularism" is in no sense atheistic: the functions of both Church and state have, after all, been determined by Divine Providence. But with both Christ and the Devil provisionally eliminated, Providence becomes a rather abstract concept: the God Who assigns parallel functions to His "ministers" is the natural God of Aristotle, and of Plato, the God of the Philosophers, far more than the God of Abraham, of Isaac, of Jacob—and of Jesus. Below the surface, however, this cool and detached parallelism is, of course, highly precarious: for the demonic aspects of the world and the radically redemptive nature of the Christ-event can never be fully suppressed within a Christian structure. This is why, even on the surface, "divine" and "human law," "affairs of religion" and "affairs of state," "the princes and bishops of the Church" and "the judges of this world" are so carefully balanced against one another. The stylistic dualism reflects the fact that the dialectical relation between world and Christ-event, though not allowed to control the foreground of Origen's exegesis, is nevertheless felt as playing an essential role behind the scene. Exactly how foreground and backdrop are reconciled, however, is not fully evident at this particular point.

For the moment the important point to remember is that this sort of balanced parallelism must be attributed to the influence of Matthew 22:21 with its dualism between God and Caesar: for, as has been noted, Romans 13:1 ff. is devoid of binary pairs of any kind. This preliminary conclusion is confirmed, moreover, by a careful examination of Origen's actual exegesis of the pericope from Matthew. As has been seen, Matthew 22:21 is analyzed twice in its proper place in the Commentary on Matthew; once in the Homilies on Luke as part of Origen's exegesis of the Lucan parallel to Matthew 22:21; and finally as part of Origen's exegesis of the pericope of the Temple Tax (Matthew 17:24 ff.); and in all these places Origen's interpretation seems at first sight quite nonpolitical, having nothing to do with the distinction between Church and state. Nevertheless, a closer analysis will reveal that these various exegeses are structurally equivalent to the political interpretation of Romans 13:1 ff.; and that the cool and "secular" dualism which impregnates the latter is in fact kept in balance by a whole series of more basic and nonpolitical dualities (such as, for instance, that between God and the Devil, soul and body, the Divinity and the Humanity of Christ), which in the exegesis of Romans 13:1 ff. do not appear at all or are present only in submerged fashion, but which become fully manifest in the parallel passages.

The discussion may properly begin with a presentation of Origen's own exegesis—as distinct from the traditional exegesis which he only rehearses in a sort of appendix—in its proper place in the Commentary on Matthew. On the surface at least, that exegesis is strictly tropological. Origen begins, to be sure, with a curiously lengthy and very carefully built introduction: the Pharisees and Herodians who sought out the Lord and tried to "entangle him in talk" at the beginning of the pericope in Matthew 22:15 ff. provide, in fact, an occasion for a masterly essay on the political situation in Judaea at the time of Christ. Much of the detail comes clearly from Josephus, but the analysis seems Origen's own. The essay begins with the typical remark that at that time "the Jews had their own way of life or state [*politeia*] of their own" and that according to the Law that *politeia* had to be kept strictly separate from that of all other nations.[61] The problem of tribute to the Romans was therefore a serious issue and divided the Jews among themselves. The Pharisees, according to Origen, had opted for the Zealot policy of tax rebellion and out of zeal for the Law refused to pay tribute and to call the Emperor "Lord":[62] the Herodians, on the other hand, rejected this policy on practical grounds, and because they collaborated with Caesar were nicknamed "Caesarians" by the Pharisees. Christ, however, was not "entangled" and refused to take sides. This, according to Origen, is the literal meaning of the text, its *voluntas loci* (Gr.: *to boulēma tēs lexeōs*).[63]

When he comes, however, to the Lord's *logion* in Matthew 22:21, Origen does not, in point of fact, seem in the least interested in that literal meaning. On the contrary, he immediately embarks on a lengthy and fairly elaborate tropology. He begins

61. *Com. Mat.* 17.25, 653: "Voluntas loci praesentis secundum textum [Gr.: *To boulēma tēs ekkeimenēs lexeōs kata to rhēton*] talis mihi videtur: Iudaei propriam habentes conversationem ex lege extraneam ab omni conversatione gentium [Gr.: *idian echontes tēn kata ton Mōseōs nomon didaskalian kai politeian apexenōmenēn tēs tōn ethnōn agōgēs*] et habentes praeceptum quod ait: 'usque ad mortem certa pro veritate' (Ecclesiasticus 4:28 LXX) . . . ideo contradicebant gentibus dominantibus sibi ut non transgrederentur legem dei. Et frequenter radicitus interire periclitati sunt sub Romanis volentibus statuam Caesaris introducere in templum dei resistentes . . . ." The source of much of this is Josephus, *Antiquities* 18.1 f. and *Jewish War* 2.8 f.; see Klostermann's notes on the text of Origen, ibid., 653.27 ff.

62. Ibid., 654 f.: ". . . Et in tempore ergo Christi quando tributum [Iudaei] iussi sunt dare Romanis, cogitatio et consilium erat apud Iudaeos utrum deberent qui dei populus erant . . . tributum dare principibus aut potius pro libertate bella suscipere. . . . Et refert historia, quod Iudas quidem Galilaeus, cuius memor est et Lucas in Actibus Apostolorum, avellens multam multitudinem Iudaeorum docebat non oportere Caesari dare tributum neque dominum [Gr.: *kurion*] Caesarem appellare; qui autem erat in tempore illo tetrarcha suadere populo festinabat, ut . . . non voluntarie contra fortiores susciperent bellum, sed adquiescerent dare tributum. Et sermo quidem evangelii praesentis non quidem manifeste tamen haec ipsa ostendit." Origen here is combining Luke's account in Acts 5:37 with Josephus, *Antiquities* 18.1 f.; see Klostermann's note, loc. cit., 655.2 ff. See also below, next note.

63. Ibid., 26, 655 ff.: "Et vide nisi manifestatur historia illa ex eo, quod volentes [Pharisaei] Christum 'capere in sermone' non solum miserunt 'discipulos suos' interrogantes de censu, sed cum 'Herodianis.' Forsitan enim in populo tunc qui quidem docebant dare tributum Caesari vocabantur 'Herodiani' ab his qui hoc facere recusabant; qui autem prospectu libertatis dare tributum vetabant, videbantur esse Pharisaei subtilitatem Iudaicarum disciplinarum cautius observantes, ut si quidem Christus responderet non oportere Caesari dare tributum traderent eum Romanis [Herodiani] quasi recessionis [Gr., *apostasia*] auctorem, si autem iuberet dari, Pharisaei accusarent eum 'quasi personas hominum' aspicientem. . . . Unde et dominus . . . dixit: '. . . reddite ergo quae sunt Caesaris Caesari, et quae dei sunt deo.' " For the phrase *voluntas loci* and its Greek equivalent, see above, the beginning of n. 61.

with a remark that is strikingly reminiscent of the literal exegesis in the Commentary on Romans: but from the context the resemblance seems at first simply fortuitous. The Lord's *logion*, Origen starts his exegesis, can be "tropologized" as follows: all human beings consist of body and soul (at least, he hastens to add, if for the moment one is willing to overlook the "spirit"). All men, he continues, must therefore pay "tribute to Caesar": that is they must give unto the body food, clothing, sleep and everything else that is necessary for its sustenance. All these bodily things, Origen stresses, "bear the bodily image of the Prince of Bodies" (Gr.: *echonta tēn eikona tou tōn sōmatōn archontos sōmatikēn;* Lat.: *habentia imaginem principis corporum corporalem*). The soul, however, was created according to the Image of the King its Maker: all that is in accord with the soul's true nature (all the roads, for instance, that lead to virtue) must therefore be "rendered unto God."[64] Those, Origen continues, who claim to teach the Law of God, but in fact follow it beyond measure to the point of believing that Christians must take no care of the body, and must abstain even from what it needs for survival, are thus like the Pharisees of the pericope. Such are, for instance, the heretics against whom the Apostle warns in 1 Timothy 4:3 ff., those who "forbid marriage and enjoin to abstain from foods which God created to be received with thanksgiving." Those, on the other hand, who believe in indulging the body beyond measure are like the Herodians of the pericope who served Herod beyond measure. The Lord, however, made an illuminating separation between what is reasonably due to the body and the spiritual needs of the soul. This distinction He drew by saying "render unto Caesar the things which are Caesar's and unto God the things that are God's." Indeed, all bodily things bear the image of Caesar, while every virtue bears the image of God: *imaginem enim Caesaris habet omnis res corporalis et imaginem dei habet omnis virtus.*[65]

64. Ibid., 17.27, 658 f.: "Potest aliquis moraliter intellegere locum istum hoc modo. Omnes consistimus ex anima et corpore (differamus nunc dicere quoniam et ex spiritu) et debemus quaedam dare quasi tributum corporum principi qui dicitur 'Caesar' [Gr.: *sōmatōn archonti legomenō*[*i*] *'Kaisari'*], id est necessaria corpori et habentia imaginem principis corporum corporalem [Gr.: *echonta tēn eikona tou tōn sōmatōn sōmatikēn*], hoc est escas et vestimenta et somnium et quaecumque necessaria sunt ad repausationem simplicem naturae carnalis, sine quibus consistere non potest carnis natura. Item quoniam anima, quantum ad naturam suam, secundum imaginem est dei regis sui, quaecunque sunt convenientia animarum naturae, id est viae omnes quae ducunt ad virtutem . . . debemus ea Deo offerre. Qui ergo . . . [below, next note] . . . ."

65. Ibid., 659 f.: "Qui ergo supra modum docent legem dei et de rebus corporalibus

To this lengthy "moral" interpretation, Origen appends a short note, in which he apparently seeks to reassure the reader: despite the perhaps novel tropology which he has propounded, he is fully aware of a more traditional exegesis, according to which the word "Caesar" in the Lord's *logion* stands not for the body or its needs but directly for the Prince of this World, "since all the princes of the Gentiles bear the person of the Prince of this World." If Christians, this more traditional interpretation pursues, keep within themselves anything that properly pertains to the World and its Prince—vices, for instance—they cannot "render unto God the things that are God's." Thus, before Christians can offer to God what is due unto God, they must first (Gr.: *proteron;* Lat.: *prius*) give up all vices and, in this fashion, "render" or "give back" unto Caesar (that is to the Prince of this World) "the things which are Caesar's." This is why the Lord—Who is the True King of the Ages and not merely "king in symbol" (Gr.: *tōn aiōnōn basileus en oudeni sumbolō*[*i*]) as are the kings of the Gentiles—asked to see the coinage and image of Caesar and said: "Render unto Caesar the things which are Caesar's and unto God the things that are God's."[66]

---

et debitis corpori nihil curare praecipiunt, ipsi sunt 'Pharisaei' qui reddere 'Caesari tributum' vetabant, id est qui . . . suadent . . . abstinere ab omnibus quae sunt corporalia . . . ut nihil ex nobis corporis principi tribuatur: quales sunt de quibus ait apostolus [1 Tim. 4:1] 'in novissimis temporibus recedent quidam a fide, adtendentes spiritibus erroris et doctrinae daemoniorum . . . prohibentium nubere et iubentium abstinere a cibis, quos deus creavit ad percipiendum cum gratiarum actione fidelibus.' Alii autem sunt qui supra modum aestimant oportere corporibus indulgere et per omnia satisfacere principi corporum; et ipsi sunt secundum similitudinem 'Herodianorum' dicentium oportere 'Caesari' dare tributum. Salvator autem noster 'verbum Dei' dilucide separans [Gr.: *chōrizōn*] rationabilia corporis debita a debitis spiritalibus animae, dicit: 'Reddite Caesari quae Caesaris sunt et quae dei sunt deo'; imaginem enim Caesaris habet omnis res corporalis [Gr.: *eikona gar echei Kaisaros kai sōmatikōn pragmatōn ho phoros*] et imaginem dei habet omnis virtus." The Greek version here is much shorter than the Latin: the last phrase is found only in Latin.

66. Ibid., 17.28, 661: "Scio et huius loci aliam tradit[am exposit]ionem [Gr.: *Oida de kai allēn eis ton topon toiautēn pheromenēn diēgēsin*] quoniam princeps mundi moraliter dicitur Caesar [Gr.: *ho men archōn tou aiōnos toutou en tropologia*[*i*] *kaleitai Kaisar*], sicut et omnium gentium principes in persona principum mundi ponuntur [last phrase not in Greek but see *Hom. Luc.* 39, 220, cited below, next note]. Rex autem omnium saeculorum deus non in uno mysterio [Gr.: *en oudeni sumbolō*[*i*]] sed ubique est deus. Quoniam ergo habemus quaedam in nobis quae sunt principis huius mundi, id est diversas malitias et non possumus prius [Gr.: *ou proteron*] reddere 'deo quae dei sunt' nisi reddiderimus principi quae principis sunt, id est nisi deposuerimus malitiam universam, ideo dominus, ostenso sibi nomismate et imagine eius respondit: 'Reddite Caesari quae Caesaris sunt et deo quae dei sunt.' " Hanson, *Allegory and Event,* 133, also believes that this is a traditional allegory which was not invented by Origen; Crouzel, *Théologie de l'Image,* 194, seems to ignore the point. See also below at nn. 71 and 72.

In his exegesis of the parallel passage in Luke 20:20 ff., which is to be found in the Homilies on Luke, Origen stresses that since the literal meaning of the passage is so obvious—for what Christian would deny that tribute was due to Caesar?—another "secret and mystical" interpretation must be sought. Using the language of 1 Corinthians 15:49—but reversing the Pauline order of temporal priorities—he points out that two images are to be found in man. One comes from God's creation "in the beginning" since, in the words of Genesis 1:26, man was created "according to the image and likeness of God." The other, and latter (Gr.: *husteron;* Lat.: *postea*) image is the Image of Dust of 1 Corinthians 15:49, which man "assumes" because of his sin and disobedience. For just as a coin bears the image of the Ruler of the Gentiles, so he who performs the works of the Prince of this World bears his image. This is why Jesus in this particular pericope orders the Christian to give back and reject that image and assume in its stead the Image in accordance to which he was created "in the beginning."[67] Luke 20:20 ff. (: Matthew 22:15 ff.) is thus the equivalent of 1 Corinthians 15:49: "render unto Caesar the things that are Caesar's and unto God the things which are God's" means the same as "even as we have borne the image of the dusty, we shall also bear the image of the heavenly."[68]

67. *Hom. Luc.* 39, 219 f.: "Haec de quaestione quam Sadducaei Domino proposuerunt. . . . Porro quia adiectum est de imagine Caesaris, etiam super hoc debemus pauca perstringere. Putant quidam a Salvatore dictum esse simpliciter: 'reddite quae sunt Caesaris Caesari' id est: tributum reddite, quod debetis. Quis enim nostrum de tributis reddendis Caesari contradicit? Habet igitur locus quiddam mystici atque secreti. Duae sunt imagines in homine: una, quam accepit a Deo factus in principio, sicut in Genesi scriptum est 'iuxta imaginem et similitudinem' Dei [Genesis 1:26] altera choici postea, quam propter inoboedientiam atque peccatum eiectus de paradiso assumpsit principis saeculi huius suasus illecebris. Sicut enim nummus sive denarius habet imaginem imperatorum mundi [Gr.: *eikona echei tou basileuontos tōn ethnōn*], sic qui facit opera rectoris tenebrarum istarum portat imaginem eius, cuius habet opera: quam praecepit hic Iesus esse reddendam et proiciendam de vultu nostro assumendamque eam imaginem, iuxta quam a principio ad similitudinem Dei conditi sumus." On the Grecism *'choicus'* see below, next note.

68. Ibid., 220 f.: ". . . 'Ostendite' inquit 'mihi nummum' pro quo in Matthaeo scribitur 'denarius.' Quem cum accepisset, ait: 'cuius scriptionem habet?' Qui respondentes dixerunt: 'Caesaris.' Ad quos rursum: 'Reddite' inquit 'quae sunt Caesaris, Caesari, et quae sunt Dei, Deo.' Quorum consequentiam et Paulus locutus est dicens: 'Sicut portavimus imaginem choici, portemus et imaginem caelestis' (1 Cor. 15:49). Quod ergo ait 'Reddite, quae sunt Caesaris, Caesari' hoc dicit: deponite personam 'choici,' abjicite imaginem terrenam, ut possitis vobis personam caelestis imponentes reddere 'quae sunt Dei, Deo.' " On the importance of the "image of the Terrestrial" or the "image of Dust" in the whole theology of Origen, see below, n. 70. Here it should simply be noted that Jerome, for whatever reason, refuses to translate the *choikos* of 1 Corinthians 15:47 ff. (which means here "dusty" or even "dust" and is

There are thus three separate interpretations of the pericope of the tribute money that Origen offers *in situ* either in margin of Matthew 22:15 ff. or in margin of Luke 20:20 ff.: a long and rather puzzling tropology in the Commentary on Matthew; a much briefer and apparently traditional exegesis as a sort of appendix to that rather daring tropology; and an almost equally short discussion in the Homilies on Luke. The two shorter exegeses are relatively simple and can be taken up together. First, both passages clearly—and rather surprisingly, considering Origen's theology of politics as a whole[69]—identify Caesar with the Devil. Second, even though the appendix in the Commentary on Matthew seems to oppose the True King of the Ages with those who are only kings in symbol, the Homilies on Luke make clear that the primary opposition is that between the Image of God and the Image of the Devil which Christians must renounce. Third, the reader should perhaps be reminded that in accordance with Origen's basic theology, *the* Image of God is the Word, in accordance with which Man (or at least his soul) was created "in the beginning." Fourth, the apparent contradiction between the two shorter passages can be easily reconciled. As Crouzel has noted in this very context, Origen, when discussing postlapsarian man from an existential point of view, as he now is, normally follows the temporal order of 1 Corinthians 15:48 f.: the Image of Dust, of the Earthly, of the First Adam, or indeed of the Devil, comes first and must be rejected or "surrendered" before the new Christian can put on Christ and thus assume the Image of God. But when Origen thinks of man from a prelapsarian, cosmological, or metaphysical viewpoint, the Pauline order is naturally reversed: "in the beginning" Man was created "in the image and likeness" of God and it is only after sinning that he "assumes" the Image of Dust. What happens at conversion is thus a true *apokatastasis*, a restoration of the state that prevailed before the Fall.[70]

---

obviously related to the "dust" [*chous*] out of which man is formed in the "Second Creation" of Genesis 2:7) as *terrenus* even though he does so in the Vulgate.

69. See above, the first part of this whole chapter, particularly at nn. 16–26. Crouzel, *Théologie de l'Image*, 196, puts too much political emphasis on this identification of Caesar with the Devil. See also the concluding pages of this chapter below, pp. 171–181.

70. On the role of 1 Corinthians 15:47 ff. in Origen's theology of the Image, see Crouzel, *Théologie de l'Image*, 182–89; on the Image of the Devil in his theology, see ibid., 189–97. The relation between the *choikos* of 1 Corinthians 15 and the "dust" (*chous*) of the Second Creation (and the First Adam after the Fall?) in Genesis 2:7 is perhaps insufficiently stressed by Crouzel. It is because of this connection that I

Finally, the appendix in the Commentary on Matthew has many of the earmarks of the sort of traditional baptismal allegory with which Origen was perfectly familiar, and which, it may be recalled, he has used in his exegesis of the Sihon episode in the Book of Numbers and of the Hazor episode in the Book of Joshua.[71] *Apodidonai, reddere,* "render," is understood in the sense of "to give back" and Origen clearly suggests that it is no accident that in the Lord's *logion* the phrase "render unto *Caesar*" has temporal priority. According to this baptismal exegesis—whose original *Sitz am Leben* may well have floated between the present pericope and the episode of the Coin Found in the Mouth of the Fish in Matthew 17:24 ff.[72]—Christians before (Gr.: *proteron;* Lat.: *prius*)[73] putting on Christ, that is to say the Image of God, must surrender to the Devil the coin that bears his image and inscription: in the words of the old baptismal formula, they do this by renouncing the Devil and all his pomp. By giving up all their former vices they surrender to the Devil their former allegiance and thus "render unto Caesar the things that are Caesar's." This apparently traditional interpretation is rehearsed, but not explicitly endorsed, by Origen, and he certainly fails to develop it in this particular context. It does not really clash with his own lengthy and rather puzzling interpretation which precedes the appendix, but as usual (and indeed as in his exegesis of the Sihon and Hazor episodes) he is more interested in tropology than in traditional baptismal allegory and is thus satisfied with a simple summary.

To return to the lengthier exegesis in the Commentary on Matthew: in the light of the discussion of the baptismal appendix and of the parallel passage in the Homilies on Luke, the idea that all "bodily things bear the bodily image of the Prince of Bodies" should have acquired a more definite meaning, yet must still seem a little odd.[74] The counterpoint to that notion, namely, that Christ is *the* Image of God and that the soul is the image of that Image is, of course, traditional enough. That

have preferred "Image of Dust" to the more common "Image of the Earthy" (KJ, cf. also Confraternity) or "Image of the Terrestrial" (the simplest translation of the Vulgate, cf. Crouzel's "Image du Terrestre," *Théologie de l'Image,* 182 ff. passim); on the other hand, "Image of the Man of Dust" (RSV, see also Jerusalem Bible), though quite allowable as a translation of Corinthians, makes the connection with Genesis 2:7 perhaps too palpable for this text of Origen's. Cf. also Ladner, *Idea of Reform,* 87 ff.

71. Above, n. 66, and chapter 1 at nn. 52 f. and 67 f.

72. See below at nn. 87–100.

73. See above at n. 66.

74. See above at n. 64.

the Word was the Image of God (and therefore the exact equivalent and nevertheless only "second" to His Father) was a central part not only of Origen's Trinitarianism but of that of a good many of his contemporaries. Equally broadly based was the doctrine that because of his soul (or at least because of the rational part of that soul) man can be said to have been created "in the image of God," that is to say according to the pattern of God's Word. Distinctly Origenist, however, is the hypothesis of double creation, according to which the account in Genesis 1:26 ff. refers to the creation of a purely "spiritual" man without an earthly body, while the second account in Genesis 2:7 ff. refers to the formation of that earthly body out of "dust," as the result of a cosmic Fall in which all of the spiritual or rational creatures of the First Creation (with the single exception of the human soul of the pre-existing Jesus) fell together with the Devil.[75]

Only within this purely Origenist framework does the idea that the Devil is the Prince of Bodies, and that all bodily things bear his bodily image, become comprehensible. For Origen, the Irenaean view according to which the body as well as the soul participates in the image of God in Man, because of the Incarnation in which God may be said to "truly manifest His Image by becoming what his image was," is not only rejected, it is actually reversed.[76] Far from being the Image of God, the body, the Image of Dust of the Second Creation, is the Image of the Devil. This reversal is made possible by Origen's gnosticizing (though emphatically not Gnostic) doctrine of matter (or at least earthly matter), as well as by the somewhat peculiar role which the Devil is made to play in his theology. On the one hand, earthly matter is formed by God and ultimately in some sense perhaps redeemed by Christ through the resurrection of the flesh.[77] On the other, the appearance of earthly matter is

75. Crouzel, *Théologie de l'Image,* 75–128, on the Logos as the Image of God; ibid. 143–80 on the soul as the image of that Image; on the two creations, see ibid., 148–53, and Daniélou, *Origen,* 212; on the soul of the pre-existing Jesus, see Crouzel, 129–42.

76. On the citation by Irenaeus, see *Adversus Haereseos* 5.16.2, ed. Harvey, vol. 2, 368, cited by Ladner, *Idea of Reform,* 84, n. 9. On the rejection of the Irenaean doctrine by Clement, as well as by Origen, see Ladner, 85 ff., and Crouzel, *Théologie de l'Image,* 135 f.

77. All creatures are "corporeal" or material, at least in an ethereal sense. That the *logikoi* before the Fall when still in "Heaven" were nevertheless composed of *pneuma* ("spirit"), *nous* ("mind"), and *sōma* ("body") is clear from *De Principiis* 2.2.2, 112 (Butterworth, 81 f.); see the comments by Crouzel, *Théologie de l'Image,* 247, n. 6;

nevertheless both a result of and a punishment (though, no doubt, also a remedy) for the Fall. Though God created it, so to speak as an afterthought, and then made use of its negative qualities for educational purposes in accordance with Origen's doctrine of Divine *Paideia*, earthly matter nevertheless bears the mark of the Devil.[78] For Origen, therefore, not only vices or evil men (such as before their conversion Matthew the tax collector or Paul the persecutor of the Church) may be said to bear the image of the Devil,[79] but also the flesh as such; and this despite the fact that God is the author of bodies and not merely of souls, and despite the additional fact that He ultimately was willing to take flesh presumably in order to redeem it.[80] Yet this rather negative view of earthly matter is allied with a theology in which the Devil is seen in slightly more positive terms than in fully orthodox Christianity. The mature Origen may have denied that the Devil would ultimately be saved, but it remains significant that at an earlier age he had at least been able to envisage the possibility of a salvation so universal that it would in the end include even the Demon himself.[81] In the meantime, as in the Book of Job, the Devil remains

---

contra Daniélou, 217 f. On the redeeming of the Flesh through the Incarnation and ultimately the Resurrection, see Crouzel, 140 ff. and 247 ff., and Henry Chadwick, "Origen, Celsus and the Resurrection of the Body," *Harvard Theological Review* 41 (1948) 83 ff. Yet Crouzel, 247 and 263, suggests that the *corpus gloriosum* of the Resurrection is merely a return to the "body" of the *logikoi;* in that case, can one really speak of a genuine Redemption of the Flesh, i.e., of the earthly matter or the "Dust" of the Second Creation? And while Chadwick, loc. cit., 99, rightly emphasizes that even from the citations of Origen's enemies it is evident that for him there is some sort of continuity between the pre-Resurrectional bodies of, say, Peter and Paul and their (still individual) post-Resurrectional bodies, from the material he cites (ibid., 90 f.) it is equally clear that the post-Resurrectional body—since it will lack the needs of its prior existence—will not be provided with the same organs as in its previous existence; in what sense is it then really the same body that is being redeemed? But see below, nn. 104 and at 102.

78. On the paideutic role of matter, see Ladner, "The Philosophical Anthropology of Gregory of Nyssa," *Dumbarton Oaks Papers* 12 (1958) 63, and *Idea of Reform*, 72, n. 39; on the paideutic role of the Devil almost nothing to my knowledge has been written, but cf. Koch, *Pronoia und Paideusis*, 103 f., 118 ff., 126 ff., and 142 ff. See also 1 Timothy 1:20 (cf. Bauer, Arndt, and Gingrich, *Lexicon of the New Testament* ad v. *paideuein*).

79. Origen, *Hom. Gen.* 1.13, 18: "Matthaeus publicanus erat et utique imago eius diabolo similis erat, sed veniens ad imaginem Dei . . . et sequens eam transformatus est ad similitudinem imaginis Dei. . . . Paulus ipsius imaginis Dei persecutor erat; ut autem potuit decorem eius et pulchritudinem contueri, visa ea . . . ad eius similitudinem reformatus est . . . ." The passage is cited by Ladner, *Idea of Reform*, 88, and n. 21.

80. See above at n. 77, and below, nn. 104 and at 102.

81. Contrast the letter by Origen cited by Rufinus in his *De Adulteratione librorum*

the great Tester of Mankind; and because of this testing process, which he carries out in part in his role as Lord of Bodies, the Devil plays an important though unwitting role in the never-ending process of Divine *Paideia* through which the Logos educates Mankind.[82] From this point of view, the Devil thus becomes almost a stepbrother of Christ.

At first glance the body/soul contrast which is the main theme of Origen's lengthy interpretation of Matthew 22:21 in the Commentary on Matthew seems to have nothing to do with the political and ecclesiological exegesis which he gives of the same verse in the Commentary on Romans. Yet even on the surface there are some curious parallels. In the one, to be sure, the main point is the distinction between body and soul; in the other, that between state and Church. Yet even in the context of the exegesis of Romans 13:1 ff., the analogy between the powers that be and the power of the body seems to suggest that "the bishops and princes of the Church" are in some sense analogous to the powers of the soul or spirit.[83] Again, in the Commentary on Romans, the Devil plays no part, at least in the foreground; while even in the longer exegesis of the Commentary on Matthew (and not only in the baptismal appendix)

Origenis, PG 17.624 ff., with *De Principiis* 1.6, 3, 83f. (Butterworth, 57). On the question whether Rufinus in his translation of *De Principiis* "softens" Origen's position by leaving the salvation of the Devil an open question for the reader to decide and on whether the so-called letter of Origen's reproduced in *De Adulteratione* is a forgery or not, see Butterworth, *On First Principles*, xxxix–xli and 57, n. 1; on the other side of the question, see Crouzel, *Théologie de l'Image*, 210, and n. 219.

82. For the *Paideia* of the Logos, see above, chapter 2 at n. 87. On the Devil, see also *Hom. Ez.* 13.2, 443–48. The passage in Ezechiel laments over the prince of Tyre (Ezechiel 28:11), of whom it could once have been said, "Thou wast the seal of resemblance and the crown of beauty" (28:12 LXX), who "from the day in which he was created" (28:14 LXX) "amidst the delights of Paradise" (28:13) "was with the Cherub on the Holy Mountain of God" (28:14 LXX), but who "because his heart was lifted up with his beauty, has lost his wisdom and his beauty and was cast to the ground" (28:17). Origen has thus good grounds to identify the prince of Tyre with Lucifer and (p. 443) cites Isaiah 14:12 LXX: "How has he fallen from Heaven, Lucifer, who rose in the morning?" In this context the point is that ontologically the Devil can be called "the seal of resemblance" because God "was truly his Father" (445). This "seal" with which even the Devil was once "signed" is the same that is now borne by the faithful, once they reject the Image of Dust which they receive from the Devil as he now is and replace it by the Image of God given to them by Jesus (445 f.; see below, n. 95). As for the Devil, "how happy was he when he was the 'seal of resemblance': what he now lacks is that he shall never grow into the 'likeness of the seal' " (446, ll. 4–5). Thus, in origin the Devil as the "seal of likeness" was almost the counterpart of Christ, the Image of God. Crouzel, *Théologie de l'Image*, does not seem to discuss the Devil as the "seal of likeness."

83. Above at nn. 52 and 55; also above, p. 147 f.

he plays an important role, though under the guise of "the Prince of Bodies." Yet, as has been seen, in his exegesis of Romans, Origen at least assumes some sort of eschatological opposition between God and World,[84] an opposition that is simply rendered more explicit in the Commentary on Matthew.

Despite the felt presence of the Devil, however, in the longer exegesis of the Commentary on Matthew the usual eschatological *psychomachia* against the Devil, the flesh, and their vices, has taken on a curiously tame coloring. The excesses of the flesh must no doubt be resisted; but so must the exaggerated puritanism, the immoderate zeal for the spirit, which refuses to grant to the body what is its lawful due. Eschatology has somehow been civilized into the Golden Mean. This too suggests that the exegesis in the Commentary on Romans and the longer exegesis in the Commentary on Matthew are very closely linked, in at least two ways. For one thing, it may be hazarded (though at this stage only as a preliminary hypothesis) that the triadic structure with which the longer exegesis in the Commentary on Matthew both begins and ends had its analogue in the exegesis of Romans. In the Commentary on Matthew, the behavior of Christ is seen in the historical introduction both as the only "right" behavior in opposition to that of Pharisees and Herodians and yet also as mediating between these two extremes; while at the end of the same exegesis it is the behavior of orthodox Christians which is seen as both opposed to and yet mediating between the behavior of self-indulgent pagans and immoderate ascetics alike. And in the Commentary on Romans, it will be recalled, Origen ends his exegesis by opposing the nonresistance of orthodox Christians both to the violence of pagan authorities, who through persecution serve the state beyond measure, and to the equal violence of those overly zealous (and Zealot) Christians who might usurp the function of the state by unrighteously resisting unrighteous persecution through material force. Perhaps, moreover, it is no accident that Origen should have begun his exegesis of Romans 13:1 ff. with an opposition between "soul" and "spirit," which, as has been shown, is in fact part of a trichotomous anthropological structure. In both politics and morals, orthodox Christian behavior is clearly identified with the more positive "pneumatic" or "spiritual" of two antagonistic

84. Above, p. 150 and pp. 151 f.

poles. Yet from a noneschatological perspective, the same behavior is seen as both in opposition to and at the same time mediating between these two extremes: extremes which by ignoring the necessary duality between body and soul or between state and Church also ignore the special requirements of the "time in-between." Yet the exact nature of these identifications, oppositions, and mediations is by no means clear: it is only the exegesis of Matthew 17:24 ff. (that is to say of the pericope of the Temple Tax) that will provide the necessary clue.[85]

Moreover, this taming of eschatological antagonism is strongly reminiscent of the process of "secularization" which, it has been argued, is such a marked feature in the exegesis of Romans. Though the body in the Commentary on Matthew "bears the bodily mark of the Prince of Bodies," the body is there perceived primarily not as antagonistic to the soul but as in some way a parallel structure: both body and soul have parallel "rights" which must not be allowed to impinge upon each other. As has been seen, a similar parallelism between Church and state was the main characteristic of the exegesis of Romans. The world and the flesh can—from an exaggeratedly eschatological perspective—simply be identified with the Devil their Prince and thus with absolute evil. From a more correct viewpoint, the world and the flesh are the stage on which the Devil and Christ engage in their eschatological struggle. But from still a third perspective, the world and the flesh are the stage on which both Christ and the Devil play the role assigned to both by God. If the Devil can from an admittedly limited point of view function as almost the stepbrother of Christ, it should cause no surprise if for certain purposes state and Church should be perceived as twins! In the Commentary on Romans, this taming of eschatology is achieved through the exclusion of both Christ and Devil: neither the redemptive nature of the Church or of the Christ-event nor the demonic aspects of both world and state are allowed to come to the surface.[86] The exegesis of Matthew 22:21 shows that the same effect can be achieved even though the Devil is explicitly present: for if one may say so, the demonic aspects of the Devil are—at least in the longer exegesis of the Commentary on Matthew—subordinated to his God-given role as the Lord of

85. Below at nn. 97–99, and pp. 165–174.
86. Above at nn. 60 and 82.

Bodies and the Tester of Mankind. Origen's exegesis of Matthew 17:24 ff. (the pericope of the Temple Tax or of the Coin Found in the Mouth of the Fish) will reveal that the same "neutral" or "secular" effect can be achieved even in the redemptive presence of the Lord Himself.

Because the biblical passage is brief and because of the importance of each of its details for Origen's exegesis, the King James Version should for once be cited in full:

And when they were come to Capernaum, they that received tribute money [Gr.: *didrachma*, 'twopence'] came to Peter and said: 'Doth not your master pay tribute?' He saith: 'Yes.' And when He was come into the house, Jesus prevented him, saying: 'What thinkest thou, Simon? Of whom do the kings of earth take custom or tribute? Of their own children or of strangers?' Peter saith unto him: 'Of strangers.' Jesus saith unto him: 'Then are the children free. Notwithstanding, lest we should cause scandal, go thou to the sea and cast an hook, and take up the fish that first cometh up. And when thou hast opened his mouth, thou shalt find a piece of money [Gr.: *statēra*, a fourpenny coin]: that take and give unto them for me and for thee.'

At the time of Jesus, the Temple Tax was a religious tribute levied on all Jews by their own hierarchy for the upkeep of the Temple and the worship of God; it had nothing to do with tribute to Caesar. The Lord's simile was meant to suggest that just as the sons of the kings of this earth were free from earthly tribute, so the Son of God should by rights be free from a tax levied in the Name of His Father. He nevertheless paid but only in order to avoid scandal and to preserve the Messianic secret.[87]

With the destruction of the Temple and the subsequent secularization of the Temple Tax into tribute to Rome, the point of the pericope tended to be forgotten and Matthew 17:24 ff. to be assimilated to Matthew 22:21. Origen is perhaps still dimly aware of the religious purpose of the original Temple Tax: but as is the case of almost all later exegetes the process of confusion has already gone very far.[88] The confusion, moreover, leads to difficulties in understanding even the literal meaning

87. See *The Interpreter's Bible*, ed. George Buttrick et al. (New York, 1951), vol. 7, 465 f.; *The Jerome Biblical Commentary*, ed. Raymond Brown et al. (Englewood Cliffs, N.J., 1968), vol. 2, 94.123.

88. For Origen, see below, n. 94. In the West at least the only commentator who does not confuse the two levies is Hilary of Poitiers, *Commentarius in Matthaeum* 17.10, *PL* 9.1017: "Dominus didrachma solvere postulatur: hoc enim omni Israel lex pro redemptione animae et corporis constituerat in ministerio templi servientium . . . ." See above, chapter 3, n. 8.

of the pericope: for if the tribute in question is an "earthly" tribute to Caesar, why should those who are "strangers" to "the kings of this earth"—and emphatically no longer their "sons"—be exempt from earthly tribute? And if they have to pay, what is the point of the Lord's simile, and why all the complications about fishes and the fear of scandal? Origen is so troubled by these difficulties that he does something rather unusual even for him: he suggests two quite separate literal constructions. The first, more or less, preserves the simile, but only at the cost of totally ignoring the fact that the Lord paid only in order to avoid scandal; the second, on the contrary, emphasizes the business about scandal but only at the cost of destroying the simile.

The second construction is of relatively little interest in this context. The Greek version (which may be fragmentary and is in any case hard to follow) seems to take advantage of the fact that the Lord in His answer to Peter did not say "Then are the children *of kings* free" but simply "Then are *the children* free." Origen thus can distinguish those who are children of the kings of the earth from those who are children "absolutely" or "simply." The former are not free, for in the words of John 8:34 "everyone who commits sin is a slave to sin." The latter can apparently be equated to the "strangers" of the pericope who must be considered as children of God or at least as children of one of the sons of God: these are free "in essence." Nevertheless, being free, they take care not to scandalize "the kings of the earth" or their "children" or those "that receive tribute money." What "nature" is represented by each of these categories, Origen adds with some irony, is a question that should be asked of "those who enjoy myth-making about the forces of nature." Christ at any rate paid the tribute money in order to avoid scandal, but took it from the mouth of a fish in order to show that "their nature was not a praiseworthy one."[89]

89. Origen, *Com. Mat.* 13.11, 208 f. The Greek is just a little confusing. For those who are children absolutely (*apolelumenōs huioi*), see 209 l.5; for he who is simply a child (*huios haplōs*), see 210 l.13. Those who are strangers to the kings of the earth are said to be free children according to their essence: *hoitines allotrioi eisin tōn basileōn tēs gēs kai dia ton einai eleutheroi huioi tugchanousi* (209 ll. 19 ff.). About the question that should be asked from those that enjoy mythmaking about nature, see 210 ll. 24 ff.: *puthoimēn d'an tōn chairontōn tē(i) peri phuseōn muthopoiiā(i), poias phuseōs ēsan eite 'hoi tēs gēs basileis' eite 'hoi huioi autōn' eite 'hoi ta didrachma lambanontes,' hous mē bouletai skandalizein ho sōtēr.* About their nature not being praiseworthy, see ibid., ll.31 ff.: *phainetai dē . . . hoti ouk epainetēs eisi phuseōs.*

The author of the Latin version (who may be forgiven for finding some of this a little hard to follow) does not stress the distinction between those who are children of kings and those who are children "absolutely." Like the Greek, however, the Latin version sharply distinguishes "the children of the kings of this earth" from "the children of the King of Heaven" and emphasizes that the Lord's response "then are the children free" applies to the latter only because the "children of the kings of this earth" "are in bondage to sin."[90] Both versions thus ignore the simile that is basic to the pericope. The Latin version, however, has nothing about nature or mythmakers, and adds some political material that is not found in the Greek. In the Latin Origen, Matthew 17:24 ff. becomes a special and extreme case of Matthew 22:21: if as a part of "the mystery of iniquity," the kings of this earth exact a coin bearing the "image of Caesar"—that is to say any earthly possession—the children of the King of Heaven should meekly give in, even though the exaction be unjust. The children of the King of Heaven, to be sure, are free (and therefore presumably unlike the children of the kings of this earth not really subject to unjust exactions), but they must be careful not to scandalize anyone, not even the unrighteous.[91] Whatever the meaning of the Greek, in the

90. Ibid., 208 f.: "Ista diximus secundum unum modum [cf. below, nn. 97–99], quoniam duplicem sensum habet hic sermo. Secundum alterum autem talia dici possunt: filiorum sunt quidam 'filii' regum 'terrae,' alii autem propter hoc ipsum quod alieni sunt a filiis regum 'terrae' nullius quidem eorum qui sunt super terram 'filii' sunt, sed . . . filii dei aut alicuius filiorum dei. Quando ergo salvator interrogat Petrum, dicens, 'reges terrae a quibus accipiunt tributum vel censum? a filiis suis aut ab extraneis? dicente' Petro: non a suis filiis sed 'ab extraneis,' quod dominus dicit de illis qui extranei sunt a regibus 'terrae': 'ergo filii liberi sunt,' tale aliquid aestima dictum, quoniam 'liberi' sunt qui 'filii' sunt dei, 'filii' autem 'regum terrae' liberi non sunt, 'quoniam omnis qui facit peccatum servus est peccati' [John 8:34] . . . ."

91. Ibid., 210: "Si ergo in mysterio quodam 'reges terrae' a filiis dei liberis constitutis exigunt 'didrachma Caesaris' habentia imaginem, consequens est intellegere quoniam et quotienscumque exsurgunt quidam, qui per iniustitiam tollant nostra terrena, reges huius terrae eos transmittunt ut exigant a nobis quae sunt ipsorum." This whole sentence is missing from the Greek version. I have taken the liberty in my paraphrase to explain the *mysterium quodam* (in the context of *iniustitia*) by means of the *mysterium iniquitatis* of 2 Thessalonians 2:7. The Latin version then goes on, ibid., 210 f.: "Quicumque ergo filius est simpliciter [Gr. *huios haplōs*, above, n. 89] et non filius regum 'terrae,' ille est liber. Tamen cum sit liber, sollicite agit, ut ne scandalizet vel ipsos reges 'terrae' vel filios eorum. . . . Et quamvis essent iniqui, tamen sollicite egit Christus, ut ne scandalizaret eos, et suo exemplo prohibet aliquod scandalum fieri etiam huiusmodi hominibus sive ut ne amplius peccent scandalizati, sive ut salventur suscipientes eum, qui pepercit eis quominus scandalizentur." See Crouzel, *Théologie de l'Image*, 174, and n. 188.

Latin Origen the first part of the pericope is thus literally (though incorrectly) interpreted: Christians must pay not only lawful taxes, as in Matthew 22:21, but even unjust exactions, as in Matthew 17:24. After all, all earthly things (whether justly or unjustly required by the state) "bear the image of Caesar"; and in any case Christians must be careful not to scandalize even the unrighteous.

The remainder of the pericope—and here Greek and Latin more or less coincide—Origen interprets figuratively as both a baptismal allegory and a tropological warning against avarice and iniquity in general. "Capernaum" means "field of comforting," and each disciple is comforted, for he is "free" and a "child" and has received the power to fish from the sea and to bring comfort to those whom he has fished out. Indeed, this is why the coin is removed from the open mouth of the fish and given back to those who demand the coin as their own.[92] Moreover, before they are fished out of the sea by Peter, men are immersed in the billows of avarice and in the salty brine of the cares of this world; but Peter, the Teacher of Truth, catches them by means of the hook of the Word, extracts from their mouths the coin of avarice and apparently through his preaching of the Word replaces the coin with the Image of God.[93] Finally (and here there is perhaps a distorted reminiscence of the religious purpose of the Temple Tax), Origen concludes with reminding the reader that according to Numbers 3:47 LXX the Temple Tax consisted not simply of two pennies but of two *sacred* pennies. Therefore, when the tax collectors demanded not these sacred pennies but pennies that defile, the Lord ordered Peter to take the money out of the mouth of a fish: this was done so that Christians should remember to keep

92. Ibid., 211: "Et sicut in AGRO CONSOLATIONIS [Gr.: *PARAKLĒSEŌS*]—sic enim interpretatur Capharnaum—consolatur omnem discipulum et liberum eum et filium esse pronuntiat et dat ei virtutem piscandi 'piscem primum,' ut ascendente eo consolationem accipiat Petrus super eum quem piscatus est. Et propter hoc quod ablatus est stater de ore ipsius aperto, dandus eis quorum proprius est stater et [qui] exigunt huiusmodi nomisma quasi suum."

93. Ibid., 12, 211 f.: "Convenienter poteris uti hoc textus adversus avaros, qui nullam habent in ore suo loquelam nisi pecuniae. Cum autem videris huiusmodi hominem ab aliquo Petro correptum, qui abstulit non solum de ore eius verbum pecuniae sed et de toto adfectu concupiscentiam pecuniae, dices eiusmodi hominem in mari fuisse et in salsis rebus huius vitae et in fluctibus sollicitudinum avaritiae et habuisse in ore suo 'staterem' quamdiu infidelis extitit et avarus, ascendisse autem de mari ad hamum rationabilem [Gr.: *logikos*] et conprehensum atque salvatum (ab aliquo Petro qui eum docuit veritatem) ut ne habeat aliquando in ore suo 'staterem,' sed pro eo habeat imaginem dei, eloquia dei [Gr.: *ta echonta tēn eikona logia tou theou*]."

away from everything that bears the image of Caesar. One should note, moreover, that the same tribute was paid for Peter as for Christ: this shows that Peter was greater than the other disciples.[94]

The literal exegesis of this second construction—found really only in the Latin version—confirms the political exegesis of Matthew 22:21 given by Origen in the Commentary on Romans. Matthew 17:24 is treated as an extreme case of Matthew 22:21: Christians must pay their taxes, even if Caesar's exactions are unjust. The spiritual exegesis, on the other hand, combines the traditional baptismal allegory, rehearsed but not specifically endorsed in the exegesis of Matthew 22:21, with a tropological contrast between earthly avarice and Heavenly Image; an allegorical emphasis on the role of the preacher who fishes the sinner out of the sea of this world, and an eschatological slant that seems to equate "the kings of this earth," their "children" and those "that receive tribute," with the cosmological forces of nature that in some sense are still ruled by the princes of this world. This latter element is absent from the Latin version and only hinted at in the Greek, but seems confirmed by a passage in the Homilies on Ezechiel. Here it is stressed that Jesus takes a coin from the mouth of the fish in the sea because the fish is similar to the dragon that is king of all that is in the water.[95] The stress on the kerygmatic function

94. Ibid., 13, 212 f.: "Et signa tibi ex Numeris (Numbers 3:47 LXX), quoniam pro sanctis secundum legem dei non simpliciter didrachmum datur, sed didrachmum sanctum. Scriptum est enim: 'Accipe quinque siclos secundum [caput, secundum] didrachmum sanctum' . . . . Quoniam ergo non licet sanctis dei cum sanctis didrachmis habere didrachmum inquinatum [Gr.: *didrachma . . . bebēla ton hagion tou theou*], ideo accipientibus non sancta 'didrachma' et interrogantibus Petrum et dicentibus: 'Magister vester non solvit didrachmum?' praecepit salvator dari 'staterem' (in quo erant duo didrachma) qui inveniebatur in ore piscis. . . . Quod dedit magister et dant semper discipuli eius pro sua salute et gloria Christi, ut longe faciant a se omnia quae imaginem Caesaris habent." Ibid., 14, 214: "[the *statera* was given] pro se [i.e., Domino] et Petro . . . quasi per hoc iudicasset eum ceteris discipulis meliorem . . . ." (The context here is the next pericope in Matthew 18:1 ff.: "Who is the greatest in the Kingdom of Heaven?")

95. *Hom. Ez.* 13.2, 445 f.: (The context is Ezechiel 28:1–12, where the prince of Tyre is threatened with punishment, though he was once "the seal of resemblance, full of wisdom and perfect in beauty." For obvious reasons, Origen identifies the prince of Tyre with Lucifer himself; see above, n. 82.) "Signat autem [i.e., diabolus] singulorum corda considerans et imprimit in eis 'figuram terreni' per peccata, per vitia 'ut portent imaginem terrestris' [1 Corinthians 15:49]. Audi Iesum, quid respondeat, quando 'imaginem et inscriptionem Caesaris' [Luke 20:24] postulatur. . . . Nam quia non habebat eam 'imaginem' quam petebatur, neque ipse neque discipulus suus, docet, ubi valeat repperiri 'imago' quae quaeritur: 'vade' inquit 'ad mare et mitte hamum et primum piscem . . . tolle, et aperies os eius et, cum inveneris staterem . . . dabis

of the Teacher of Truth is, of course, fairly typical of much of Origen's allegorism.[96] These various elements are not, however, related to each other and in this second construction of Matthew 17:24 ff. the exegesis of Matthew 22:21 remains in the end as disjointed as before.

Origen's first construction of Matthew 17:24, on the other hand, unites all the various strains of his exegesis of Matthew 22:21. While the second construction misconstrued the simile in order to preserve the point, the first construction preserves the simile but shifts the focus of the pericope so as completely to assimilate Matthew 17:24 to Matthew 22:21. (In the process, Origen of course has to ignore the Lord's claim that He was paying tribute only in order to avoid scandal.) Christ's response, "then are the children free," is here construed correctly and taken to refer to the children of the kings of this earth. But Origen shifts the focus of the simile, for among those, he suggests, who seem to be "strangers" and not "children of the kings of the earth" there are some who only appear to be in bondage but are in fact the children of kings and thus "free" by nature. This piece of Hellenistic romanticism is then inserted by Origen into a biblical framework: for among those who only appeared to be in bondage but were in fact free and the children of a king there were, for instance, the children of Israel during their sojourn in Egypt. Indeed, it was for the sake of such children in bondage, Origen pursues, that the Son of God (in the words of Philippians 2:7) "took upon him the form of a servant." It is therefore as one who had the form of a servant—and not as Son of God—that the Master in Matthew 17:26 paid the same tribute as the disciple.[97]

---

pro me et te. [Matthew 17:24 ff.] Neque ego habeo hanc 'imaginem et superscriptionem' neque tu, si tamen vere discipulus meus es, si 'portae inferorum non praevalent adversum te' [Matthew 16:18]. Ergo Iesus aliter dat pro se 'imaginem' de 'mari' illam accipiens, quae in 'pisce' fuerat inclusa, simili his piscibus de quibus hodie lectum est, qui 'adhaerent in squamis draconis, qui sedet super flumina Aegypti' [Ezechiel 29:4]. . . . Quanti et hodie 'pisces' sunt, quorum rex est iste qui in aquis regnat? Scriptum est quippe de invisibili 'dracone' quia 'ipse sit rex omnium quae sunt in aquis' (Job 41:25) . . . ." See Crouzel, *Théologie de l'Image*, 195 f.

96. See, for instance, above, chapter 1, pp. 7f.

97. *Com. Mat.* 13.10, 206 f.: "Sunt ergo aliqui 'reges terrae' et eorum filii, qui non dant 'tributum vel censum' et alii praeter filios eorum extraeni a regibus 'terrae,' ex quibus 'accipiunt reges terrae tributum vel censum' et sunt 'filii quidem' eorum 'liberi' apud reges 'terrae' sicut apud patres filii: extranei autem extra terram quidem liberi sunt, propter eos autem, qui dominantur eorum et deprimunt eos, sicut 'Aegyptii filios Israel' [Exodus 1:13 f.] servi. Propter quos servientes 'formam servi' suscepit filius dei [cf. Philippians 2:7] qui nullum opus fecit luteum et servile. Quasi ergo habens

Moreover, Origen emphasizes, the coin could not be found in the house of Jesus: but had to be extracted from the "mouth of a fish from the sea." Nor was it an accident that the fish should be caught from the hook of the same Peter whom the Lord had made a "fisher of men." Figuratively, therefore, Origen continues, the fish represents the Christian of today, from whose mouth the coin that bears the image of Caesar must first be extracted before he can join the ranks of those who have fished him out of the sea. Thus, he who has still within himself "the things which are Caesar's," Origen concludes, must "render" or "give them back" to Caesar before he can truly "render unto God the things that are God's."[98] Therefore:

> quoniam [autem] Jesus non habuit imaginem Caesaris (princeps enim saeculi huius nihil habebat in eo) propterea non ex proprio sed ex convenienti loco maris imaginem Caesaris accepit eam, ut det regibus terrae pro se et pro discipulo suo, ut nec arbitrentur . . . esse eum debitorem [eorum] [Gr.: *hina mēde hupolambanōsin . . . opheiletēn autōn einai*]. . . . Reddit enim debitum [Gr.: *apedōke gar tēn opheilēn*], non suscipiens [Gr.: *analabōn*] eum, neque possidens, neque adquirens, neque faciens eum sibi possessionem, ut ne sit aliquando imago Caesaris apud imaginem invisibilis Dei.[99]

Jesus, however, had no image of Caesar's; for as He said in John 14:30, "the prince of this world has nothing in me." He therefore took up a coin bearing the image of Caesar not from anything that belonged to Him but from a fitting place in the sea. This He did that He might pay tribute to the kings of this earth (in both His Name and that of His disciple) without their thinking that He owed them anything at all (Gr.: *hina mēde hupolambanōsin opheiletēn einai*; Lat.: *ut nec arbitrentur esse eum debitorem eorum*), for He gave them back the coin that was owed to them (Gr.: *apedōke gar tēn opheilēn*; Lat.: *reddit enim debitum*) without picking it up Himself, nor ever having it in His possession, nor making lawful acquisition of it, nor

formam servi illius tributum et censum dedit non aliud ab eo, quod dedit discipulus eius: ipse enim stater sufficiebat et unum nomisma, quod dabatur pro Iesu et pro discipulo eius."

98. Ibid., 207 f.: "Hoc autem nomisma in domo quidem Iesu non erat, in mari autem erat et erat in ore piscis marini, quem ipsum piscem arbitror adiuvatum ascendisse ad hamum Petri et conprehensum ab eo, qui hominum piscator fuerat factus, in quibus erat qui nunc moraliter dicitur piscis, ut tollatur ab eo nomisma quod habebat imaginem 'Caesaris' et fiat inter eos qui piscati sunt eum. Qui ergo habet quae sunt 'Caesaris' 'Caesari' ea reddat, ut post hoc valeat reddere 'deo quae dei sunt.' "

99. Ibid., 208. See Crouzel, *Théologie de l'Image*, 195.

turning it in any way into His legal possession, lest at any point the image of Caesar should be found upon Him Who is the Image of the Invisible God.

At first sight the passage may seem to raise more problems than it solves. For one thing, the way in which the traditional baptismal allegory (which here, as in the second construction, Origen seems to make his own) is sandwiched between two christological passages may present something of a puzzle. To be sure, the transition between the first christological passage and the baptismal allegory is traditional (though perhaps a little gnosticizing) and reasonably clear: the Son of the King of Heaven lowered Himself and "took upon Him the form of a servant" so that He might free the other children of the King from their bondage in "Egypt." Thanks to this subjection on the part of Christ Christians at baptism are rescued from the "sea" of the world and enter into freedom by renouncing their former bondage to "Caesar." The connection of the baptismal allegory with the second christological passage seems, however, less clear; and the passage itself may on first inspection seem rather self-contradictory. It opens resoundingly with a citation of John 14:30: "the prince of this world hath nothing in me"; and it ends on the same note with the statement that "at no point was the image of Caesar found upon Him Who is the Image of the Invisible God." In between, however, there lies the puzzler: in the space of less than ten words and using the very same term (*opheiletēs / opheilē* in the Greek, and *debitor / debitum* in the Latin version), first in the negative and then in the affirmative mode, Origen manages to say at one and the same time both that the Lord "owed" the kings of this earth "nothing at all" and that He "gave them the coin that was owed to them."[100] What then is the purpose of this second christological passage and what is its connection with the baptismal allegory that precedes it? Is it to affirm that Christ was free and that at baptism Christians enter into that same freedom, or is it, on the contrary, to remind the Christian that even Christ remained in subjection of a kind?

To raise the problem is in a sense to solve it: Origen's pur-

100. Ibid., 208. The Latin here is an almost exact translation of the Greek: "Hina mēde hupolambanōsin . . . opheiletēn . . . einai . . . tōn basileōn tēs gēs ton Iēsoun; apedōke gar tēn opheilēn, ouk analabōn autēn . . . ." (*analabein* does suggest "picking up" in the physical sense more clearly than *suscipere.*) See above, text at preceding note.

pose is obviously both. This christological solution will, moreover, integrate the various elements in Origen's exegesis of Matthew 17:24 ff., Romans 13:1 ff., Luke 20:20 ff., and Matthew 22:21. For Origen, the Incarnation is quite literally that: the taking on of flesh, the assumption of a body and nothing more. He does not, to be sure, deny that Christ had a human soul: but for him that soul existed and had been fused with the Word since the beginning of Creation. For Origen, therefore, the Incarnation consisted of the taking on of a body by an already human though disembodied Christ; the so-called Logos-Flesh theology, which was to culminate in the fourth century in the Apollinarian heresy and which denied that Christ had a human soul, cannot in all fairness be attributed to him, but it was no accident that almost all of his followers were in fact to subscribe to that doctrine.[101] But if all bodies bear the bodily image of the Prince of Bodies, it follows that by "taking on the form of a servant" the Lord subjected Himself to the Prince of this World. The case of Christ is, to be sure, peculiar, "as is immediately apparent from a consideration of his virgin birth." Admittedly he ate and drank after His resurrection and showed the disciples his pierced "hands, his feet and his side; yet he can pass through . . . doors, and while breaking bread can vanish out of . . . sight. And even before the resurrection certain things . . . do not in any way correspond with our normal physical experience, as for example in the Transfiguration."[102] It was voluntarily that the Lord subjected Himself to the flesh, just as He voluntarily underwent death (first figuratively in the form of baptism and then in reality) and through that voluntary assumption of death paradoxically triumphed over the Lord of Death. Voluntary subjection, however, both is and is not subjection. Unlike other men, the Lord does not—and in a sense cannot—sin, just as he does not *have* to die: from that perspective He can truly say "the prince of this world has nothing in me." Yet His form as a Servant nevertheless bears the bodily mark of the Lord of Bodies: like other men, Christ is subject to temptation, to hunger, to cold, to

101. On the christology of Origen and of his followers, see, for instance, Kelly, *Early Christian Doctrines*, 153–62. On the influence of Origen on the Logos-Flesh christologies of the fourth century and ultimately on the heresy of Apollinaris of Laodicea, see ibid., 280–95. On the soul of Jesus, see also Crouzel, *Théologie de l'Image*, 129–42.

102. Chadwick, "Origen, Celsus and the Resurrection of the Body," 100. See above, n. 77, and below, n. 104.

sleep, and to all the other necessities of the body (even though because His subjection is voluntary He may on occasion escape from some of these restrictions). This is why Christ both "gives to the kings of the earth the coin that was their due" and yet may be said "to owe them nothing at all." Though Origen should not be ranked among the docetists (who believed that the humanity of Christ was nothing but appearance), there is a docetic element in his christology of the Flesh. In his corporeal form as a servant, Christ paid tribute to the kings of this earth; but to indicate the far greater "spiritual" reality—which in this context refers both to the human soul of Christ which, unlike that of other men, has remained completely "rational"[103] and to the Logos with which it is fused—He took care to pay them with a coin that was never in His possession and that in fact He never even touched.[104]

The christological exegesis of Matthew 17:24 ff. thus integrates the tropological exegesis of Matthew 22:21, the political exegesis of Romans 13:1 ff., and the baptismal exegesis of the first two passages into a single and unified structure. Christ paid tribute to Caesar but in a peculiar way to symbolize both the freedom that was truly His in His capacity as Logos as well as in that of a purely rational soul, and yet also the subjection which He nevertheless observed because of the "appearance" He had assumed in His form as a servant. Christians at bap-

103. Crouzel, *Théologie de l'Image,* 132 ff.

104. Above at nn. 98–100. Relevant here may be *Hom. Gen.* 1.13, 17: "Ad huius [i.e., Verbi] imaginis similitudinem homo factus est et propterea Salvator noster, qui est imago Dei misericordia motus pro homine, qui ad eius similitudinem factus fuerat, videns eum deposita sua imagine maligni imaginem induxisse, ipse motus misericordia imagine hominis assumpta venit ad eum, sicut et Apostolus contestatur dicens: 'cum in forma Dei esset . . . semet ipsum exinanivit formam servi accipiens, et habitu repertus ut homo, humiliavit semet ipsum usque ad mortem' [Philippians 2:6–8]." See the brief discussion by Crouzel, *Théologie de l'Image,* 141, and above, n. 79, where a passage that comes only some twenty lines later has been cited. For Origen the *kenōsis* of Philippians 2:6 ff. has to do quite specifically with the Incarnation: the emptying, the humiliation, consists in the taking on of the "appearance" of flesh, not in the fusion between the human soul of Christ and the Word that had taken place before the creation of the material world. On the other hand, the "image of Man" which the Word assumes is therefore quite clearly the Image of Dust of 1 Corinthians 15:47 ff. which is in fact the Image of the Devil (here called the *imago maligni;* cf. Crouzel's translation "image du Malin," *Théologie de l'Image,* 141; cf. also above, n. 70). The passage from the Homilies on Genesis thus confirms and gives soteriological significance to Origen's interpretation of Matthew 17:24 ff.: by assuming the Image of the Devil, Christ allows man to reassume the Image of God according to which he had first been created. Against this, see Crouzel, *Théologie de l'Image,* 137, who—for no reason that I can see—applies the exegesis of Philippians 2:6 ff. found in *Com. Rom.* 5.10, 1051C–1052A, to the fusion of soul and Logos.

tism enter into Christ's freedom by assuming Christ and renouncing their former bondage to "Caesar": the Old Man has become the New Man. Yet, as has been seen, the diachronic and biographical contrast between Old and New Man is through baptism merely transformed into a synchronic duality and that on two levels. On a "sociological" plane (and I am here speaking of theological sociology), the pneumatic elite is to the mob of psychic Christians as the spirit is to the letter and the New Man is to the Old. From that point of view, those who have followed Christ's counsels of perfection, who have given up all possessions and lead a life of perfect asceticism, have nothing through which they may be subject to Caesar, while those who still have "something of the world"[105] must—even after baptism—"render unto Caesar the things that are Caesar's." On a deeper level, however, the diachronic contrast between Old and New Man and its sociological counterpart, the synchronic duality between psychic and pneumatic, have been internalized into another and more pervasive synchronic pair, the "anthropological" distinction between body and soul. From that point of view, no one—whether psychic or pneumatic—can fully give up the world as long as he remains in the flesh, for as long as he remains a rather disjointed composite the Christian still belongs to the time in-between, is still under the lordship of the Lord of Dust. Thus, even a pneumatic remains dependent on "Caesar" for his food and his clothing, be it only a single tunic: and this has both political and eschatological consequences. Compared to the psychic, the pneumatic may in a loose sense be said to have given up all possessions and the cares of this world and thus to be free from subjection to the emperor, the body, and the Devil. Absolute poverty is an ideal which he attempts to fulfill; but from the point of view of the time in-between it is an ideal which, strictly speaking, remains incapable of absolute fulfillment.

Because of this pervasive dualism, the pneumatic must remember that his spirituality, his pneumaticism, remains in some sense proleptic and eschatological: from the point of view of the time in-between, he too remains in a way a psychic, a member of the common flock. As has been seen, Origen is fully aware of this—at least in his less elitist and gnosticizing moments. The pneumatic who does not remember that he

105. See above, n. 50.

shares the common lot of all men is, in fact, transformed into an Encratite or other puritan, a Pharisee, or a spiritual Zealot. This indeed is the Devil's last temptation: a temptation to which Origen was peculiarly subject, but also a temptation of which he was acutely aware. Out of pride in the spirit, out of an "immoderate lust for purity," such pseudo-pneumatics despise the humility of the flesh: they forget that in doing so it is Christ Whom they despise.[106] From this point of view, the orthodox Christian must remember that he is not only a citizen of Jerusalem but, alas! still a denizen of Babylon. He mediates between the body and the flesh, the world and the Church, this world and the next, while he is crucified by these disjunctions. Though as a citizen of Jerusalem he has the freedom of the pneumatic, humility requires him to recognize that from the point of view of the time in-between he still corresponds to the second and not the third term of the hylic-psychic-pneumatic progression. In a less crude but far more dangerous fashion, the puritan heretic or Christian Zealot is therefore as much a sinner as his pagan converse, the self-indulgent Epicurean or the persecutor of Christians. In one sense, the orthodox Christian mediates between these two errors: in all humility he acknowledges that in spite of his pneumatic freedom he remains in the flesh and still belongs to the common flock of psychics. In another, he is equally opposed to materialistic paganism and to pseudo-spiritual heresy. Indeed, the two extremes touch: for the Devil is clever and the overweening spiritualism of many a heretic has a way of turning into a materialism of its own. What begins with contempt for matter and the flesh—something that up to a point is simply a Christian duty—turns all too easily into fleshly and therefore violent abuse of the flesh. What begins with contempt for the world and all worldly powers turns all too easily into violent and therefore worldly resistance to the world.

As Origen's first commentary on Matthew 17:24 ff. makes clear, moreover, this curious position of the Christian is itself rooted in Christ: the Son of God "took upon Him the form of a Servant" for the sake of His brethren in bondage. It is because Christ voluntarily entered into slavery of a sort that Christians at baptism enter into the freedom of the Spirit. Conversely, the dual nature of Christ means that the Christian—before the resurrection of the flesh—must lead a fractured existence:

106. See above, chapter 2, n. 46.

despite his freedom, he remains enslaved. It is to signify this paradox that Christ both gave the kings of this earth "the coin that was their due" and yet made it clear that he owed them "nothing at all." The fracture that characterizes Christian existence in the time in-between (that is to say before the Second Coming and the Resurrection of the Flesh) is thus prefigured by the still incomplete fusion of the two natures of Christ before His Resurrection.

To an extent this persistent dualism in Origen's conception of the earthly Jesus is due to the unorthodox peculiarities of his christology. Later orthodoxy will avoid the danger of both monophysitism (too much emphasis on unity between the Two Natures) and Nestorianism (too much emphasis on their duality) by asserting that the Humanity and Divinity of Christ remain distinct but not separate entities. Origen achieves the same effect by distinguishing two moments in the process of God becoming Man. The union of the Logos with the soul of Jesus at the beginning of Creation is pretty much a "monophysite" fusion: the two, he asserts, become united like fire and iron in a red-hot lump. The insertion of this red-hot lump into its envelope of flesh is, on the other hand, a rather "Nestorian" affair. Origen, as has been seen, is always a little uneasy with the fleshly Jesus. And the dichotomy within the earthly Christ is for him not so much that between the Divine and the Human as that between Flesh and Spirit—the latter including the human soul of Jesus since the beginning of time already fused with the Divine Logos. Thus both orthodox christology and that of Origen preserve the dialectic between God and Man: the radical distinction between the two both is and is not sublated by Christ.[107]

From the point of view of Christian anthropology, the main consequence of Origen's somewhat peculiar christology is that through their souls Christians are more conjoined with God than in orthodox theology; while through their bodies they remain more disjoined. Beyond this, Origenist anthropology implies that the flesh (and through the flesh the whole of the material world) is less redeemed and less capable of redemption

107. See, for instance, *De Principiis* 2.6.6, 145, Butterworth, 113. Cf. also *De Principiis* 2.6.3, 141 ff., Butterworth, 110 f. See Kelly, *Early Christian Doctrines*, 155, n. 5, and Crouzel, *Théologie de l'Image*, 136 f. Crouzel notes that in modern times Origen's christology has been called "Nestorian" as well as "Monophysite." Is it possible that what I have said in the preceding paragraph explains at least some of that double apprehension?

than in later orthodox theology. Origen, of course, does not deny the resurrection of the flesh. Yet the resurrection of Christ to the contrary notwithstanding, there is for him a veritable chasm between the "spiritual flesh" of the resurrection and the all too fleshly flesh of today; and in one passage at least he can forget himself to the point of suggesting that the resurrected Christ should no longer be considered a man.[108] Earthly matter and fleshly flesh no doubt play an important role in the process of redemption: but that role is essentially external and primarily negative. The flesh is sanctified not so much because Christ was to take flesh but rather because earthly matter, "dust" and flesh form the first step in the educative process of Divine *Paideia.* This is why, after the Fall, God created earthly matter and allowed the Devil to put his seal upon it. This is why at a later stage God allowed His Son to lower Himself and by taking flesh subject Himself to the Devil. In order to redeem the inner core—the souls—of those who were in bondage, the Son of God assumed an envelope of flesh.[109] But the consequences of such an external incarnation can themselves only be external. In his exegesis of Matthew 17:24 ff., Origen speaks not of the fusion of the soul of Jesus with the Word of God but of what to him is no doubt an important (but still essentially secondary, and at any rate external) process: the Incarnation according to the flesh—if the tautology can be forgiven. As a result, what is stressed in that exegesis is not so much the redemption of man (which has primarily to do with the soul), but the lesson in humility which can lead to that redemption. If Christians wish to be free, as their Lord was free despite His voluntary subjection to the flesh and its Lord, they must humbly take up that subjection and recognize that, like Christ, they are weak and thus subject to temptation; and in particular that because of their weakness they are still subject to the needs of the body, and because of these needs incapable of "giving back" (at least in the absolute sense) all possessions and thus become totally free of their subjection to Caesar. Despite his rejection of Gnosticism, the unease which earthly matter and the flesh inspire in Origen is thus extended even to the Flesh of Jesus. If the exegesis of Matthew 22:21

108. *Hom. Jer.* 15.6, 111 f., cited by Kelly, *Early Christian Doctrines,* 158. But see above, n. 77, for a more positive assessment of Origen's doctrine of the Resurrection.

109. See above at n. 97 and pp. 176 f.

demonstrated that the Devil can be made to play a commanding role even when his demonic and eschatological aspects are more or less suppressed, the exegesis of Matthew 17:24 shows that the redemptive dimension may stay in the background even in the presence of Christ—or at least of the earthly Jesus.[110]

These restrictions on both the antithetical or eschatological and on the mitigated or incarnational frames of reference are due, no doubt, to the peculiarities of Origen's theology, which explains at least in part the cool, balanced, and, as has been said, "secular" aspects of his political exegesis. Yet more or less the same effects can (but need not) be achieved in orthodox theology through the interaction of the four levels of meaning, as well as through some special features of tropological exegesis. Tropology refers essentially to the life of Christians: it is the second of the spiritual meanings and thus mediates between the allegorical or christological and the eschatological or anagogical levels. Eschatology, as has been seen, is either "consequent" or "realized." If the former, it tends to look at everything from the point of view of a never-ending struggle between Christ and the Devil: the various dualities of the Christian life, such as those between body and soul or between Church and world, tend to become exaggerated under the influence of that paradigm. If eschatology is "realized," on the other hand, it tends to look at everything from the point of view of an already triumphant Christ: it thus tends to merge with christology and with the first level of spiritual meaning.[111] At this "realized"—and christological—level, the various dualities of the Christian life are thought of as already resolved; through the Incarnation and Redemption they tend to mirror the union (without confusion) of the Two Natures of Christ. The body is thus reconciled to the soul, and the world to the Church. Though it has not usually been noted, tropology, like eschatology, can also be subdivided into either "realized" or "consequent." If it is the former, the three levels of spiritual meaning tend to merge into one; tropology becomes mystical (and therefore christological as well as eschatological), and the soul of the individual Christian becomes more or less identified with the Triumphant Christ. If it is "consequent,"

110. Above at nn. 61–82, and at nn. 88–100.
111. See above, n. 42.

tropology tends to turn into a quasi-naturalistic or quasi-secular morality. The dualities will survive but will tend to become reduced to an "illuminating distinction" between parallel but by no means antagonistic structures, both of which are thought of as created by God. What is stressed is no longer the heroism of eschatological struggle but the "bourgeois" virtues of noninterference and of give-and-take.[112] The need for mediation also survives; but the tendency is to stress reconciliation through God the Creator (and therefore through a merely "naturalistic" God) rather than through Christ. In behavioral terms, the mystical union with Christ the Mediator has been civilized into the Golden Mean.[113] But for the tropology to remain alive and Christian, this process of secularization—in structural terms, a process of isolation by which the other levels of spiritual meaning are in effect kept out of the surface of the exegesis—must not be allowed to spread too far: other and less "secular" dimensions should at least lurk beneath these cool and civilized pairs of dioscuric twins.[114]

In *Contra Celsum* Origen presented his theology of politics from the eschatological vantage point of the theology of history. This allowed him to emphasize either one of two aspects. When he had to argue as a polemicist, he stressed the never-ending struggle between God and the Devil and tended to equate the Church with the former and the Empire with the latter. On the contrary, in his more frequent and apologetic mode, he tended to stress the reconciliation of the world through Christ: from that point of view the Empire could be seen as operating in the sacramental penumbra of the Church.[115] In his exegetical writings, on the other hand, a theology of politics that is neither demonic nor christological, but instead cool, moderate, and, in some sense at least, distinctly "secular," tends to come to the fore. As has just been seen, however, these three theologies of politics—though some of the details are due to the peculiarities of Origen's private stance—do not contradict one another, but rather fit together through the complex interrelationship among the three levels of spiritual meaning.

Indeed, from what has been said in the last few pages, it

112. On bourgeois Christianity, see above, chapter 3, n. 4.
113. On the "taming" of eschatology, see above, pp. 140 f. and at nn. 105–06.
114. See above at n. 60.
115. See above at nn. 2–31.

should be clear that both the demonic and the christological strands in the theology of politics of *Contra Celsum* must be understood as operating under rather rigid restrictions. As has been said before, Origen is no Hippolytus of Rome. Even when he is forced to stress the demonic aspects of the state, he acknowledges its providential role as an instrument of Divine *Paideia:* nor is this a paradox, for such is after all the role of the Devil himself.[116] But if Origen is no Hippolytus, neither is he Eusebius of Caesarea, even though in the end he may lead to Eusebius.[117] To say that from a certain point of view Origen sees the Empire as operating in the sacramental penumbra of the Church is correct; but then one must remember that for Origen the sacraments, insofar as they reflect the flesh of the earthly Jesus, remain themselves in the penumbra of the True Church, that is to say the Church of the Spirit.[118] At best, the state is therefore the fleshly envelope. The state has a redemptive function, but that redemptive function is purely external: it helps the spread of the redemptive process by providing the modicum of external peace that makes it possible for the Church to do its work of "godliness and charity" in relative "peace and quiet." It remains an "external power" appointed primarily for the "utility of the Gentiles," inasmuch as its functions have to do with avenging crimes and defending external possessions.[119] The Christian who has truly put on Christ and fully shed the outer man has no need for it: yet Christians must remember that even Jesus put on an outer garment of flesh and thus from an external point of view that did not really affect the inner Christ subjected Himself to Caesar and the Devil and that He did this in order to save His brethren in bondage. From one point of view the externality of the state puts it outside the redemptive process. From another, that very "secularism" is seen as an external means of redemption; and voluntary subjection to this external power is a form of humility and thus an imitation of Christ and an inner part of the redemptive process.

116. See above at nn. 78–82.

117. On Hippolytus see above at nn. 34–37. On Eusebius' political theology and the connection with Origen, see, for instance, Ladner, *Idea of Reform,* 115–25; Beskow, *Kingship of Christ,* 261 ff.; and Ehrhardt, *Politische Metaphysik* 2.282 ff.

118. For Origen's view of the Eucharist, see above, chapter 2 at nn. 15 f. and 29–33.

119. See above at nn. 43 and 44.

CONCLUSION

The two main themes of this book have been Origen's exegetical method and his theology of politics. In counterpoint to these two motifs, the reader has heard in the background repeated, though intermittent, echoes of the later medieval theory of the two swords. The first theme has been elaborated concretely in terms of carnal swords in the first, in terms of spiritual swords in the second chapter; while it has been developed on a more theoretical level in the third. The fourth chapter has dealt with Origen's theology of politics. The book as a whole has attempted to establish the existence of an internal harmony between these two themes. Origen interprets the Phineas episode, the pericope of the two swords, and the pericope of the tribute money, as allegories about letter and spirit, allegories about allegory itself. For Origen, the carnal sword of Phineas is to the spiritual sword of the Old Dispensation, as exegetical letter is to exegetical spirit, as Caesar is to God, and ultimately therefore as state is to Church.

The later political interpretation of the sword pericope is thus grounded in the interrelation between Origen's exegetical method and his theology of politics. Much of Origen's theology will, to be sure, not be transmitted to the medieval West. *Contra Celsum,* the main vehicle of that theology, was never translated into Latin. Moreover, those elements of Origen's theology of politics that are based on his peculiar theological stance—his views on the Devil or on the Flesh for instance—even if transmitted tend to be neglected, because they do not fit into later orthodoxy. Finally, so many of the pre-Constantinian conditions, the radical pacifism of Christianity or the necessary paganism of all "powers that be," on which much of Origen's theology of politics rests, were totally foreign to medieval times; while many medieval categories of political ecclesiology, the sharp distinction between cleric and layman or that between kingship and priesthood, were basically foreign to Origen's political vocabulary. Yet despite these factors the structure of Origen's theology of politics is so embedded in an exegesis that is not only transmitted and understood but is heavily exploited by the medieval West, that the radical change in social conditions and the loss or neglect of much Origenist material does not significantly lessen its impact.

The interrelation between Origen's exegesis and his theology of politics is realized on at least three levels. First, his own, actual, exegesis of the sword pericope—a point at which hermeneutics and theology of politics naturally meet—provided the foundation stone for all later interpretations of the passage. Second, at a structural but relatively superficial level, his exegetical method, so heavily influential in the West (in part through the intermediaries of Hilary, Ambrose, Jerome, and much more indirectly Augustine), allowed later exegetes to deepen and when necessary change the surface while preserving the foundations of his exegesis. Third, at a deeper level, the interpenetration between hermeneutics and theology of politics meant that even quite radical changes in the conditions of Church and of world, the christianization of the Empire, the substitution of clerical for Christian pacifism, the sharper and sharper distinction between layman and cleric, the integration of kingship into the Church or again its relegation back into the world, and finally the conflict between kingship and priesthood, could all quite easily be integrated into the hermeneutics of the Pauline circle.

These developments will be the subject of another book, the history of the two swords from the fourth century to the third quarter of the twelfth. That book will attempt to trace the slow evolution, and then in the period just around 1075, the coalescence of four distinct elements: first, the growth on the basis of Origen's exegesis of a proto-political interpretation of the sword pericope; second, the surprisingly late appearance of the rebuke of Peter—the fifth moment of the sword pericope—as an authority for clerical pacifism; third, the evolution of what may be called a nonexegetical tradition of the two swords; and fourth and finally the development of an equally nonexegetical doctrine of two powers, first within the world, then within the Church, and then again within the world.

With the Constantinian Revolution, the "spiritualizing" tendencies that had already been marked in Origen's exegesis of the sword pericope move to the foreground. Origen had never denied that the rebuke of Peter at the end of the pericope was at a literal level an *auctoritas* for Christian pacifism; but he had been more interested in a "tropological" interpretation that saw in that rebuke a denunciation of spiritual strife. With the fourth and fifth century, from what is probably an address by Constantine himself to Augustine's Tractates on John, Matthew 26:52 is seen as a denunciation of either self-help and self-defense[1] or as a condemnation of anger not of war.[2] In the same period, Hilary and Jerome emphasize that the sword which Christians are forbidden to use—or the sword by which those that disobey this injunction will perish—is not necessarily a physical sword (and indeed that one can "perish" in a number of senses).[3] At the same time Ambrose and Ambrosiaster both distinguish the power of self-defense, which neither the Lord nor his disciples had lost, from the will to make use of that power: in the rebuke of Peter, the Lord forbids His disciples to use a power which they (like He) have nevertheless kept.[4] Finally, Ambrose gives the allegorical interpretation of Luke 22:38 that will enter later tradition. The two swords represent the Old and the New Testament: together they "suffice" or are "enough" to defend Christian doctrine.[5] The Origenist scheme, the dialectic between letter and spirit, has thus remained unchanged; and in most of the authors the influence of Origen

1. [Constantine], "Oratio ad Sanctorum Coetum" 15, in Eusebius of Caesarea, *Opera*, *GCS* 7, 175 ll.15 ff. See Altaner, *Patrology*, 265 on the authenticity of the speech.

2. Augustine, *In Iohannis Evangelium Tractatus* 112.5, *CC* 36, 635.

3. Hilary of Poitiers, *Commentarius in Matthaeum* 32.2, *PL* 9, 1071 and Jerome, *Commentariorum in Matthaeum Libri* IV (26.52), *CC* 77, 258, see above, chapter 2, nn. 106 and 130.

4. Ambrose, *Expositio Evangelii secundum Lucam* 10.53, *CC* 14, 361 and Ambrosiaster, *Quaestiones Veteris et Novi Testamenti* 104.4 *CSEL* 50, 229, see above, chapter 2, n. 117.

5. Ambrose, *Expositio Evangelii secundum Lucam* 10.55, *CC* 14, 361.

is plain.[6] The patristic commentaries are filtered through Bede, who while keeping the basic scheme intact, suggests that one of the two swords represents the power of self-defense never used by Christ or his disciples, the other the will not to make use of that power.[7] Carolingian exegesis is rich, plentiful, and diverse. For Alcuin the two swords may represent body and soul or else works and faith.[8] Paschasius Radbertus, developing the suggestion of Hilary and Jerome, proposes that one of the two swords is the sword of excommunication or damnation; the other the sword of life, that is, the word of God, by which Christians "die" to this world only to live really and truly in the spirit.[9] These are all transformations that follow the rules outlined in chapter 3: but the deep structural level has remained the same. The only thing that is a bit surprising is that a fully political dialectic of state and Church, or at least of material and spiritual power, of kingship and priesthood, of layman and cleric, has not yet been grafted onto the exegetical structure.

An at least implicit distinction between layman and cleric (and by extension between kingship and priesthood) begins to appear in the margins of the exegesis of the sword pericope among Italian reformers of the tenth and eleventh centuries. In the tenth century, Atto of Vercelli seems to have been the first to link clerical pacifism with the rebuke of Peter: it is clerics and clerics alone who in Matthew 26:52 are strictly enjoined from making use of the sword.[10] Among a group of eleventh century reformers, possibly followers of Peter Damian, Matthew 26:52 reappears as an *auctoritas* for clerical pacifism and in an interesting construct clerical pacifism is closely linked to clerical celibacy.[11] The appearance of this new interpretation

6. The influence is plainly visible in Hilary, Jerome and particularly Ambrose. It is more indirect in the case of Ambrosiaster and Augustine. Cf. above, chapter 2, n. 124.

7. Bede, *In Lucae Evangelium Expositio* (22:38), *CC* 120, 384.

8. Alcuin, *Epistola* 136, *MGH, Epistolae* 4, 207f.

9. Paschasius Radbertus, *Expositio in Matthaeum* 12.26, *PL* 120, 916–19, see also above, chapter 2, n. 106.

10. Atto Vercellensis, *De Pressuris Ecclesiasticis* 1, *PL* 134, 60 ff.

11. Pseudo-Innocent in Deusdedit, *Collectio Canonum* 3.250, ed. V. Wolf von Glanvell (Paderborn, 1909), 537. See already *membra disjecta* of the same text in Wido Ferrarensis, *De Scismate Hildebrandi*, 2, *MGH. LdL.* 1, 554 and 554 f., the first passage attributed to Jerome, the second to Innocent. The text of Pseudo-Jerome begins with a sentence from Peter Damian's letter to Bishop Oldradus of Fermi, the main manifesto of eleventh-century Italian clerical pacifism (Peter Damian, *Epistolarum Liber* 8.9, *PL* 154, 313 ff.). In Deusdedit, the Pseudo-Innocentian canon appears in close proximity to the genuine letter to Oldradus, *Collectio Canonum*, 3.246, 532. For a later extract of

is explicable in part by the aims of certain segments of the Reform Movement, in part by the fact that for centuries already a material or corporeal sword had been opposed to a sword of the spirit in a nonexegetical framework, or at least in a framework that was quite detached from the sword pericope. The opposition between a carnal sword of the Old Testament, a sword that carries out executions or just wars, and a spiritual sword of the New Testament that merely excommunicates or anathematizes seems to go back at least to St. Cyprian.[12] In the ninth century, the opposition becomes widely current in papal letters: in those for instance of Nicholas I[13] and in a quite different way (leaving out the historical opposition between Old and New Dispensation) in those of John VIII.[14]

Exegetical and nonexegetical usage must both be understood within the framework of a developing theology of the two powers: a theology that receives its classical formulation in the fifth century by Pope Gelasius I, in terms that may have had their roots in Origen's exegesis of Matthew 22:21.[15] As is well known, for Gelasius the "power" of kingship and the "authority" of Priesthood are within the world; with the Carolingian period (actually already in Visigothic Spain with Isidore of Seville) both powers are usually seen as existing within the Church; the Reform Period from the eleventh century on sees both a survival of the Carolingian or Isidorian viewpoint and a revival of Gelasianism, in which kingship is no longer—or no longer entirely—perceived as an office within the Church.[16]

Pseudo-Innocent (surely not based on the text in Deusdedit) see the *palea* in Gratian C.23 q.8 c.2. (See also below, nn. 20 and 23.)

12. Cyprian, *Epistola* 4.2, *CSEL* 3.2, 473.

13. E.g., Nicholas I, *Epistola* 47, *MGH Epistolae* 6, 327, *Epistola* 123, ibid., 641 and most significantly the *responsum* contained in *Epistola* 156, ibid., 674: "Sancta Dei Ecclesia mundanis numquam constringitur legibus; gladium non habet nisi spiritalem atque divinum; non occidit, sed vivificat." (See above, chapter 3, n. 21.)

14. E.g., John VII, *Epistola* 41, *MGH Epistolae* 7, 39 and *Epistola* 249, ibid., 218. (The Pope threatens the Amalfitans *non solum visibili sed etiam invisibili gladio.*)

15. Gelasius I, *Epistola ad Anastasium Imperatorem, Epistola* 8 in Eduard Schwartz, *Publizistische Schriften zum Acacianischen Schisma,* 19 ff. and *Tomus De Anathematis Vinculo,* ibid., 14 (see above, chapter 3, n. 16). The language of the *Tomus* (usually known as *Tractatus* IV) emphasizes that the Lord's ruling in Matthew 22:21 was a *magnifica dispensatio* by which He set bounds (*temperavit*) and separated (*discrevit*) distinct dignities (*dignitates distincta*). There are similarities of language with Hilary of Poitier's exegesis of the same passage *Commentarius in Matthaeum* 23, *PL* 9.1044 f., and that exegesis is in turn almost surely based on that of Origen.

16. See Gerhart B. Ladner, "The Concepts of 'Ecclesia' and 'Christianitas' and their Relation to the Idea of Papal 'Plenitudo Potestatis' from Gregory VII to Boniface VIII" in *Miscellanea Historiae Pontificiae,* vol. 18 (*Sacerdozio e Regno da Gregorio VII*

After 1075, with the outbreak of the Investiture Controversy, the new political interpretation of the sword pericope suddenly comes to the fore. It was, at one and the same time, a retrospective reading of the new clerical interpretation of the rebuke of Peter into the earlier moments of the pericope; an application of the old nonexegetical tradition of the two swords to the heretofore more conservative demands of biblical exegesis; a further development of the Pauline dialectic, already at work within the traditionally Origenistic exegesis, allowing the duality between kingship and Priesthood to be assimilated to the Pauline pairs; and the result of a new emphasis on theology of politics, resulting in part from the sudden confrontation of the by now traditional Isidorian or Carolingian ecclesiology with a revived Gelasian ecclesiology.

During the Investiture Controversy and for perhaps half a century after its conclusion, the atmosphere is electric and conducive to a whole series of exciting new re-interpretations of the sword pericope that are nevertheless based on the basic Origenist tradition, and vibrate with the resonances of the Pauline dialectic. Thus at the very beginning of the controversy, the court of Henry IV interprets the pericope within a strictly "Isidorian" framework: the two swords are distinct, neither must usurp the functions of the other, yet both clearly operate as offices within the Church, and the priesthood must not be deprived of "the honor of kingship" any more than the kingship of "the honor of priesthood."[17] At about the same time, an otherwise unknown chaplain at the court of Matilda of Tuscany puts curialist restrictions on the clerical pacifism for which Matthew 26:52 had become the main *auctoritas:* the rebuke of Peter means that priests may not make use of the

---

a Bonifacio VIII) 1954, 49 ff. For my purposes I do not distinguish between what Ladner has called "Carolingian" and "inverted Carolingian." For Isidore of Seville, see the often cited passage, *Sententiarum Libri* 3.51.4, *PL* 83, 723: "Principes saeculi nonnumquam intra Ecclesiam potestatis adeptae culmina tenent, ut per eamdem potestatem disciplinam ecclesiasticam muniant. Ceterum intra Ecclesiam potestates necessariae non essent, nisi ut, quod non praevalet sacerdos efficere per doctrinae sermonem, potestas hoc imperet per disciplinae terrorem."

17. Henry IV, *Epistola* 13, in *Die Briefe Heinrich IV*, ed. Carl Erdmann, *MGH, Deutsches Mittelalter* 1, 19. I have to disagree with the otherwise excellent translation given in Theodor E. Mommsen and Karl F. Morrison in *Imperial Lives and Letters of the Eleventh Century* (New York, 1962), 152 ff. *Dum nec sacerdotii regnum, nec sacerdotium regni honore privaretur* cannot possibly mean "as long as neither the kingship is deprived of honor by the priesthood, nor the priesthood is deprived of honor by the kingship," but only "as long as neither the kingship is deprived of the honor of priesthood, nor the priesthood of the honor of kingship."

"worldly sword" with their own hands, but the Vicar of Peter rightly delegates that sword to the powers of this world.[18] After the Concordat of Worms, Rupert of Deutz, Gratian and Bernard quite independently and in quite different ways stress the importance of the *thy* in the Lord's, "Put *thy* sword back into its sheath." For Rupert, the material sword is Peter's because it is emphatically not the Lord's, who is the Lord of spiritual warfare only.[19] For Gratian—at least in one *dictum*—the sword is Peter's because "so far" it had belonged to Peter and to his predecessors, the leaders of the Israel of Old; now however he and his successors are to be restricted to the sword of the spirit.[20] For Bernard, the pericope means that the Church has indeed two swords, one of which is delegated to the Emperor, but in his capacity as protector of the Church, not in his capacity as secular king.[21] For Rupert, in addition, a christological and eschatological dimension that had only been hinted at in the previous tradition is now fully developed: the sheath into which the material sword (which is also the sword of wrath) is put, is the sheath of Jesus' humanity, for until the Second Coming the sword wielded by the Church is the sword of mildness and the sword of humility.[22] Finally, it remains for Gerhoch of Reichersberg to pick up Rupert's suggestions as well as the clerical pacifism found in the Italian Reform Movement (and reflected in several of Gratian's *dicta* in *Causa* XXIII) and for the last time play all the changes on, and give monumental expression to, the traditional exegesis. "So far", that is, until the Coming of Christ the Lord's Priests had been allowed to fight with the material sword; but with His Coming that sword is to be relinquished to the world. The possession of regalian rights that brings with it the right to wage war and

18. John of Mantua, "Commentary on the Song of Songs (1:16)," in Bernhard Bischoff and Burkhard Taeger, *Ioannis Mantuani 'In Cantica Canticorum' et de Sancta Maria Tractatus ad comitissimam Matildam, Spicilegium Friburgense* 19 (Fribourg, 1973) 52. I owe the reference to the kindness of Miss Beryl Smalley of Saint Hilda's College, Oxford University.

19. Rupert of Deutz, *Commentaria in Evangelium Sancti Johannis* 13 (18:11) *CCCM* 9, 718.

20. Gratian, *Decretum* C. 23 q.8 *dict. Grat. in princ. qu.* This is one of the *dicta* where Gratian seems to be influenced by the clerical pacifism of Pseudo-Innocent; see above, n. 11 and below, n. 23.

21. Bernard of Clairvaux, *De Consideratione* 4.3.7, *Sancti Bernardi Opera,* ed. J. Leclercq, vol. 3, 454. See above, chapter 2, n. 117.

22. Rupert of Deutz, *De Victoria Verbi Dei* 12.17, ed. R. Haacke, 391; see above chapter 2, n. 149.

make judgments of blood had thus introduced hopeless confusion into the Church of Christ.[23] The two powers are distinct, in the same way as world and Church and Old and New Dispensation are and must remain distinct. Diachronic relations are now consciously translated into synchronic ones.

In other respects, the new political interpretation—or interpretations—of the sword pericope is rapidly turning into a cliché, or perhaps into three separate and distinct clichés. For the defenders of the monarchy, the sword pericope becomes the main *auctoritas* for a thoroughgoing and largely defensive dualism: there are two swords, the two must remain distinct, and the spiritual power has no business interfering in secular affairs. For curialists, on the other hand, in a misinterpretation of Saint Bernard that seems to go back to John of Salisbury, Peter has both swords, and the fact that he may not use the material sword only demonstrates that he delegates that power to emperors and kings who become simply his delegates or vicars.[24] Finally, for the neutralists of the center, the sword pericope is simply evidence that there are indeed two powers, though the relationship between the two is carefully avoided.[25]

For Origen and for most of the Fathers, as for most of the Early Middle Ages, theology of politics did not consist of an isolated, distinctive, and somehow frozen political stance. Origen could hold at one and the same time a theology of politics that saw the Roman Empire as having a christological dimension, as being a purely secular good established by God essentially for the sake of non-Christians, and yet as also being an instrument of the Devil.[26] Similarly Gregory VII, in a single letter, saw kingship as being so worldly that it could be conceived as essentially an invention of the Devil, and yet at the same time as capable of functioning as an ecclesiastical office.[27]

23. Gerhoch of Reichersberg, *De Investigatione Antichristi* 35, *MGH LdL.* 3, 343 f. and in numerous other passages. For the *dicta* of Gratian that seem influenced by the clerical pacifism of Pseudo-Innocent and the Italian wing of the Reform Movement see C. 23 q.8 *dict. in princ. qu.* (above, n. 20); also C. 23 q.8 *dict. Grat. post* c. 20 and *post* c. 28. Cf. also *dicta Grat. post* c. 6 and *post* C. 18.

24. John of Salisbury, *Policraticus* 4.3, ed. J. Webb (Oxford, 1909), vol. 1, 239.

25. This is the sense in which the "argument des deux glaives" is used, for instance, by Odo of Deuil, in *De Profectione Ludovici in Orientem*, ed. Virginia G. Berry (New York, 1948), 1, 14 and 2, 20. There are countless similar usages.

26. See above, chapter 4, pp. 139 ff.

27. Gregory VII, *Registrum*, 8.21, ed. E. Caspar, *MGH, Epistolae Selectae* 2.1, 552 *versus* ibid., 561. Cf. Ladner, "The Concepts of 'Ecclesia' and 'Christianitas,'" art. cit., 51 n. 10 for a slightly different interpretation of the two passages.

Until the Investiture Controversy, political thinking had been part of a mode of thought in which such features as generations of new pairs based on the Pauline circle, biblical associations, and reverberations allowed by the deep structures of exegetical "grammar" played an essential role. Under those conditions, the sword pericope could be used creatively, in ways that deepened without ever destroying its traditional meaning, and in ways that gave a glimpse of the complex theological interrelations among a whole gamut of political stances. With the freezing of political positions as a result of the controversy, and, more importantly, owing to the slow growth of scholastic and legal modes of thinking, the second half of the twelfth century slowly lost this sort of flexibility. The development of a mode of thinking that was analytical, and emphasized clarity and distinctions rather than interrelationships, caused the two swords to lose their flexibility and their exegetical resonance and harden instead into slogans that could be used with equal facility by opposing political parties that then shouted at each other without any hope of mutual understanding.

Until the middle of the twelfth century, on the contrary, political parties within the Church had spoken in symbols that struck deep roots in the Bible and in the grammatical structure of exegetical thinking. Symbols could of course be interpreted in different ways, but multifaceted surfaces are part of the nature of symbols and are fully expected by those who engage in symbolic discourse. For Origen, the carnal sword of Phineas both is and is not rejected; for the chancery of Henry IV the two powers are strictly divided, but strict division does not preclude the admission that bishops share not only in the Priesthood but even in the Kingship of Christ; and for Gregory VII, royal power has both a demonic and an (admittedly subdued) christological dimension. During the Investiture Controversy, imperialists and curialists could hurl invectives at one another, but the symbolic network that both parties share suggests that at some level at least both sides remain aware of the sacred claims of royal power, of its demonic aspects, and of a cool, detached, neutralist, and, in some sense, "secular" theology of power. The resonances built into the symbolic network and into the structure of exegetical grammar assure that when one surface of the symbol is in focus, the other surfaces are at least fuzzily present in the background. With the growth of scholastic and legal modes of thinking, on the other hand, there is a tendency for questions to be reduced to a clear and simple either/or; *either* the Emperor has his sword from the Pope, *or* he does not! The arguments on center stage are illuminated with startling clarity; but the other sides, the other surfaces, have become opaque, and everything that is not clearly visible has been plunged into utter darkness. This new structure of thought works well for any kind of argumentation, for legal and scholastic modes of thinking, where the law of the excluded middle is a necessary tool. But when the network that sustained the older symbolism collapses, when the unity of exegesis and politics is dissolved, the symbols that remain in use cease in effect to function as genuine symbols. They no longer resonate, they are no longer translucid, the facets that are not in the light have become darkened. From multifaceted and transparent symbols, they have become one-dimensional and opaque emblems; they are turning into slogans, into rather dreary political clichés. They had illuminated; now they merely obscure.

BIBLICAL INDEX

INDEX OF ORIGEN'S TEXTS

INDEX OF EARLY CHRISTIAN* AND MEDIEVAL AUTHORS

*For purposes of this index Philo and Josephus have been annexed to the Early Christian period.

GENERAL INDEX

Designer: Dave Pauly
Composition: Freedmen's Organization
Lithography: Braun-Brumfield, Inc.
Binder: Braun-Brumfield, Inc.

Text: Compugraphic Paladium
Display: Compugraphic Paladium
Paper: 50 lb. P&S offset Vellum B32
Binding: Holliston Roxite B 53537